MW00466303

Native Features

Also available from Continuum

*Me and You and Memento and Fargo: How Independent
Screenplays Work*
J. J. Murphy

The Historical Epic and Contemporary Hollywood: From Dances with
Wolves *to* Gladiator
James Russell

Toward a New Film Aesthetic
Bruce Isaacs

The Strange World of David Lynch: Transcendental Irony from
Eraserhead *to* Mulholland Dr.
Eric G. Wilson

A New History of Documentary Film
Jack C. Ellis and Betsy A. McLane

*Directed by Steven Spielberg: Poetics of the Contemporary
Hollywood Blockbuster*
Warren Buckland

*The Films of Tim Burton: Animating Live Action in
Contemporary Hollywood*
Alison McMahan

The Films of Krzysztof Kieslowski: The Liminal Image
Joseph Kickasola

The Films of Peter Weir
Jonathan Rayner

Native Features

Indigenous Films from Around the World

Houston Wood

continuum

NEW YORK • LONDON

2008

The Continuum International Publishing Group Inc
80 Maiden Lane, New York, NY 10038

The Continuum International Publishing Group Ltd
The Tower Building, 11 York Road, London SE1 7NX

www.continuumbooks.com

Copyright © 2008 by Houston Wood

All rights reserved. No part of this book may be reproduced, stored in a retrieval
system, or transmitted, in any form or by any means, electronic, mechanical,
photocopying, recording, or otherwise, without the written permission of the
publishers.

Continuum is a member of Green Press Initiative, a nonprofit program dedicated
to supporting publishers in their efforts to reduce their use of fiber obtained from
endangered forests. We have elected to print this title on 50% postconsumer
waste recycled paper. For more information, go to www.greenpressinitiative.org.

Printed in the United States of America

Library of Congress Cataloging-in-Publication Data

Wood, Houston, 1944–
Native features: indigenous films from around the world / Houston Wood.

  p. cm.
Filmography: p.
Includes bibliographical references and index.
ISBN-13: 978-0-8264-2844-8 (hardcover: alk. paper)
ISBN-10: 0-8264-2844-4 (hardcover: alk. paper)
ISBN-13: 978-0-8264-2845-5 (pbk.: alk. paper)
ISBN-10: 0-8264-2845-2 (pbk.: alk. paper)
1. Indigenous films--History and criticism.
2. Indigenous peoples in motion pictures. I. Title.

PN1995.9.I49W66 2008
791.43'655--dc22

                  2007040409

For Anna and Charlotte,
my guides to the new generation of moviegoers

Contents

Acknowledgments

I began writing this book with Vilsoni Hereniko, who subsequently decided to pursue other projects. Hereniko's inspiration as an Indigenous filmmaker still permeates every chapter; no doubt the book would have been better had our collaboration continued. I also had help from producer and raconteur Jeannette Paulson Hereniko and from Heather Zwicker, who kindly guided me through a difficult transition from an academic to a more public prose. Several filmmakers generously provided information and, sometimes, hard-to-find copies of their work. These included Barry Barclay, Chris Eyre, Rodrick Pocowatchit, Ian Skorodin, and Lars-Göran Pettersson. I thank my colleagues at Hawai'i Pacific University, Kathy Cassity, Phyllis Frus, Laurie Leach, and, especially, Catherine Sustana, who helped me discover an appropriate voice, and Mark Tjarks, who pressed me to explain why Indigenous cinema deserved a book of its own. I also received help from Brian Baldwin, Ernie Blackmore, Kristin L. Dowell, Alan Howard, Jan Rensel, Freya Schiwy, and Naomi Wood.

My wife, Susan, edited chapters cheerfully, even though they contained no unsolved crimes to puzzle out.

Thanks as well to those who provided permission to reproduce images. These include Alan Howard, Igloolik Isuma Productions, imagineNative, Kristy Griffin, Larry Estes, South Pacific Pictures, and Te Maka Productions. The cover art is by permission of Jason Walker, www.sharp shooterinc.com. The original context of the cover image can be seen in chapter 13, "Future Indigenous Films."

Introduction

If fate had reversed the play
And a hard black boot pressed on your white throat
When released—what would *you* say
Friends and pal forever together in a new fair dawn?
Or meet like you and I shall meet
With flames and daggers drawn.

Kevin Gilbert, "The Flowering"

Indigenous-made feature films are as varied as the native peoples who make them. Their extraordinary diversity is attracting an increasingly broader audience, but this same diversity also creates multiple challenges. How can films such as *Atanarjuat: The Fast Runner* (2001) and *The Journals of Knud Rasmussen* (2006), made by the Indigenous people in the Arctic, be compared to films like *Once Were Warriors* (1994), *Whale Rider* (2002), and *The Maori Merchant of Venice* (2002), made by the Indigenous people of New Zealand? Even Indigenous people living on the same continent frequently share too few commonalities to make their films seem well suited to be grouped together. So, for example, such a widely seen Indigenous North American film as *Smoke Signals* (1998) seems to share little with the less-well-known *The Business of Fancydancing* (2002) written by the same scriptwriter, Sherman Alexie. Both of these films are also much different from the director of *Smoke Signals*, Chris Eyre's, later film *A Thief of Time* (2004).

Collecting Indigenous-made films under a single label is useful, nonetheless, as a way to call attention to the common relationship all share to the various national cinemas for which they offer alternatives. To greater and lesser degrees, every Indigenous film reflects the specific storytelling traditions of the native peoples being represented. Though these traditions and the resulting films are often very different from one another, all offer alternatives to movies based entirely on non-Indigenous traditions. Indigenous films thus share not content but rather a similar relationship to the dominant cinematic traditions that they, to various degrees, oppose. It is primarily this common relationship to non-Indigenous films, then, that gives coherence to the label *Indigenous film.*[1]

Indigenous peoples appeared in thousands of films made by outsiders before they began to make feature films representing themselves. Beginning with a pioneering handful in the 1980s, now fifty or so Indigenous features have appeared. Within another decade, there will likely be hundreds more, although, of course, Indigenous film output will never be as large as that produced in film centers such as China, India, and the United States. Still, the importance of these films for both Indigenous and non-Indigenous peoples far exceeds their number.

The United States National Science Foundation estimates that about half of the 6,000 to 7,000 languages currently in use in the world will be extinct or near extinct (no longer taught to children) by the end of the twenty-first century. Most of these threatened languages belong to Indigenous peoples, and, for most of these peoples, the loss of their language will also mean the loss of much of their cultural distinctiveness. As the number of languages and their associated customs disappear, the range of human diversity shrinks and so shrinks, too, the cultural multiplicity necessary for a healthy human future.

Of course, Indigenous feature films cannot by themselves save Indigenous languages and cultures from extinction. In some places, however, Indigenous films have already proven their power to strengthen Indigenous cultures. Indigenous feature films are, in addition, helping increase awareness among non-Indigenous audiences about Indigenous issues and needs. This book aims to encourage both these projects, to strengthen Indigenous cultures and to educate audiences about them.

A Non-Indigenous Perspective

I focus only on Indigenous feature films, although the archive of documentaries and short fiction films by Indigenous peoples is much larger. These other works, too, have done much to strengthen Indigenous identities and to inform non-Indigenous audiences. Still, including these many thousands of non-fiction and short films would have required a book many times larger than I was prepared (or qualified) to write. Such a book would also have forced me far from my own interests. Instead, *Native Features* reflects my personal fascination with Indigenous movies. It embraces what André Bazin called an "appreciative criticism," a criticism that aims not to diminish but rather to celebrate the films it examines.

My expertise, such as it is, rests mostly in my enthusiasm for these films and, a bit, in my academic training in media analysis. I lack anthropological training and have done no fieldwork into even one of the many diverse cultures out of which these films have emerged. I do here, however, endeavor to observe community-specific protocols, to avoid topics and films not open to the public, and to write in ways that acknowledge how completely my opinions are based in experiences rooted outside Indigenous worlds. Still, I fear, breaches of custom, large and small, may yet remain. That thought has made me sometimes think I should not go forward with this book. Finally, however, I concluded that no one could ever really know enough about hundreds of distinct peoples as different from one another as the Inuit are from the Yolngu, as Rotumans are from the Navajo. The choice seemed finally between publishing this book with probable unforeseen protocol mistakes and not publishing it at all. I hope that it is not vanity alone that led me to make the former choice.

Readers may be surprised to find that I do not assign value here either to how much it cost to make a film or to how much revenue it generated. So, for example, I examine Blackhorse Lowe's digitally made *5th World* (2005), produced with his friends and family, with the same respect I accord to the multimillion-dollar, professionally acted and Miramax-released *Smoke Signals* (1998). Omitting low-budget films would have implied that production costs and distribution profits help define a film's worth. Instead, I seek here to explain why many Indigenous filmmakers do not embrace the values of commercial cinema. Different values demand a different way of thinking about these films.

I use *Indigenous* throughout to refer to the world's First Peoples, using uppercase to signal that Indigenous is a proper noun, such as, for example, Chinese, English, and Inuit. I reserve the lowercase *indigenous* for the local films of nations, as in the phrase the "indigenous film industry of Canada." This type of nation-state indigenous film may be made by both Indigenous and non-Indigenous people.

Looking Ahead

Native Features is divided into three sections that can be read independently and in any order. Part one contains three chapters that examine the overlap between Indigenous and non-Indigenous films. Chapter 1 focuses on four of the best-known films generally considered to be Indigenous, *Rabbit-Proof Fence* (2002), *Whale Rider* (2002), *Smoke Signals* (1998), and *Atanarjuat: The Fast Runner* (2001). The following chapter looks at the career of Chris Eyre, the most prolific Indigenous director in North America and, possibly, the world. Chapter 3 focuses on the long career of Aboriginal actor David Gulpilil, whose films provide a vivid illustration of the differences in representations to be found in Indigenous and non-Indigenous films.

Part two employs a broader perspective on Indigenous films as it seeks generalizations about the current and probable future archive of First Peoples cinema. Chapter 4 examines problems associated with the divergent knowledge and expectations that Indigenous and non-Indigenous viewers bring to watching these films. Chapter 5 considers some of the uses and abuses that have been associated with Indigenous features, while chapter 6 explores five dimensions of differences found among them.

Part three, the book's longest section, contains six chapters that closely examine the four regions where most Indigenous feature films have appeared. These regions include, in their order of presentation, North America, the Arctic, Oceania, and Australia. Most of the Indigenous films made in each of these regions are described, along with interpretations that aspire to encourage further watching and discussion. Chapter 13, a final chapter, offers a brief description of the state of Indigenous filmmaking in the regions not reviewed in part three, along with some conjectures about the future of Indigenous feature films.

Part One

Indigenous Films Come of Age

Chapter 1

Four "Indigenous" Hits

We all belong to the story of our people.

John Trudell, *A Thousand Roads*

In 2004, at age thirteen, Keisha Castle-Hughes became the youngest ever Oscar nominee for Best Actress for her role in *Whale Rider*. Castle-Hughes did not win, but that publicity-winning nomination, along with many film festival awards, helped *Whale Rider* earn a worldwide box office gross of over sixty million dollars (U.S.), a spectacular return on its production cost of about four million dollars.

Whale Rider's success followed earlier significant but more modest successes by *Atanarjuat: The Fast Runner* (2001), *Rabbit-Proof Fence* (2002), and *Smoke Signals* (1998), films—like *Whale Rider*—generally considered to be Indigenous by audiences and reviewers. These four films were not the first features to be made by or closely associated with Indigenous people. Earlier path-breaking feature films included *House Made of Dawn* (1972), *Pathfinder* (*Ofelas* [1987]), *Ngati* (1987), *Mauri* (1988), and *Tukana: Husat i Asua?* (1983). Still, collectively, *Atanarjuat: The Fast Runner*, *Rabbit-Proof Fence*, *Smoke Signals*, and *Whale Rider* signaled that films labeled "Indigenous" could now regularly reach and please audiences beyond the specialized festivals where most Indigenous films previously had been screened.

Though increased attention to Indigenous peoples is generally a good thing, the perception that these four films offer Indigenous self-representations simultaneously creates problems. As the first feature films that many people have seen that foreground the lives, respectively, of the Inuit, Australian Aborigines, Native Americans, and Māori, these films are often assumed to picture Indigenous people as they "really are." Logically, of course, viewers understand that no single film—or even a set of films—provides an accurate portrait of any culture or people. Even films totally controlled, produced, and distributed by Indigenous people can offer only partial perspectives. Nonetheless, audiences tend to put logic aside and accept film images as "authentic" guides to the peoples presented. So, for example, audiences tend to see Victor and Thomas in *Smoke Signals* as typical not just of Coeur d'Alene men but of contemporary Indian men associated with hundreds of diverse tribes across North America. Similarly, mainstream audiences commonly believe, mistakenly, that Pai and Koro in *Whale Rider* provide useful knowledge about all Māori people.

There is no easy way to specify exactly how Victor and Thomas are not representative, for to do so would require describing the variety among hundreds of American Indian tribes. Similarly, to try to explain how Paikea and Koro differ from other Māori would require exploring differences between the Ngati Porou and other Māori tribes, as well as differences between rural and urban Māori, between Māori communities that have continuously occupied ancestral land and those who have not, as well as much more. Such investigations could fill many volumes and still fail to specify what different tribes of contemporary American Indians and Māori are "really" like.

Another, more achievable task, however, may help viewers of these films. Since *Rabbit-Proof Fence, Whale Rider, Smoke Signals*, and *Atanarjuat: The Fast Runner* each adapts a previously existing story, we can look at how each film deals with its sources. In general, it seems, the more a film's adaptation is controlled by Indigenous people, the more likely it is to stay close to its source. Also, these four films indicate that, in general, the more filmmakers transform Indigenous stories to fit the expectations of non-Indigenous audiences, the more popular their films become.

Rabbit-Proof Fence

The production of *Rabbit-Proof Fence* involved fewer native people than any of the other three films to be considered here. Though based on Doris Garimara Pilkington's biography of her Aboriginal mother, *Follow the Rabbit-proof Fence*, the screenplay was written by white Australian Christine Olsen and directed by white Australian-born but now Hollywood-based director Phillip Noyce.[1] Noyce and Olsen, along with John Winter, another white Australian, also acted as producers. Aboriginal actors and some Aboriginal crew were employed, but most creative decisions remained in non-Indigenous hands.

Noyce's previous directing included such political thrillers as *Patriot Games* (1992) and *Clear and Present Danger* (1994), as well as *Dead Calm* (1989), *The Bone Collector* (1999), and *The Quiet American* (2002). In *Rabbit-Proof Fence*, Noyce returned to topics broached in his first feature film, *Backroads* (1977), which explored white-Aboriginal relationships in the remote Australian countryside. *Rabbit-Proof Fence* foregrounds related themes, this time focusing on Australia's "Stolen Generation," the name given to the estimated 100,000 Indigenous children who were separated from their families under a government policy in effect from 1905 to 1970. (*Bringing Them Home* [1997], the official Australian government report, estimates that no less than 10 and perhaps as many as 30 percent of all Aboriginal children born in the first seventy years of the twentieth century were forcibly removed from their communities.[2])

Rabbit-Proof Fence focuses on fourteen-year-old Molly (Everlyn Sampi), captured by white authorities while her mother and grandmother helplessly shriek. The abductors cage Molly with her eight-year-old sister, Daisy (Tianna Sansbury), and their ten-year-old cousin, Gracie (Laura Monaghan), then ship them by train and truck 1,200 miles south to the Moore River Native Settlement, near the city of Perth.

The Settlement is a detention prison for youth overseen by A. O. Neville (Kenneth Branagh), the Western Australia Territory's Chief Protector for all Aboriginal and part-Aboriginal children under the age of sixteen. The Aborigines Act of 1905 had changed the status of Australia's Indigenous population so that these individuals were no longer treated as "wildlife" but more as prisoners or wards of the government. By law, Chief Protectors such as Neville henceforth controlled every aspect of all Aboriginal children's existence: where they might live; what training they received; if, who, and when they could marry; and what jobs they would be given, both at the facility and upon release into adulthood. In the film, Neville argues that whites must do all they can to save Aborigines from themselves. The more they resist, the more harshly he feels he must treat them. "If they would only understand," he laments, "what we are trying to do for them."

Molly bristles under the humiliations visited upon children at the Settlement. The detainees are told, for example, that they left no mothers behind. They are forced to embrace a British-based version of Christianity. Resistors are put into solitary confinement.[3] Molly coaxes her younger sister and cousin to join her in escaping, and much of *Rabbit-Proof Fence* chronicles the girls' attempt to walk home while avoiding the police and Moodoo (David Gulpilil), the Settlement's Aboriginal tracker.[4] When news of the girls' escape reaches their homeland, Molly and Daisy's mother (Ningali Lawford) and grandmother (Myarn Lawford) begin enacting spiritual rituals to help guide them home.

Molly displays great ingenuity in eluding Moodoo and various local police. Her strategy centers on following a rabbit-proof fence that was, when new, the longest continuous fence in the world. Its promoters had touted the fence as a modern wonder, as white Australia's answer to China's Great Wall, though its purpose was in fact an attempt to correct an earlier, massive white error. Government workers had constructed these two barrier fences—1,139 miles and 724 miles—from sea to sea in an effort to keep out of Western Australia the descendents of rabbits that whites had earlier mistakenly introduced to the continent. By the early decades of the twentieth century, these foreign rabbits had become a rapidly expanding vector that threatened the profits of white ranchers and farmers throughout Australia's east and south regions.

1-1 Molly, Grace, and Daisy stand at the rabbit-proof fence

Knowing that one fence passes near her family's homeland, Molly leads her sister and cousin week after week as they walk homeward across isolated bush and desert lands. The fence, symbol of settler efforts to appropriate Aboriginal lands and bring modern commerce to Australia, works for the girls as a lifeline although, ironically, it failed utterly at keeping out the rabbits. Jokers claimed that after the fence was built there were more rabbits on the Western Australian than on the South Australian side.

The white workmen who constructed and repaired the fence had succeeded, however, in one pursuit: They impregnated hundreds of Aboriginal women.[5] "My dad was a white man working on the fence," Molly says at the opening of the film. "They called me half-caste." The government policy of child abduction and resettlement, in fact, was focused particularly on "half-castes," understood then in Australia as children born of Aboriginal mothers by white fathers. Children born of white mothers by Aboriginal fathers were not spoken about. The government policy of child removal focused only on mixed-race children born of Aboriginal mothers in part since it was believed that full-blooded Aboriginals lacked sufficient intelligence to be trained to become the domestic servants and low-wage laborers that white Australian desired.

The power of *Rabbit-Proof Fence* derives in part from the screen presence of the three principal girls, especially Molly, played by Everlyn Sampi, the clear hero of the film. Sampi's real-life mother had herself been transported to the Moore River Native Settlement when she was a child. In acting as Molly, then, Sampi reenacted some elements of her own family's story. Sampi's screen charisma, and the performances of most of the other Aboriginal child actors in *Rabbit-Proof Fence*, reflects a particular casting strategy that Noyce and his white assistants executed in their three weeks of auditioning hundreds of Aboriginal children for the film. Searching contemporary rural areas of Australia for inexperienced young people he could transform into actors, Noyce says, was like "finding a needle in a haystack."[6] Noyce explains, "I wanted kids who people all over the world would want to adopt as their own children." Noyce elaborates that "they had to be identifiable as aboriginal children. . . . And yet they had to have a certain charisma that would allow white Australians to say, 'They are my children.'"

Noyce's strategy worked, as non-Indigenous audiences and reviewers have strongly identified with Sampi's Molly as well as with the other girls. It seems likely that white audiences would not have empathized as deeply had Noyce selected leads with features that emphasized Aboriginal rather than white ancestors. The tagline for Miramax's North American publicity for *Rabbit-Proof Fence* proclaimed, "What if the government kidnapped your daughter?" The line amplifies Noyce's desire to reach the broadest possible audience by representing the film as portraying a situation even a non-Indigenous parent might face.

These choices of emphasis in the directing, casting, and publicity of *Rabbit-Proof Fence* seem to reflect the goals of the non-Indigenous people making the film more than the perspective of Australia's Indigenous peoples. Similarly, even though *Rabbit-Proof Fence* features Aboriginal actors and tells a story based on a biography written by an Aboriginal writer, the screenplay alters Pilkington's book in ways that deemphasize its Indigenous origins.

The first half of Pilkington's *Follow the Rabbit-proof Fence* offers the history of post–white-contact Australia from an Indigenous perspective. Pilkington includes substantial excerpts from letters, telegrams, newspaper articles, and official government documents to establish a broad context for the horrors perpetrated on thousands of Aborigines. The second half of *Follow the Rabbit-proof Fence* then offers an account of the girls' long walk home from the Moore River Native Settlement. This story is told sparingly, without any of the intercutting of what the film suggests was a parallel story involving the white authority's futile search. The book treats the girls' trek as a sufficient subject in itself while the film offers a story that is as much about white as about Aboriginal Australia. While the book *Follow the Rabbit-proof Fence* is part of a broader movement by Aboriginal people to assert the validity of their radically alternative experiences of modernity, the film *Rabbit-Proof Fence* reaffirms the white settler tendency to frame how Indigenous lives are understood.

Rabbit-Proof Fence concludes with the triumphant return of sisters Molly and Daisy to their family. (The third girl, their cousin Gracie, goes off on her own and is captured. "I lost one," are Molly's first words to her mother once they embrace.[7]) *Rabbit-Proof Fence* thus illustrates the common Hollywood requirement of ending films with upbeat conclusions. Even commercial films about genocide such as *Schindler's List* (1993) offer audiences optimistic ends. *Rabbit-Proof Fence*'s cinematic triumph, too, is more about creating wide audience appeal than about representing reality.

The last ten minutes of *Rabbit-Proof Fence* are built from shots using handheld cameras and night filters. The edited scenes emphasize shadows and a surrealistic blue light, increasing the audience's experience of suspense as well as its sense that the film is moving toward a familiar cinematic conclusion. For several minutes a lone white officer, acting out of some undefined motive, menacingly prowls through the Jigalong Aborigine camp. He brandishes a rifle, though guns have played little part in the film until then. The officer's presence provides a final Hollywood-style threat hinting that the girls may be captured only moments before completing their desperate nine-week walk. Then, triumphantly, the officer is frightened away by Aboriginal spiritual powers and Molly and Daisy run through blue shadows to embrace their mother and grandmother. Exultant music composed by Peter Gabriel fills the screen.

Audiences see that individual tenacity and Indigenous wisdom can conquer bigotry.

In Pilkington's book, as well as in a voice-over coda to the film, readers and audiences are told the truth, that a few escapes here and there did not alter the government's half-century-long exercise of legalized kidnappings. Even Molly's own epic escape earned her but a brief triumph. She later bore two children, Doris and Annabelle, and, in accord with the continuing half-caste policy, in 1940 all three were transported to the Moore River Native Settlement. Doris, then four years old, was immediately taken away from her mother and forced to live in a dorm with other girls. When Molly escaped again soon after, she could not retrieve Doris from the dorm and had to leave her behind. Mother and daughter never lived together again.

During this second escape, Molly carried eighteen-month-old Annabelle, week after week, as she again followed the fence that had guided her nine years before. She once more avoided capture and trekked 1,200 miles back to her homeland. Decades later, Doris, the child left behind, sought and found her mother, became an author, wrote one earlier book, and then *Follow the Rabbit-proof Fence*. The younger daughter, Annabelle, was captured once more, however, when she was five. Molly never saw her again. "You told the wrong story," Molly complained to Noyce when she saw his film.[8] The second escape and separate losses of her two daughters seemed more important to Molly.

Of course, this true story, ending with one daughter lost for decades and a second lost for life, does not lend itself to triumphant filmmaking nor to international box office success. Such success is necessary for films to reach large audiences, and probably few would wish that *Rabbit-Proof Fence* in its present form had never been made. "I've learned the lessons in marketing and casting that Hollywood teaches," Noyce explains. And so in *Rabbit-Proof Fence* Noyce aimed "to use these skills to sell an Indigenous story to the mainstream. It's not overtly political but covertly."[9] Happily, Noyce's considerable commercial filmmaking skills produced a film that has inspired many throughout the world to learn more about Aboriginal and white settler history. Still, *Rabbit-Proof Fence* likely tells most audiences at least as much about the conventions of dominant commercial cinema as about Australia's Indigenous peoples.

Documentary footage of the real-life, now-eighty-five-year-old Molly Craig concludes *Rabbit-Proof Fence*. She walks with her sister, Daisy Kadibill, now seventy-nine, leaning on a stick, crossing a bush landscape that could be part of the film. Molly's wrinkled face is shot to look wise and beautiful. Her eyes avoid the camera and she is lit so that she seems almost to glow, to look wondrously victorious. The aged Molly Craig's appearance on-screen is included to increase the credibility of the fictionalized story that has come before. And yet, as Molly told Noyce, *Rabbit-Proof Fence* is not her story as she would tell it. Perhaps it is not, either, a story much like any Aboriginal director and screenwriter would tell. The films by Aboriginal directors described in chapter 12 certainly include none with stories following Noyce's lead.

Whale Rider

Whale Rider, like *Rabbit-Proof Fence,* was produced, directed, and scripted by non-Indigenous people adapting a previously published book by an Indigenous author. In this case, however, the book, *The Whale Rider,* by Māori writer Witi Ihimaera, was fiction, not a historical memoir like Pilkington's *Follow the Rabbit-proof Fence.*[10] *Whale Rider*'s screenplay, fashioned by white New Zealander Niki Caro, who also directed the film, included more input from Ihimaera and other Māori than was provided by Aborigines for *Rabbit-Proof Fence.* Even so, some Māori[11] maintain this participation was insufficient and that *Whale Rider* should not be regarded as a Māori or Indigenous film.

Whale Rider is built on an origin tale associated not with all Māori but with the Ngati Porou tribe mostly located in and around the village of Whangara on the east coast of Aotearoa New Zealand. Ihimaera is from this tribe (as well as from two others) and his fiction, *Whale Rider,* adapted this tribe-specific story for young, modern readers of English. His novel seems aimed at readers with little, if any, specialized Indigenous knowledge. Caro consulted with Ihimaera on the script, and the writer has expressed satisfaction with the film.[12] Elders from the Ngati Porou tribe also were involved in the film's production and have similarly been publicly supportive of the result, as have many Māori who acted in the film.[13] In a sense then, the issue may be more whether *Whale Rider* is an authentic or proper Ngati Porou film rather than if it is an Indigenous or Māori film.

Still, it is understandable why some Māori from other tribes feel an investment in how *Whale Rider* is perceived. Most audiences do not understand the tribal distinctions that make Māori groups different from one another and, indeed, Caro's script encourages thinking that the

Māori are a single people. Caro's film makes no effort to inform viewers that the tale of a human arriving in Aoatearoa on the back of a whale is not a widely shared Māori genealogical narrative. *Whale Rider* also alters Ihimaera's novel in other ways that, together, suggest that Caro was as interested in telling a story familiar to non-Indigenous audiences as in filming a region-specific Ngati Porou tale.

1-2   Paikea greets a beached whale ©Kristy Griffin, South Pacific Pictures

Caro, for example, eliminated an important parallel story that is foundational to Ihimaera's *The Whale Rider*. The novel intertwines a tale about a pod of whales swimming complex paths across the Southern Hemisphere with a second tale focused on an extended family of people living in the tiny community of Whangara. Pod and people share a common memory of the time when, as a youth, the old bull whale carried on his back a young man, Kahutia Te Rangi (aka Paikea), the ancestor for whom Kahu, the girl, is named. Kahutia Te Rangi finally left the ocean and whale to become chief at the human settlement that Koro and his family now occupy. In Ihimaera's novel, the whale has grown old and is increasingly unable to lead the pod. Simultaneously, Koro, too, is struggling to find a new leader to guide next generations in the village. Pod and people, in the novel, resolve their parallel problems by reuniting to create a second whale rider many generations after the first.

Caro transformed this story into a narrative more familiar to viewers of Hollywood films. Though it includes several breathtaking scenes of swimming southern white whales, Caro's film omits the whale pod story so central to Ihimaera's novel. *Whale Rider* does not identify a whale leader or present the whales as creatures that think or communicate in ways humans understand. The novel, by contrast, builds a sense that animals and humans are equals, meant to live in a peaceful unity. The film's elimination of this partnership story encourages the sense that, while the tribe's distress produces anxiety in the whales, these emotional effects do not work in reverse.

Caro also notably altered the family dynamics at the center of the film. Ihimaera's novel assumes it takes a village to raise a Ngati Porou child and, in the book, the village is functioning fairly well. Adults come and go in the novel, but, since all take responsibility for one another, there is little sense that Kahu is neglected. In the film, on the other hand, Paikea, the young girl, much resembles the "poor orphan" familiar to western stories. For instance, while Porourangi, Paikea's father, is present and actively involved with the tribe and with Paikea in the book, he is alienated from family and tribe in the film, has abandoned his daughter, and lives in Germany, pointedly on the other side of the world.

The film's shift away from representing the functioning extended village family of the novel is especially evident in Caro's changes to the character of Rawiri, Paikea's paternal uncle. Rawiri narrates the human portions of Ihimaera's novel, providing readers with the perspective of one of several loving members of the extended family who nourish Paikea. In the film, however, Caro transforms Rawiri into an idle, drug-using young Māori of little use to his family. Caro even adds a scene with a car full of tattooed, vaguely threatening young Māori males that will seem familiar to audiences who have viewed earlier films such as *Once Were Warriors* (1994) and *What Becomes of the Broken Hearted?* (1999).

Caro's most striking alteration of the novel may be her addition of the *waka*, the huge, unfinished traditional canoe that has no counterpart in Ihimaera's fiction. In the film, Paikea's father is said to have begun and then, upon the death of Paikea's mother and twin, to have abandoned this very large canoe. The unfinished hull looms in the background of many scenes in *Whale Rider*, a symbol of the troubles the village is experiencing. Paikea retreats to stand or sit in this *waka* when she is upset. Both her father and her grandmother offer her advice and comfort there. It is from the *waka*'s platform that Paikea develops her ability to sense and to communicate with the distant, unseen whales. And, at film's end, the completion of this *waka* and its celebratory maiden voyage with Paikea and her grandfather surrounded by dozens of village paddlers suggests to audiences that the village's troubles may end.

The *waka* used in the film was manufactured in Auckland, using non-traditional methods and materials. The completed *waka*, nonetheless, was donated to the people of Whangara and has become a tourist attraction. Though a movie prop, it has helped spark new interest in traditional Māori canoes. The Whangarei District Council subsequently decided to support the building of a real *waka* by master carver Wallace Hetaraka. Glenda Bostwick, council parks manager for the Whangarei District, pushed the plan by invoking *Whale Rider*. "I have just seen the film," she said, "and now I know what it means to Māori."[14] Caro says she included the *waka* because it seemed to her to be an apt symbol for the contemporary situation of the Māori.[15]

Films that tell Indigenous stories can change local traditions on a scale inconceivable within dominant cultures. So, *Whale Rider* has shaped how millions conceive of all Māori, not just those Māori who trace their genealogy to the Ngati Porou. Because they wield economic and media power far greater than the Māori themselves, non-Indigenous audiences are likely to use the "knowledge" gained from *Whale Rider* to influence how Māori represent and even think about themselves. Stories of whale riders and of empowered children, especially of girls, are now (and, likely, will for a long time) be sold in Aotearoa New Zealand tourist shops and hotels. Guided tours of the "real" Whanagara, the "real" *marae* (a sacred place serving both religious and social purposes), and the "real" *waka* are already altering these places and things to make them more like the film that arriving visitors hope to experience.[16]

No filmmaker, either Indigenous or non-Indigenous, can realistically expect that the films they produce will create effects as great as *Whale Rider*. And yet, perhaps, no filmmaker should craft a film that tells an Indigenous story without considering what impact the movie might have should it, too, become a global hit.

Smoke Signals

Few films have entered theaters carrying greater burdens of expectation than did *Smoke Signals*. Though several Indian-made films had preceded it at festivals or on television (see chapter 7), *Smoke Signals* was the first widely distributed feature film created by the native people of North America. It was thus often mistakenly treated as the first cinematic Indian response to thousands of earlier films that had shown Native Americans as others view them. These non-Indigenous films commonly flipped history on its head, presenting European invaders as heroes and their Indian victims as barbarians. No single film or even dozens of films by Native

Americans could reverse this topsy-turvy history, yet *Smoke Signals* was celebrated as an important start.

Like *Rabbit-Proof Fence* and *Whale Rider*, *Smoke Signals* adapts a previously published book. In this case, however, Sherman Alexie, the Spokane and Coeur d'Alene author, was able to transform his own fiction into the screenplay.[17] *Smoke Signals* also had an Indigenous director, Chris Eyre, of Cheyenne and Arapaho descent. (Eyre's other films are discussed in chapter 2.) With both an Indigenous screenwriter and director, then, *Smoke Signals* is clearly further toward the Indigenous end of the continuum described in chapter 4 than is either *Rabbit-Proof Fence* or *Whale Rider*. Still, as we shall see, *Smoke Signals'* non-Indigenous producers (Larry Estes and Scott Rosenfelt) and Miramax, its distributor, also shaped the film in ways that, perhaps, neither Alexie nor Eyre would have accepted had they possessed more artistic control.

Smoke Signals traces the evolving relationship between two young Coeur d'Alene men, Victor (Adam Beach) and Thomas (Evan Adams), as events challenge their very different ideas about Victor's father. Victor remembers his father, Arnold (Gary Farmer), as an abusive drunk who abandoned Victor and his mother after an especially bad domestic quarrel when Victor was twelve. Thomas, on the other hand, remembers Arnold as the hero who saved Thomas when he was thrown from a burning house by his doomed parents just before they perished inside. Thomas spins tall tales about the absent Arnold and about much else, infuriating Victor and many of their peers.

Victor is a handsome, ex–high school athlete struggling to find a way to maturity while living with his mother and memories of a long-absent father. Thomas is an outcast, a nerd with few friends besides the grandmother (Monique Mojica) who has raised him. He seems to supply his own companionship through incessant talking. The film follows these contrasting characters as circumstances lead them off their reservation in Idaho to retrieve Arnold's ashes and sparse patrimony from a mobile home outside of Phoenix, Arizona.

"Do you guys got your passports?" a character asks as Victor and Thomas near the reservation's edge. Though Victor protests, "But it's the United States," he is told, "That's as foreign as it gets. I hope you two got your vaccinations." This joke highlights how fundamentally Victor and Thomas both are, and are not, like non-Indian youth their age. They do resemble North American youth in playing to type as, respectively, a popular jock and an isolated, loner geek. The centrality of sports in their young lives mirrors similar themes associated with mainstream culture, as does the young men's quest to explore and heal relationships with a father figure. Simultaneously, however, Victor and Thomas do not fit into the dominant white culture that surrounds the reservation. They may not need passports, but the film demonstrates they do require special skills to survive in a country that has very definite expectations of what young Indian men should, and should not, do.

During a pickup basketball game early in the film, one player asks Victor who is "the best basketball player ever." Victor answers, "That's easy. Geronimo." This sparks repartee about the relative shortness of Apaches, the comparative athletic abilities of Custer and Chief Joseph, and speculation about "old Pokey" (Pocahontas) as a possible cheerleader or point guard. Such basketball court banter evokes how players trash-talk one another across North America. Yet this talk is unfamiliar, too, in its reliance on historical and popular cultural figures unlikely to be part of non-Indigenous joking. Similarly, we see and hear that the reservation radio station broadcasts traffic reports, as do radio stations throughout North America. The reporter, Lester Fallsapart, however, sits under a beach umbrella atop the KREZ traffic van, "broken down at the cross-roads since 1972." He reports, "A couple of cars drove by earlier. And you know old Mrs. Joe; she was speeding. Kimmy and James were in a yellow car and they were arguing. Ain't no traffic, really."

A similar blending of the familiar and unfamiliar shapes *Smoke Signals* throughout. The film echoes earlier road and also buddy movies, as the "opposites" Victor and Thomas pursue a quest through unknown territories that transforms them. *Smoke Signals* explicitly invokes the classic revisionist road/buddy movie, *Thelma & Louise* (1991), through the introduction of Velma (Michelle St. John) and Lucy (Elaine Miles), two women who drive their beat-up car in reverse to transport Victor and Thomas as they commence their journey. Alexie also points to *Midnight Cowboy* (1969), another classic road movie, as influencing his writing of the screenplay.[18]

In *Smoke Signals*, as in many cinematic predecessors, the travelers return home from their journey having won insights. *Smoke Signals*, however, undermines as often as it invokes traditional film genres. Victor and Thomas like and understand each other better at the end of their travels, but there is little reason to suppose they will become friends. Victor achieves some understanding of his now-dead father, as would be expected in a mainstream film, but *Smoke Signals* does not end with any unequivocal image or action. Thomas earlier predicts such a Hollywood-inspired ending. He foresees that throwing Arnold's cremation ashes into Spokane Falls will provoke this father to "rise like a salmon." Victor, on the other hand, says he expects disposing of the ashes will be "like cleaning out the attic . . . Like throwing things away when they have no more use." Neither prediction pans out, as viewers see Victor crying out in anguish and anger as he flings the ashes near the end of the film, triggering neither salmon nor cleanliness but a dusty swirl.

Thomas, in voice-over, concludes the film by reading Dick Lourie's poem, "Forgiving Our Fathers." The poem speculates about the consequences of forgiving fathers and ends with the question, "If we forgive our fathers, what is left?"[19] The film offers no answer, and, as Alexie writes in his notes to the screenplay, "Instead of a 'happy ending' we have an ending that's much more poetic, much more emotional, much more unpredictable and open-ended."[20]

The many ways that *Smoke Signals* invokes but revises past films is illustrated as well by actor Irene Bedard, who plays Suzy Song in *Smoke Signals* as a multifaceted, somewhat mysterious Indigenous woman. Bedard's voice will sound familiar to many as it is the voice of the Disney-produced *Pocahontas* (1995), an animated feature about Indians that is one of the top one hundred revenue-producing movies of all time. Bedard's face was also used by the artists to help create the cartoon-Pocahontas's face. By casting Bedard as the complex female lead and foregrounding her face on its promotion posters, *Smoke Signals* at once invokes and repudiates the most prominent cinematic representation of Indians ever made.

Smoke Signals references other earlier feature films by outsiders as well. Victor, for example, mocks Thomas for having learned how to act Indian from watching *Dances with Wolves* (1990) "two hundred times." *Smoke Signals* also ridicules the representation of the Indian shaman so influentially offered in *Little Big Man* (1970). There Old Lodge Skins (Chief Dan George) declares, "Today is a good day to die." In *Smoke Signals*, one of Victor's friends jokes, "Yeah, sometimes it's a good day to die. Sometimes, it's a good day to play basketball." And, later, Thomas remarks, "Sometimes, it's a good day to die. Sometimes, it's a good day to have breakfast." Even the use of a road journey in *Smoke Signals* invites comparisons with a similar narrative in *Powwow Highway* (1989), a film by non–Native Americans that also focuses on two contrasting contemporary males who head off the reservation to make discoveries about themselves. Gary Farmer, who plays Victor's father in *Smoke Signals*, acts the part of an eccentric Thomas-like character, Philbert Bono, in *Powwow Highway*.

Smoke Signals acknowledges its characters' immersion in North American popular culture while simultaneously asserting that Indigenous reality differs from earlier media portrayals. Thomas and Victor share characteristics with *Powwow Highway*'s Philbert and Buddy Red Bow (A. Martinez), and even with famous wannabe Indians like Little-Big-Man (Dustin Hoffman) and Dances-with-Wolves (Kevin Costner). But Victor and Thomas, like *Smoke Signals* itself, reenvision these previous cinematic representations of Native America. When Thomas tells one of his many long-winded stories to Lucy and Velma, Velma remarks, "I think it was a fine example of the oral tradition." She is joking, of course, and yet Thomas's storytelling is, indeed, an example of a contemporary Indian oral tradition, just not in a form that Hollywood films or anthropologists commonly present.

Smoke Signals draws characters and incidents from a few of the twenty-two short stories in Alexie's collection of linked fictions, *The Lone Ranger and Tonto Fistfight in Heaven*.[21] Arnold Joseph is Victor's uncle, not his father, in these stories. Smoke Signals also incorporates ideas from Alexie's later novel, *Reservation Blues*.[22] It is in *Reservation Blues*, for example, that the image of a road trip to retrieve ashes appears. In *The Lone Ranger* the trip is precipitated by Victor's desire to claim three hundred dollars from his deceased uncle's savings account. These and many other plot adjustments, however, are much less consequential than the changes in tone that Alexie made in adapting the screenplay. Alexie's fiction presents a generally pessimistic view of contemporary Indians while *Smoke Signals* offers a generally optimistic view. The sad failures and victims of Alexie's stories are transformed in *Smoke Signals* into people as likely with time as any other cinematic characters to find their rightful civic places in North America.

Alexie explains this change as resulting in part from the earlier daily drunkenness that guided his composition of *The Lone Ranger and Tonto Fistfight in Heaven*. Alexie says that he had quit drinking and was totally sober as he scripted *Smoke Signals*.[23] In *The Lone Ranger*, Alexie writes that "When a glass sits on a table here, people don't wonder if it's half filled or half empty. They just hope it's good beer" (49). Victor is an alcoholic in these stories and it costs him his job, as well as much else. Victor's perspective is summarized: "He thought one more beer could save the world. One more beer and every chair would be comfortable. One more beer and the lightbulb in the bathroom would never burn out. One more beer and he would love her forever. One more beer and he would sign any treaty for her" (88). Though alcoholism remains a problem in *Smoke Signals*, it no longer defines the condition of contemporary Indian peoples. Emblematically, in the film Victor is transformed into a teetotaler. His abstinence is so deep-seated that he tells a police chief, "I've never had a drop of alcohol in my life, Officer. Not one drop."

The shift in tone from Alexie's fiction to the final film may reflect more than changes in Alexie's own drinking habits. Alexie's "Scene Notes" appended to the published screenplay make it clear that various producers and actors, the influential distributor Miramax, personnel associated with the Sundance Institute, as well as audience responses at early test screenings, together exerted pressures that encouraged the final cut of *Smoke Signals* to present Victor, Thomas, and contemporary Indians in general as warm-hearted survivors.[24] Distributors seek films that remind audiences of earlier films that have left them feeling happy. Alexie's description of the process of creating the final cut of *Smoke Signals* suggests some decisions were made with the anticipated desires of commercial audiences in mind.

Both Alexie and director Eyre's own separate next films seem in part to have been aimed at correcting or, at least, responding to the upbeat mood that dominates *Smoke Signals*. Alexie's *The Business of Fancydancing*, discussed in chapter 8, presents a much more ambiguous and darker picture of contemporary Indian males. Similarly, while Eyre's second film, *Skins*, discussed in chapter 2, revisits many of the same themes found in *Smoke Signals*, it offers much less hope that its Sioux protagonist will escape the demons that transform him from a reservation cop into a lawless vigilante.[25]

Neither Alexie's *The Business of Fancydancing* nor Eyre's *Skins* pleased mainstream audiences nearly as much as *Smoke Signals*. Whether it is more accurate for films to adopt an optimistic or pessimistic view of contemporary Indians, I cannot say. It does seem likely, however, that Indigenous filmmakers will often face difficult choices between filming their visions and modifying those visions to earn production funds and wide distribution. Most filmmakers confront similar choices, of course, but the stakes are generally higher for Indigenous filmmakers, since their films are frequently viewed as representing "authentic" Indigenous views.

Atanarjuat: The Fast Runner

No film associated with Indigenous people has accumulated more critical acclaim than the Inuit-made *Atanarjuat: The Fast Runner*. It won the Caméra d'Or at Cannes and then received multiple reviews across North America that foregrounded words like *brilliant, classic,* and *masterpiece.* *Slate*'s David Edelstein gushed that the film provided "the most enthralling three hours you'll ever spend at the theater."[26] J. Hoberman in the *Village Voice* announced that *Atanarjuat: The Fast Runner* "could herald a rebirth of cinema."[27]

These accolades came to a film situated as far toward the Indigenous end of the Indigenous to non-Indigenous continuum of films as is possible. Igloolik Isuma, the Inuit production company responsible for *Atanarjuat: The Fast Runner,* is majority owned and controlled by the Inuit. *Atanarjuat* was the company's first feature film after a decade of producing impressive television documentaries, including a monumental thirteen-part television series, *Nunavut: Our Land* (1999). Subsequently, Igloolik Isuma produced *The Journals of Knud Rasmussen* and co-produced *Before Tomorrow* (2007), features discussed in chapter 9. *Atanarjuat: The Fast Runner* is alone among the hits discussed in this chapter in its exclusive use of an Indigenous language, Inuktitut, the first time this language had been the basis of a feature film. *Atanarjuat: The Fast Runner* also differs from *Rabbit-Proof Fence, Whale Rider,* and *Smoke Signals* in relying on a mostly Indigenous production crew. And, though an adaptation, like the earlier three films discussed, *Atanarjuat: The Fast Runner* alone offers an Indigenous tale that predates European colonialism.

1-3 Atanarjuat with his brother, Amaqjuaq (© Igloolik Isuma Productions)

The film's first half hour works as a prologue, establishing for the audience a sense of both the different culture and temporal rhythm within which the film's almost three hours reside. A voice-over near the beginning invokes the oral origins of the story and warns, "I can only say this story to someone who understands it." It requires careful attention, then, and maybe multiple viewings for non-Inuit spectators to begin to join those who understand this ancient story of two cousins, Atanarjuat (Natar Ungalaaq) and Oki (Peter-Henry Arnatsiaq), who both wish to marry Atuat (Sylvia Ivalu). Tension and verbal sparring escalate into physical fights, then into murder, banishment, more murder, plans for revenge, and a surprise ending.

Atanarjuat: The Fast Runner embeds this old tale of curses, love, and revenge within meticulously filmed ethnographic details about how the pre-contact Inuit survived in their Arctic lands. Robert Flaherty's 1922 fictionalized documentary *Nanook of the North* excited unprecedentedly large audiences in its own time for similarly dwelling on ethnographic details; *Atanarjuat: The Fast Runner* has the advantage of being shot not only in color, with a wide-screen video camera, but also by people with much more than Flaherty's outsider acquaintance with the Arctic environment. The broad sky plays so brightly across many shifting shades of snow in *Atanarjuat: The Fast Runner* that viewers may wish they were wearing sunglasses. Even the orange-lit ice-house interiors glow in ways that remind audiences they are gazing into a culture and time very far from their own.

Atanarjuat: The Fast Runner sometimes pauses in its dominant narrative to show exactly how ice is shaped for igloos, how snow is used for mortar, how sharpened stones are used to strip whale meat, how dogs are cared for and trained, and how life is passed inside closed spaces. To some degree, then, *Atanarjuat: The Fast Runner* attempts for three hours to place viewers within the very rhythms and activities of pre-contact Inuit life. The film thus works, as Roger Ebert says, as an "experience so engrossing it is like being buried in a new environment."[28]

Atanarjuat: The Fast Runner's central story was carefully chosen to be representative of hundreds of stories that have helped the Inuit for centuries understand who they are and how they should behave. The screenplay was created from interviews about this tale with seven Igloolik elders, then changed to offer an ending unlike any these elders knew.[29] The movie thus offers one more version of a tale that, like most oral stories, always exists in multiple versions. *Atanarjuat: The Fast Runner* perpetuates the tradition of creating a new story based on earlier stories but does so in a new media, film.

1-4 Atanarjuat escapes across the snow

By carefully filming and foregrounding traditional cultural practices in this first feature film by and for the Inuit, the makers of *Atanarjuat: The Fast Runner* demonstrate their conviction that many older practices should continue to ground Inuit life. Traditional Inuit ways of working were even used in the shooting of the film. As Kunuk explains:

> We went to the actual location where the story happened. We did it in the Inuit style. . . . For food, we hired hunters to hunt for us so we could eat because we had no catering trucks in the Arctic. The Inuit style of filmmaking takes lots of teamwork. We work horizontally but the usual Hollywood film is in a military style. . . . We put the whole community to work. Costumes, props, we had a two million dollar [Canadian] budget, and one million stayed with the people of Igloolik. The people learned to practice their own cultures, and language.[30]

Actors, crew, and support people enacted some traditional customs that had been neglected. The film's narrative thus celebrates some of the same Inuit practices and morality that helped shape the filmmaking. (More about Igloolik Isuma's production methods are included in chapter 5.)

As the credits roll, *Atanarjuat: The Fast Runner* breaks its story's frame to show scenes exposing some of the methods of its making. Audiences see the ancient Inuit story being enacted side by side with the new custom of Inuit video making, a practice able to create pictorial representations of both the old and the new. Juxtaposing these ancient and modern practices together on-screen for a few minutes at the end demonstrates to audiences that such practices are complementary, not incompatible, ways of being in the contemporary world. Traditional Inuit storytelling can go on around campfires and also around television and movies screens. Traditional communities can hunt together and also make feature films together, while respecting ancient Indigenous organizational forms. In these closing images, then, *Atanarjuat: The Fast Runner* foregrounds a perspective increasingly shared by Indigenous filmmakers around the world.

Future Adaptations

Indigenous feature filmmakers face the daunting task of trying to counter the effect of earlier, widely disseminated misrepresentations on Indigenous, as well as on non-Indigenous, audiences. At the same time, many Indigenous filmmakers seek to make movies that will help perpetuate cultures that previously relied primarily on oral traditions. Indigenous filmmaking is, then, for these Indigenous filmmakers as much about finding new ways of being Indigenous as about being a filmmaker. As Kunuk explains, Indigenous filmmakers seek to bring their ancient arts of "storytelling into the new millennium." There is urgency in many such projects, as Kunuk further states, for often Indigenous peoples need to "unlock the silence of our elders before they pass away."[31] In this way, movies, one of the most complicated of advanced technologies, can become tools for telling stories whose origins stretch back to human beginnings.

   Atanarjuat: The Fast Runner relies exclusively on an ancient oral tale, while *Whale Rider* adapts a traditional story to a contemporary situation. Even films like *Rabbit-Proof Fence* and *Smoke Signals* that do not rely either on older stories or on traditional ways of working can help combat earlier stereotypes and misrepresentations as well as prepare audiences to watch more challenging Indigenous films. The diversity displayed by these four film "hits" is repeated and even expanded across the dozens of lesser-known Indigenous films discussed in the chapters that follow.

Chapter 2

The Films of Chris Eyre

Most audiences want to see Indians a certain way. I want to change that paradigm.

Chris Eyre

Smoke Signals, discussed in chapter 1, was the first feature film directed by a Native American to receive a national theatrical release. The film's critical and commercial success created opportunities and, in the following ten years, *Smoke Signals'* director, Chris Eyre (pronounced "air"), directed or produced seven more features, about half of all the Indigenous movies made in the North American region during this time. Before reaching age forty, Eyre had established himself as the most prolific Indigenous feature film director in the world.

Eyre rejected opportunities to move to Hollywood and make commercial films with non-Indian stories. Instead, Eyre settled in South Dakota, where he chose projects that reflected his personal interests, whether they promised financial rewards or not. *Skins* became Eyre's first feature after *Smoke Signals* and, next, came three movies made for television, each later released as stand-alone DVDs: *Skinwalkers* (2002), *Edge of America* (2003), and *A Thief of Time* (2004). Eyre also directed *A Thousand Roads* (2005), a forty-minute, high-definition video installed at the National Museum of the American Indian in Washington, D.C.

Eyre grew up in Klamath Falls, Oregon, the adopted son of white, middle-class, Presbyterian parents. Eyre recalls that they "didn't try to provide me with a culture that they didn't know themselves, so growing up I wasn't exposed to my Cheyenne/Arapaho culture. When I left that non-Native environment at eighteen, it was a real culture shock for me. People looked at me differently than I looked at myself."[1]

Eyre traveled to Oklahoma at age eighteen to learn more about the Southern Cheyenne and Arapaho communities to which he knew his biological mother belonged. Subsequently, Eyre decided that even though he was raised in a non-Indian world, he had always been Indian. He believes, "We all have an internal genetic imprint that connects us to who we are and our past" (40).

2-1 Chris Eyre, in front of *Skins* poster

Eyre earned a degree in media arts from the University of Arizona in 1991 and tried unsuccessfully for a year to produce a feature, *Things Learned Young*, based on his experience as an Indian raised by non-Indigenous parents. In 1992, Eyre enrolled in the Graduate Film Program at New York University where he wrote and directed several fiction shorts. One, *Tenacity* (1995), shot in Onondaga Territory in upstate New York, follows two Indian boys who discover corruption and violence in an adult world they are not yet old enough to enter. This ten-minute black-and-white short won multiple awards and, eventually, an invitation for Eyre to attend the 1995 Sundance Institute's Directing Workshop. Eyre there began working on ideas that would lead to his collaboration with Alexie and to the path-breaking *Smoke Signals*. When *Smoke Signals* appeared in 1998, Alexie was thirty-two and Eyre was thirty years old.

Eyre told an interviewer, "I'm an amalgamation of two worlds, and I think looking at two sides of things that I can't separate has given me that sensibility called 'humanity.'"[2] Eyre's "two worlds" perspective influences the films he makes in several ways. It has, first, left him uncommonly at ease with telling stories from diverse contemporary Indian tribes. Rather than make films only about his own Cheyenne and Arapaho peoples, in his relatively short career Eyre has already directed and produced films foregrounding Cherokee, Coeur d'Alene, Inupiat, Mohawk, Navajo, Oglala Sioux, Onondaga (Iroquois), Spokane, and Quechuan peoples.

In his youth, Eyre recalls, "I felt like a dark man in a White world."[3] To help understand these feelings, Eyre searched media representations seeking images of people who both looked like himself and seemed at ease in the contemporary world. The absence of these models drove Eyre to become particularly interested in making films that disrupt both negative and positive romanticized stereotypes about Native Americans.

Though, as Eyre maintains, contemporary Indian peoples are among "the most diverse and complicated group of American people," producing films that represent this diversity is especially difficult.[4] Investors and producers avoid films that suggest their Native American characters live much like everyone else and so most Native parts in non-Native productions are found in "leathers and feathers," historical films that commonly look at events associated with Plains Indians in the last half of the nineteenth century. The history of Indians for most audiences, then, is associated with only one region of North America and only one particularly grisly time. With *Smoke Signals* and since, Eyre has aimed to show audiences alternative stories about, as Eyre says, "real Indians, not the romanticized icons" of nineteenth-century America that they are accustomed to seeing.[5]

After reclaiming his Cheyenne/Arapaho heritage as an adult, Eyre looked back with a new understanding at his intense interest as an adolescent in landscape photography. This passion, Eyre now believes, reflected his unconscious desire to discover and know the culture he had lost through adoption. As a teen, Eyre thinks he had been peering out from his white parental world through a camera's lens, seeking to find his biological mother, tribe, ancestors, and spirits. "In high school, I took pictures of landscapes. I spent hours trying to decode the images—trying to find something that resonated with me."[6] Eyre says he was "searching for meaning and a connection between my surroundings and my culture." Eyre's subsequent films continue this gazing as they frequently emphasize the natural environments that surround the characters almost as much as they focus on the characters themselves.

In sum, to varying degrees, Eyre's films reflect his persistent desire to accomplish three tasks: to represent contemporary Indian peoples from diverse tribes, to show them living non-stereotypical lives, and to illustrate their influential relationships with their environments. As we shall see, all Eyre's films discussed below accomplish these three goals, while doing much else as well.

Skins

Skins, a theatrically released feature, was sandwiched between a pair of made-for-television movies. These television movies, *Skinwalkers* and *A Thief of Time*, described later, were part of the popular U.S. Public Broadcasting Service's Mystery! series and so were necessarily formulaic. *Skins,* on the other hand, showed what Eyre could do working outside the boundaries of genre and without the commercial pressures that had surrounded the shooting, editing, and distributing of *Smoke Signals.*

Skins offers little of the uplift or comfort that infuses *Smoke Signals.* *Skins* does contain humor, but its laughs are intertwined with abuse, violence, and death. When a father dies in *Smoke Signals,* the event occurs suddenly and out of sight. In *Skins* a father dies slowly, agonizingly, of cirrhosis of the liver. And this father is simultaneously the central comic figure. It should not surprise, then, that *Skins* did not attract even a tenth of the audience or revenues of *Smoke Signals. Skins'* many innovations and achievements, nonetheless, made notable contributions to Indigenous films in North America and beyond.

One achievement came with its locale. *Skins* was shot entirely on or near the Pine Ridge Reservation, home to the Oglala Sioux Indians in South Dakota. Filming there was more expensive than several alternatives (for example, locations in Canada), but Eyre insisted that no other locations could duplicate Pine Ridge's reality.

Pine Ridge contains the site of the 1890 Wounded Knee massacre, sometimes—incorrectly—said to be the last battle of the four-centuries-long war between European settlers and Native Americans. Made famous through Dee Brown's *Bury My Heart at Wounded Knee: An Indian History of the American West,* Wounded Knee remains the best known though not the worst slaughter carried out by the U.S. military against Indians.[7] Contemporary Pine Ridge is one of the poorest counties in the United States, as it has been for decades; unemployment hovers around 75 percent. *Skins* was the first—and likely the last—feature to be shot on the reservation. Eyre's commitment to the site required the cast and crew to commute each day from the nearest motels an hour away. The poorly paved roads and fatiguing shooting schedule led to three serious car accidents.

Skins opens with documentary footage describing the current Pine Ridge community and with words from a speech made by President Bill Clinton on a visit to the reservation. Clinton is heard in voice-over promising that the federal government will provide the residents with whatever tools they need to succeed. The mockery of such oft-repeated official promises then plays across the screen throughout *Skins* as Eyre's camera travels the rough roads and visits the mostly run-down houses that act as a character in his story.

Pine Ridge's conditions are like those in many third-world nations, and *Skins* does not flinch at representing the realities of such a place. It shows hunger, chronic alcoholism, cruelty, random violence, domestic abuse, and systematic injustice. Many viewers looking for another *Smoke Signals* seem, indeed, to have noticed little else but these horrors the film depicts. Eyre's intention, however, was much different. Pine Ridge and *Skins*, Eyre says in the DVD commentary, demonstrate "the wealth of love, the wealth of spirit that happens in people's houses." *Skins* exposes horrors, certainly, but also glories in Pine Ridge. Eyre here moves beyond the cuteness of *Smoke Signals*. *Skins*, Eyre says, "is the most realistic Indian movie every made."[8]

Skins' complicated script was written by Jennifer D. Lyne and based on a novel by poet Adrian C. Louis, who taught on Pine Ridge. Rudy Yellow Lodge (Eric Schweig) stars as a reservation cop, and viewers ride along as he encounters the everyday problems that constitute his working day. We meet veteran actor Gary Farmer, who also worked with Eyre in *Smoke Signals* and *A Thief of Time*, playing an alcoholic who dies ignominiously in a maliciously set bear trap. Characters come and go, and subplots are often introduced then little developed. These diverse characters and fragments add complexity and texture, as do the exteriors and interiors of the diverse array of Pine Ridge houses the camera visits during the film's eighty-four minutes. Pine Ridge is poor, viewers see, but not everyone there is poor. Pine Ridge has its horrors, the audience learns, but few of its people are horrible. Indian people are a paradox, Eyre insists, and no simple formulation can accurately capture who they are.

Reservation cop Rudy Yellow Lodge is on-screen during most of the film, but it is his brother, Mogie Yellow Lodge, played by Graham Greene, whose performance centers *Skins*. Greene is a veteran Oneida actor who has appeared in over one hundred films and television programs, including the path-breaking *Powwow Highway* and *Dances with Wolves*. Greene's Mogie is a Vietnam veteran in the late stages of chronic alcoholism. Mogie's frequent public drunkenness humiliates Rudy, as when Mogie is shown in a televised interview with one more of the many reporters who occasionally descend on Pine Ridge. "And you, sir," the attractive female reporter asks the disheveled Mogie, "what would you suggest the government do to improve living conditions on the rez?" Mogie answers, "I want the Great White Father in Washington to send me a big woman and when I sleep with her she'll cover up all the cracks in my shack to stop the wind from blowing through."

Mogie displays the complications that Eyre is so interested in presenting. He is alternatively ridiculous, pitiful, comic, dignified, and lovable. Even in the last third of the film, when he appears on-screen with his face horribly disfigured with burns, Mogie laughs at, and induces audiences to laugh at, his grotesque condition. In the documentary "On the Set" included with the *Skins* DVD, Greene says of his character, "What I like about Mogie is that he always keeps his sense of humor, right up to the end. *Skins* offers people a reflection of some pretty gruesome conditions, but it takes them there gently, and with humor. It's a brutal piece to do, but a healing one, too."

Skins concludes with Rudy paying homage to his just-deceased brother. Mogie had earlier asked that the two brothers work together again, as they had before bad times came, to do something dramatic to Mount Rushmore, "for our people," Mogie has said. "Give them a good laugh. Maybe that's all we need." Rudy had rudely dismissed Mogie's request then, but at the film's end, Rudy drives the short distance from the reservation to this sacred site, seized from the Lakota after the Black Hills War in 1876–1877. Rudy climbs above the four carved faces of United States presidents to heave a bucket of red paint. Later, Rudy and the audience discover this paint has created a long red tear that runs down George Washington's cheek. Washington seems to be crying for Mogie, for the Lakota, for the long, sad history of white-Indian relations. The sight gives Rudy and viewers the "good laugh" Mogie had wanted.

2-2 George Washington cries at the conclusion of *Skins*

Skins was released into the post–September 11 hysteria that swept the United States, and some critics found this long red tear to be an irresponsible desecration of a patriotic American symbol.[9] Eyre was forced to defend the scene. It is not a defilement, he insists in the DVD commentary, as much as it is the act that Rudy chooses for honoring his dead brother. "The Black Hills were sacred and the first desecration to some people was that these presidents were carved into the stones. By putting paint on, is it possible to desecrate a desecration?" Almost a year to the day after September 11, 2001, Eyre told another interviewer:

> *Skins* is a very patriotic movie. Rudy as a trickster is making a statement. He's counting coup. Patriotism isn't about waving a flag. It's about exercising your right to challenge, to question and improve and to open up dialogues about ways to make this country better. What we are fighting for is the right to say what we want to say in this country.[10]

Edge of America

Edge of America premiered as a 2004 Sundance Film Festival "opening night" film. It later earned Eyre the 2006 Directors Guild of America award for "Outstanding Directorial Achievement in Children's Programs." Though made for television, *Edge of America* has also been well received as an independent DVD. The film differs from all of Eyre's other features in using a non-Indigenous person as its lead. This allows Eyre to once more explore the problem of stereotyping that is part of all of his films, but to do so by illustrating that these misunderstandings work both ways: A black coach falsely stereotypes Indians, and they also falsely stereotype him.

Edge of America is loosely based on the true story of Jerry Richardson, who coached the girls' basketball team on the Navajo Nation Reservation in Shiprock, New Mexico, in the 1980s. (Richardson's story was also told in the two-hour documentary *Rocks with Wings* [2002], played on national public television in the United States.) *Edge of America* changes the location, in part because the tribal leaders at Shiprock refused to allow filming in their community. *Edge of America* shifts the story to Utah and to the Three Nations Consolidated Reservation School.

Kenny Williams (James McDaniel) arrives at the reservation high school mid-year, prepared to teach English. Students and teachers are startled to discover he is black. Some students ask, for example, why his name is not Kareem. Soon Williams is convinced to begin coaching the school's much-mocked and long-losing girls' basketball team. The team gets better and better under Williams's often draconian tutelage until, finally, they make it all the way to the Utah State finals. Williams's coaching methods then grow even harsher and, on the eve of the championship game, the girls rebel.

This surprising mutiny and its aftermath are but one of many ways in which Eyre and screenwriter Willy Holtzman push the familiar coach-team plot into unexpected directions. Adults save "needy" students in films such as *To Sir, With Love* (1967) and *Hoosiers* (1986) that pioneered this genre while, in *Edge of America*, it is the outsider who enters the supposedly underprivileged community who has the most to learn.

2-3 The team waits to play in *Edge of America*

The reviewer for *Variety* praised *Edge of America* for lifting "spirits without leaving the audience feeling manhandled."[11] The film accomplishes this difficult balancing of message and entertainment in part by surrounding Coach Williams with many different characters that illustrate Eyre's persistent message about the contemporary diversity of contemporary Indians. There is, for example, the team's assistant coach, Annie, played by the veteran actor Irene Bedard, the voice of Disney's animated Pocahontas and also a featured character in *Smoke Signals*. Annie as often teaches Coach Williams through her silences as through what she says. Still when, late in the film, Williams demands, "Tell me why I'm pissed off," Annie tells him, "Because you're a black man in America." Williams answers, "That's right, I'm good and pissed off." Annie replies, offering direct advice for the first time, "You're talking to Indian people here. Get over it, get on with it, or get the hell out."

Another veteran actor, Wes Studi, plays Cuch, a jack-of-all-trades. Cuch repairs Coach Williams's often broken car at a sometimes glacial and at a sometimes comet-like pace. He offers jokes that may be advice in disguise and advice that may be mostly jokes. Together, at the end of a road far out in the high desert, Cuch tells Williams, "From here you can see forever—the past, the present, the future. See, the Creator scattered us to the four winds so we could prove that we're human by finding our way home." Williams is suitably impressed. "This is like, what, a sacred site or something?" he asks. "This?" laughs Cuch. "This is just a big rock."

Professional storyteller and actor Geraldine Keams plays a traditional weaver and a basketball player's reluctant mother. The basketball team members, too, are clearly differentiated to illustrate that these Indian teenagers are as diverse as Indian adults. *Edge of America* also includes carefully framed shots of the Utah landscape, shots through which Eyre once again suggests that the grandeur of Indian country surpasses the human dramas taking place within it.

Eyre's Hillerman Mysteries

Eyre directed *Skinwalkers* and *A Thief of Time*, two made-for-public-television movies produced about the same time as *Edge of America*. Both *Skinwalkers* and *A Thief of Time* adapt novels by Tony Hillerman, the non-Navajo author of fifteen mysteries that feature two Navajo characters, Lieutenant Joe Leaphorn (Wes Studi, seen in *Edge of America*, too) and Officer Jim Chee (Adam Beach, the co-star of *Smoke Signals*). Though *Skinwalkers* and *A Thief of Time* are necessarily solidly within the mystery genre, Eyre is able in both to continue his commitment to filming Indians from diverse cultures, to showing them to be complex characters, and to foregrounding the specific landscapes that shape who they are.

The plot and mystery of *Skinwalkers* is built on the Navajo belief in *Yea-Naa-gloo-shee*, powerful beings that travel in shape-shifting animal forms. The murders that Leaphorn and Chee must solve in this movie may, or may not, have been committed by shape-shifting beings. A more mundane crime, thefts of ancient pots, drives the narrative in *A Thief of Time*, but unique elements of Navajo culture are still woven through this film. So, for example, an unexplained Anasazi spirit woman protects an archaeological site in *A Thief of Time*. And, as is his wont, the trickster Kokopelli comes and goes, playing a flute.

2-4 Leghorn and Chee work together in *Skinwalkers* (©WGBH, Larry Gus)

Skinwalkers concludes with brief glimpses of a healing ritual for Leaphorn's seriously ill wife. Practices and rituals like this are frequently depicted in both films, with little explanation. Their meaning may raise questions for outsiders, Eyre says in the *Skinwalkers* DVD commentary, but simultaneously their presence provides "a certain level of depth for people who understand what these people [on-screen] are doing. . . . I think that's the most intelligent way to make these movies."

There are many complex Indian characters in both *Skinwalkers* and *A Thief of Time*, lawyers and criminals, for example, as well as storekeepers and doctors, medicine men, and handymen. Sometimes, in fact, both films feel more like character studies than the suspense thrillers they aspire to be. Among the wealth of characters, it is the tensions between Detective Leaphorn and Officer Chee that most ground both films, as they do, too, Hillerman's books. The films push these tensions further by making Leaphorn less knowledgeable about Navajo tradition than he is in the books. The Leaphorn of the films is urban-born and educated, a recent arriver on the reservation. He is dedicated to empirical inquiry and suspicious of spirits and skinwalkers, as he is of all forces that he cannot directly see. Chee, on the other hand, is a child and lifetime resident of the reservation. He is a novice police officer who is simultaneously training to become a medicine man. As Eyre points out, cinematic Indian healers are usually shown to be old with long white hair; making Chee a young traditionalist, however, "is as contemporary and as traditional as it can get."[12]

Skinwalkers concentrates more on Chee, while *A Thief of Time* more often foregrounds Leaphorn. In each film, the contrasts between the two men carry the narrative forward. Leaphorn is approaching the end of his career; Chee is near the beginning of his. Leaphorn is long and mostly contentedly married; his wife is alive in both films, though she is deceased in Hillerman's novel *A Thief of Time*. Chee is single and, in his own laconic way, across both films developing a romantic relationship. Leaphorn is reserved; Chee wears his feelings on his face and, sometimes, on his fists. The differences between the two men make it clear that even Indians working in modern-day law enforcement are likely to be as dissimilar from one another as they are from the diverse audiences watching these films.

Though made for television and smaller screens, *Skinwalkers* and *A Thief of Time* nonetheless display Eyre's continuing commitment to shooting landscapes as characters as important as any of the principals in the script. After much traveling and shooting at multiple locations around the reservation, *Skinwalkers* concludes with multiple views of a small Navajo healing hut carefully situated in the context of the grand Four Corners New Mexican landscape in which it stands. Leaphorn gazes down from afar as his wife (Sheila Tousey) is led inside, maybe to be helped by medicine man Chee. Leaphorn now seems a little more at ease, a little more in place, through shots of him juxtaposed with shots of the healing hut, which stands, viewers sense, itself in harmony with the hill on which it sits.

A Thief of Time similarly emphasizes its landscapes. There are, for example, multiple interior shots that frame actors in doorways, in front of windows, and silhouetted inside cars in ways that call attention to the capacious New Mexican plains and mountains that loom behind. Everyone, whether urban or rural, traditionalist or anti-traditionalist, is photographed similarly, as a small creature living within an immense landscape they can traverse but never dominate.

In *Skinwalkers*, a Navajo physician, Dr. Stone (Michael Greyeyes), tells Chee that the old Navajo ways are outdated superstitions. "It's over,"

Stone insists. "See, you and the stick wavers like you, you're a dying breed. The mumbo jumbo, the bogus rituals, it's all teetering on the edge of extinction." This sentiment, so often uttered by colonists, settlers, and imperialists, is here voiced by a western-trained and western-identified Indian doctor. Both *Skinwalkers* and *A Thief of Time*, however, reject this point of view to insist, instead, that the "mumbo jumbo, the bogus rituals" do have a place in modern life, as do Dr. Stone's own allopathic medicines and rituals. Keeping these diverse elements in harmony was the old, as it is the modern, Navajo challenge.

A Thousand Roads and Beyond

Skins was shown on the Pine Ridge Reservation as a way of thanking the community for its cooperation. This screening was a part of the "Rolling Rez Tour 2002," a unique series of showings that brought the film to eleven Indian communities across North America. Eyre traveled hundreds of miles with the semitruck that hauled a mobile cinema trailer, outfitted with a 35 mm projector, one hundred luxury stadium-style seats, surround sound, air conditioning, and a concession stand. Admission was free, and Eyre met with the audiences to discuss the film and to share his belief that *Skins* "is more than just a movie. It's a place, hopefully, for healing."[13]

Around this same time, Eyre began work with Creek writer Joy Harjo and writer, producer, and director Scott Garen to create a signature film for the National Museum of the American Indian. The Museum wanted a film to show to its visitors for many years, and so specified that the finished work 1) be shot for wide-screen super-35 mm high-definition video projection, 2) last for about forty-five minutes (so it could be shown in the Museum theater hourly), and 3) reference the experience of Indians from across both North and South America.

These daunting requirements led to *A Thousand Roads*, a forty-five-minute fiction film based on a script by Harjo and Garen, directed by Eyre. The film includes four vignettes exploring the claim, "Though we journey down a thousand roads, all our roads lead home." *A Thousand Roads* emphasizes visual storytelling over dialogue and is held together by its consistently stunning wide-screen images, prayerful tone, and poetic rhythms. *A Thousand Roads* seems, indeed, as much like an extended pan-Indian chant as a fiction film.

The first segment of *A Thousand Roads* focuses on a Mohawk stock-broker (Alex Rice) who pauses at her computer keyboard in a contemporary Manhattan office to carefully arrange a row of polished stones, thus integrating an ancient ritual with the secular sacraments of capitalism. Later, on a busy sidewalk beneath steel-and-glass canyons, the stockbroker meets another Mohawk. They discover the bond that connects them through speaking Mohawk. The stranger offers a gift, a Mohawk song the stockbroker recognizes.

In a second episode, a ten-year-old Inupiat girl (Riana Malabed) is relocated from Seattle to begin a new life in Barrow, Alaska, when her enlisted mother is deployed to join the American occupation of Iraq. The girl meets her extended family for the first time and learns that her grandfather fought in World War II and her uncle in Vietnam. A third vignette shows a Navajo gang member (Jeremiah Bitsui) tending sheep on the mesas of New Mexico. In the final segment, a Quechuan healer (Honorato Nanatay) journeys across the Sacred Valley of the Incas in Peru to heal a sick child. He enacts an ancient ceremony that includes coco leaves and condor feathers.

Despite its differences in length, format, and venue, *A Thousand Roads* maintains the same emphases as Eyre's feature films. There is much attention to landscape and to understanding human actions in the culturally specific places within which they occur. *A Thousand Roads* also demonstrates Eyre's continuing ease at working with Indian peoples from very different regions. The film, in addition, allows Eyre to once more counter romanticized images of Indians with representations of protagonists who rely on their separate traditions to help them with the challenges they face today. John Trudell, a Santee Sioux and the film's narrator, explains, "We all belong to the story of our people." As is fitting for a film that will be viewed annually by many thousands of non-Indigenous as well as Indigenous museumgoers, *A Thousand Roads* implies that non-Indian peoples belong to their cultural stories as well.

Their work together on *A Thousand Roads* inspired Eyre and Garen to found the film company Seven Arrows Signature, to assist Indian groups across North America. The National Museum of the American Indian had turned to outsiders to accomplish its goals, so, Eyre and Garen reasoned, other Native American groups might similarly have project ideas requiring professional assistance. Tribes newly flush with casino money are increasingly being solicited to provide funds for films (e.g., *Black Cloud* [2004], *Naturally Native* [1998]), but Seven Arrows Signature aims instead to help tribes originate projects with messages they wish to publicize. Eyre says he and Garen ask, "How can we produce a feature, short, or documentary to tell people what you want them to know?"[14] Once projects are developed, tribal members will be trained in all areas of production, building toward a time when each tribe can produce media without outside help.[15]

In addition to co-founding Seven Arrows Signature, Eyre has served as producer for both *The Doe Boy* and *Imprint*, films described in chapter 8. Yet another film produced by Eyre, *California Indian*, is in pre-production. As he has now already for a decade, Eyre continues to seek the resources to produce a film based on the life of Leonard Peltier, who has been imprisoned for decades in the United States. Peltier is considered by Amnesty International and many others to have been unjustly tried, convicted, and imprisoned for the murder of two FBI agents killed in a shootout in 1975.

If a big-budget film directed by Eyre telling Peltier's story were to be made and prove successful, Eyre would gain significant power, enabling him to make more tribal, regional, and local, as well as more big-budget, films.[16] Eyre has accomplished so much in his first decade of feature filmmaking that there seem few limits on what he might achieve in the rest of his career.

Chapter 3

David Gulpilil in Two Worlds

I done a lot for the people. I done a lot for Australia. I done a lot
for the outsider world. Why? Because I got culture and language.
One red blood.

David Gulpilil, *One Red Blood*

David Gulpilil is one of the best-known and most prolific Indigenous
actors in the world. He first gained international attention while still an
adolescent when he shared the lead with Jenny Agutter in Nicolas Roeg's
Walkabout (1971).[1] Gulpilil's much-praised debut performance abruptly
transformed his life. Examining that life here will reveal the changes that
have occurred in the last few decades for Australia's and many other
Indigenous peoples. Gulpilil's life story also illustrates how very difficult
making progress was and continues to be.

Gulpilil grew up among the Mandipingu, one of several Yolngu tribes
associated with Australia's Northern Territory. He seldom saw outsiders
as a boy and remembers playing in the bush with a friend when they
spotted a plane coming in to land. Once a white pilot stepped out, Gulpilil
and his friend hid, unsure if the pilot was a man or a ghost.[2] By age fifteen,
Gulpilil spoke six Aboriginal languages and was already an expert hunter,
tracker, singer, and champion dancer. Indeed, it was Gulpilil's remarkable dancing at a remote mission in Arnhem Land that caught Roeg's
attention and led to his casting Gulpilil as the unnamed "Aborigine boy"
in *Walkabout*.

His work on the set of *Walkabout* was bewildering for the young
Gulpilil, as it was painfully unlike anything he had ever tried to do.
Gulpilil desperately missed his family, his tribe, his familiar homeland,
as well as the rituals and daily life he had known before. "I didn't speak
English," he recalled years later. "I had no words. The tears were falling.
I didn't know what was going on. I had to cry for myself."[3] Later, to

promote the finished film, the now sixteen-year-old Gulpilil was put on a plane for the first time and taken on a world tour, to Hong Kong, where they rushed to find a suit for him to wear, to Cannes, and to Hollywood. Gulpilil was treated as a celebrity by some and as a primitive curiosity by others. Throngs crowded to glimpse in person the exotic, charismatic "native" Roeg had shown them romping nude across *Walkabout*'s wide screen. Gulpilil was introduced to many of the day's luminaries, too, such as Marlon Brando, John Lennon, Bob Marley, Jimi Hendrix, Muhammed Ali, and Bruce Lee, most of whom Gulpilil had never heard before.

In the following decades, Gulpilil appeared in thirteen more feature films, as well as in shorts, television series, and a few made-for-television movies. When not on a shoot or a promotion tour, Gulpilil has usually lived on or near his tribal land in Arnhem Land. During most of Gulpilil's adult life, his shelter had no electricity or running water. He collected from a watering hole about a mile away. When home, Gulpilil hunts for much of his food, as do his tribal peers. Gulpilil differed from other elders mostly in that he sometimes left for months to work on a film. On shoots, Gulpilil said in 2001, "I live in the modern world with a knife and fork. When I go back to my traditional world I live with spear and *woomera* [spear-thrower]."[4]

3-1 Gulpilil at home in *One Red Blood*

Gulpilil's frequent transitions between two such different worlds have never been easy. According to Rolf de Heer, director of *The Tracker* (2002) and *Ten Canoes* (2006), Gulpilil's understanding of white culture remains "so incomplete that it's profoundly fractured."[5] Airlie Thomas, Gulpilil's fourth wife, concurs. "I don't think he feels any more comfortable [in white culture] than he did 20 years ago. Things don't change at all in Ramingining, but things change incredibly fast in the Western world from year to year."[6] Gulpilil's struggles have included problems with alcohol, a substance not allowed on his tribal land. In 2000, at age fifty-five, Gulpilil was convicted a sixth time of drunk driving and sentenced to prison. There he suffered the additional humiliation of having his hair cut short for the first time in his life. He was further humiliated upon release after two months with an additional two-months' required residence at an alcohol rehabilitation program.

In 2002, Gulpilil won the Best Actor award from the Australian Film Institute (AFI) for his performance in *The Tracker*. "Thanks," Gulpilil deadpanned to the assembled AFI members and national television audience. "I deserve this." Indeed, Gulpilil's willingness to live for decades alternatively in two very different and often clashing worlds has made him worthy of many awards. Gulpilil's decades of film work also illustrate many of the challenges and triumphs familiar to Indigenous peoples. I review Gulpilil's career in some depth here, then, to honor his pioneering accomplishments as well as to illustrate the difficult circumstances that still confront many Indigenous actors and filmmakers around the world.

Walkabout as Path Breaker and Myth Keeper

English director Nicolas Roeg had spent only a few weeks in Australia a decade before when he arrived in 1969 to begin shooting *Walkabout*. Roeg's only prior feature, *Performance* (1970), starring James Fox and Mick Jagger, has sparked critical debates for decades, in large measure because of its psychedelic imagery and frenetic editing, a style that anticipated many music videos and film action sequences to come. Roeg's cinematic Australian landscape in *Walkabout* is similarly presented with a hallucinogenic intensity. It is poetic, beautiful, and full of food and life, radically unlike perceptions of the land as harsh, ugly, and barren that had led white Australians to call the outback the "dead heart" of their country. A visiting English filmmaker's vision thus became almost a new standard perspective for white Australians. The film, Louis Nowra claims, guided white Australians to see the outback "as something wondrous, mysterious and sensuous. It took a stranger in a strange land to reveal this to us."[7]

Walkabout broke new ground, too, in presenting Gulpilil as its emblematic Aborigine. When Aborigines had occasionally been shown on-screen before the 1970s, they were commonly depicted as "evil hordes stalling white Australia's attempts to colonize the country."[8] Settler Australians thus generally considered the continent's First Peoples to be more animalistic and repulsive than figures of beauty. Just four years before *Walkabout*, Aboriginal roles were sometimes even played by white actors in blackface, as with, for example, Ed Devereaux playing a supposedly Aboriginal tracker in *Journey Out of Darkness* (1967). Roeg disrupted these traditions of negativity by filming Gulpilil as another component of the magnificent landscape, and one similarly poetic, handsome, and full of life. And Gulpilil's graceful performances, especially his repeated dance sequences, captivated audiences around the world.

Walkabout was also much noticed because of its occasional frontal nudity. The boy (Luc Roeg, the director's son) and the two teenagers, Gulpilil and Jenny Agutter, expose their bodies in ways that in contemporary America could produce felony convictions not only for Roeg and his crew but even for audiences who might briefly gaze at these under-eighteen actors. Roeg's use of Indigenous people as a pretext for extended nudity in this film continued a long tradition in Anglo-American films, one especially prominent in films made about Africa and also the islands of Polynesia. Still, Roeg did innovate by focusing almost as much attention on Gulpilil's body as he did on Agutter's. Before and since, the male gaze of most mainstream filmmakers has seldom ogled men and black men even less commonly.

3-2 The swimming idyll in *Walkabout*

More significant than the film's admiring focus on Gulpilil's male body, however, is *Walkabout*'s depiction of Gulpilil as a typical (as the script describes him) "Black Boy." The film begins with this grossly inaccurate caption:

In Australia when an Aborigine man-child reaches 16 he is sent out into the land. For months he must live from it. Sleep on it. Eat of its fruit and flesh. Say alive. Even if it means killing his fellow creatures. The Aborigine calls it the walkabout. This is the story of a walkabout.

It is difficult to imagine how more inaccuracies could be stuffed into so few words. It is not true that most or even many young Aborigine males in 1970 or any era were sent away from their communities on a quest for months or even for days. It is not true that "walkabout" is an Aborigine concept; it is a settler idea created in part to express colonial disapproval of Aborigines who did not commonly share their settler bosses' devotion to wage-labor and who, instead, sometimes left their jobs on white homesteads and missions to return to their own communities for visits and ceremonies. Even today in Australia, when one loses one's concentration or fails to complete a task, one is sometimes said to have gone "walkabout."

The formal, faintly biblical language of *Walkabout*'s opening caption anticipates the film's embrace of the familiar western myths of paradise and of humankind's supposed fall from grace. Gulpilil begins the film possessing none of civilization's "sophisticated knowledge," especially of the difference between what westerners think of as good and evil. In the logic of the film's fable, once Black Boy glimpses the white people's knowledge, he must die. As Nowra writes, Black Boy's death at the end of the film produces the "terrible feeling" that it "means more than his own death. It seems to represent the death of Aboriginal culture itself."[9] Indigenous people are of the past, *Walkabout* suggests, while the future belongs to people such as the filmmaker and others from industrialized cultures around the world. Echoing Rousseau and many others, Roeg's film laments this triumph of western culture while nonetheless perpetuating the myth that the earth's Indigenous noble savages are fading away.

Though now honored in Australia as a screen classic, *Walkabout* provided a disquieting beginning for Gulpilil's career. He would have to appear in several decades of subsequent films that often repeated many of these same colonial myths before finally being offered roles that presented Australia's First Peoples more as they understand themselves. Still, throughout these decades, as Aboriginal anthropologist Marcia Langton says, "in his own ironic and charismatic way," Gulpilil was always working in his film roles to undermine "the stereotypes that were forced on him."[10]

Exploring Stereotypes

Walkabout's success led to Gulpilil being given third billing in director Philippe Mora's low-budget *Mad Dog Morgan* (1976), starring Dennis Hopper as Daniel Morgan. The film adapts the American western genre to tell a violent, true fugitive-chase story from Australia's colonial past. Gulpilil plays a tracker, Billy, a role he would reprise in *Storm Boy* (1976), *The Tracker,* and *Rabbit-Proof Fence* (discussed in chapter 1). Gulpilil also performs Indigenous songs and added music from a didgeridoo to the sound track. He dances, too, in *Mad Dog Morgan,* and it is probably in part because he danced in both of his first two films that Gulpilil has continued, as he says, to think of his acting as a form of dance performance. Gulpilil continues to dance in tribal ceremonies and for fun whenever he returns to his homeland. As a tribal elder, Gulpilil is obligated to lead some of the ritual performances. The polish that international audiences find in Gulpilil's screen appearances seems in part an effect of Gulpilil's many years of traditional dancing.

As in *Walkabout,* the plot of *Mad Dog Morgan* draws upon a simplistic contrast between a western-imagined version of Gulpilil's supposedly unchanging, "primitive" tracker world and the dynamic, historical world that Hopper represents. Still, Gulpilil's Indigenous character is granted a personality; he is more than just an emblematic Black Boy, as he was in *Walkabout.* And, significantly, Gulpilil has many English-language lines in *Mad Dog Morgan,* the first of many English-speaking roles to come.

In *Gulpilil: One Red Blood* (2002), a documentary created at Gulpilil's request by Aboriginal filmmaker Darlene Johnson, Gulpilil recounts the struggles he continues to face in learning English dialogue. His first exposure to the language did not come until he was fifteen. Since then, he has still been around English speakers mostly in irregular spurts, while filming or promoting a film. Even after decades of filmmaking with English directors, actors, and crews, then, Gulpilil cannot read English well enough to study a script. He depends on others to read and reread his lines. Still, even in his speaking parts in *Mad Dog Morgan,* it is apparent that Gulpilil is on the way toward English oral fluency. By the time of Gulpilil's third film, *Storm Boy,* shot soon after *Mad Dog Morgan,* Gulpilil's pronunciation on-screen had become impressive.

Like *Walkabout, Storm Boy* is now considered a classic of Australian cinema. *Storm Boy* was much more commercially successful than either of Gulpilil's earlier films and made the actor into a celebrity throughout

Australia. "This was the film that departed from every other Australian film in which something about Aboriginal people appeared," Marcia Langton explains.[11] As Fingerbone, Gulpilil befriends and becomes a mentor to a lonely ten-year-old boy living, motherless, with his reclusive fisherman father. As in *Walkabout* and *Mad Dog Morgan*, Gulpilil plays an Indigenous man with both valuable knowledge of and intimacy with the natural world. And once again, as in the earlier two films, *Storm Boy* encourages the idea that good Aborigines should be available to assist settlers in their substantial material and spiritual need. This time, however, Gulpilil's Indigenous character is even more individualized. He is, as Langton explains, "absolutely adorable. Thousands of people fell in love with him, mostly children. So David became the Aborigine mascot for Australian school children."[12]

Gulpilil's next film was director Peter Weir's complicated *The Last Wave* (1977). As Chris Lee, Gulpilil again played a stereotypically spiritually wise Aborigine, but the film also countered other stereotypes. Gulpilil and other Aborigines here are placed within a contemporary urban environment, Sydney, thus for the first time acknowledging the presence of Australia's Indigenous peoples beyond rural settlements. Cities, too, the film suggests, are tribal lands. And, most important, *The Last Wave* was the first of Gulpilil's features to attempt to present Indigenous beliefs both accurately and appropriately. Aboriginal elders were consulted and agreed to allowing some ideas, rituals, and costumes to be shown while prohibiting others.

Abruptly, however, after steady progress both in the sophistication of Gulpilil's roles and in the overall representation of Australia's First Peoples from *Walkabout*, to *Mad Dog Morgan*, to *Storm Boy*, through *The Last Wave*, for almost twenty years the progress stopped. Gulpilil's films became little more than attempts at commercial exploitation of Aboriginal stereotypes.

Gulpilil made a small appearance as an Aboriginal man in Philip Kaufman's international blockbuster, *The Right Stuff* (1983), and then found himself again as a stereotype, though now as part of a joke, in *Crocodile Dundee* (1986), probably Australia's best-known and certainly its most commercially successful film.

Gulpilil makes his entrance bare-chested and in ceremonial paints in *Crocodile Dundee*. He peers menacingly out from behind a tree at night, frightening Sue (Linda Kozlowski), Crocodile Dundee's citified girlfriend. Dundee eases her panic by inviting his "old friend" Neville Bell

(Gulpilil) to join them at the campfire. Soon after, Kozlowski raises her camera. Gulpilil protests, "Oh, no, you can't take my photograph." Kozlowski apologizes, "I'm sorry. You believe it'll take your spirit away." And Gulpilil replies, "No. You got lens cap on."

Crocodile Dundee grossed over $300,000,000. Though Gulpilil received prominent billing for his small part and also worked as a chore-ographer for some scenes, he was paid only $10,000. The notoriety that the film brought to both Australia and to Gulpilil, along with the scant pay with no residuals, pained Gulpilil for years after. His meager contract may have been a result of poor negotiations, racism, or both. But the fact that his scene in the film was shot near his house, in his homeland, served to increase his sense that he was much taken advantage of.[13]

3-3 Mates together in Crocodile Dundee

Gulpilil appeared a year later in the mostly forgotten Dark Age (1987), an Australian-based film that hoped to take advantage of the interna-tional popularity of Jaws (1975), which was, the producers knew, to be followed by Jaws: The Revenge in 1987. Dark Age reprised Jaws' plot with the outback taking the role of the menacing ocean and crocodiles playing the part of murderous sharks. The killer monster croc in Dark Age is finally captured but, rather than being destroyed, is placed on a flatbed truck and used as the focus for an extended car chase. As this absurdity suggests, Dark Age's lack of commercial success probably did not result from outdated stereotypes of the outback or of Aborigines.

Gulpilil seems to have forgotten or repressed working on Dark Age, for in 2002 he remembered, "After Crocodile Dundee, it just cut. There was no filming, no script for me. Not even a tour. There was nothing. I feel bad. I thought I would be an international star by now. . . . But they left me out."[14] He had completed eight feature films in his first sixteen years in the business, but after *Dark Age,* for the next fourteen, Gulpilil appeared in none. He concluded, "I always think I did a lot of work, a job, for the people and the people didn't turn back and pay me back, payback."[15]

Eroding the Myths

In 1987, Australia presented Gulpilil with his first official government honor, the Member of the Order of Australia. In 2001, he received a second official honor, the Centenary Medal. In the intervening years, however, Gulpilil was offered no significant roles. He felt personally rejected and was especially despondent since it seemed to him that he had sacrificed much more to participate in moviemaking than had most of those with whom he had worked. To make each film, Gulpilil had had to leave his growing family, his wives and children, his community, and his ancestral land to travel for days, sometimes by foot, sometimes swimming rivers. Then Gulpilil would be surrounded by people that he was expected to understand but who made little effort to understand him.

Finally, the long drought in roles was broken with an offer to work in Wim Wenders's *Until the End of the World* (1991). Gulpilil was gratified to be working again, especially with a director whose reputation was as large or larger than any Gulpilil had acted for before. Gulpilil's role in the film, however, was small and repeats the cliché that Australia's Indigenous people possess the "primitive" knowledge that westerners lack. In *Until the End of the World,* that knowledge includes how to directly communicate telepathically, without relying on "modern" mediated images such as those provided by computer, television, and the very movie screens that Wenders is using to communicate with his audiences. In *Until the End of the World,* once again, too, Australia's Indigenous people are represented as eager to share their knowledge with invading westerners.

Five years later, in Gulpilil's next film, *Dead Heart* (1996), the representation of Aboriginal culture finally began to move beyond the level of stereotypes presented in Gulpilil's films over the preceding two decades. Both settlers and Aborigines are struggling in *Dead Heart* to find their places in modern Australia's outback, the "dead heart" of the title. Neither group is shown to be associated entirely with good or evil, and neither seems to have a firm understanding of which parts of their cultures, European and Indigenous, they want to retain. There are tradition-based

Aborigines and post-tradition Aborigines; Aborigines who like white settlers, who hate them, and who are indifferent. *Dead Heart* thus counters the message of so many of Gulpilil's and other earlier Australian-based films. Indigenous culture is here not presented as an alternative to modern western culture, existing in a timeless realm separate from history. Aborigines do not possess secrets that westerners lack, nor are they people eagerly waiting for outsiders to invade their communities so they can share what they know. Perhaps in part because it broke so many stereotypes, *Dead Heart* received a lukewarm critical and box office reception, both in Australia and beyond.

Gulpilil next had a small role in *Serenades* (2001), a pioneering film that found even less of an audience than *Dead Heart*, in large measure, no doubt, because it tells the story of a minority within a minority: the story of the daughter of an Aboriginal woman and an Afghan man. The man was one of many hundreds of camel drivers who immigrated to Australia in the 1860s when the use of these desert-hearty animals was at its peak. Though set in the nineteenth century, *Serenades* continues the trend toward greater complexity and specificity of representation initiated in *Dead Heart*.

Then came the watershed year of 2002, when five Aborigine-themed films appeared. Gulpilil played a prominent role in one, *Rabbit-Proof Fence*; then, for the first time since *Walkabout*, he played the lead again in *The Tracker* (2002). With these two films and the three others also released in 2002—*Australian Rules*, *Black and White*, and *Beneath Clouds*—the trend toward complexity, specificity, and appropriateness in representations of Australia's First Peoples reached a long overdue maturity.

The Tracker

Gulpilil's role as Moodoo, the tracker, in *Rabbit-Proof Fence* was path-breaking in at least three respects. For decades, Gulpilil had appeared in films that told white people's stories; *Rabbit-Proof Fence* was the first of his films to be based on an Aboriginal story. The film was also a departure from Gulpilil's earlier films because, for the first time, Gulpilil himself was not the primary on-screen face of Aboriginal Australia. The focus of the story, instead, is Everlyn Sampi and, to a lesser extent, her sister and cousin, played by Tianna Sansbury and Laura Monaghan. For the first time, too, Gulpilil plays a villain or, at least, a close ally of a villain. There are hints in *Rabbit-Proof Fence* that Gulpilil is not pursuing the fugitive girls with all his skills, that he is permitting their escape. Still, in most scenes Gulpilil is closely associated with the white Australian authorities the audience is positioned to root against.

Gulpilil's performance in *Rabbit-Proof Fence* earned him a nomination for Best Actor in a Supporting Role from the Australian Film Institute (AFI). He did not win this lesser award, however, perhaps because he was that same year also nominated for AFI's Best Actor in a Leading Role award for his part in *The Tracker*. For this, his first starring role as an adult after thirty years of professional acting, Gulpilil not only won the AFI award and additional awards from other organizations, he also won gushing reviews from writers around the world. Even reviewers who did not like the film commonly offered something like Walter Addiego's recommendation in the *San Francisco Chronicle* that audiences "[s]ee the film mainly for the quiet and powerful work of Gulpilil in the title role."[16]

The Tracker was written, directed, and produced by white Australian filmmaker Rolf de Heer, who also wrote the lyrics for the many songs that sometimes make the film operatic. *The Tracker* is de Heer's film at many levels, then, and so certainly should not be thought to present an Aboriginal point of view. Nonetheless, *The Tracker* signaled important changes in Gulpilil's career even beyond providing him at last with a vehicle through which he could display his matured acting skills.

The Tracker begins, like Gulpilil's earlier films, in a world dominated by white people, laws, and customs. Gradually, however, that familiar world fades and, by film's end, Aboriginal peoples, laws, and customs dominate. Early on, long takes of the Flinders Mountain Range show a profound emptiness, but as time passes first one, then a few, and finally entire small tribes emerge to fill that emptiness. The situation seems clear in the opening scenes: a white posse and hired Aboriginal tracker are pursuing an Aborigine fugitive. However, the situation becomes more ambiguous and complex. Finally, it is not clear who is chasing and who is chased, who is fugitive and who is the representative of white laws. Even the very idea of justice undergoes transformations.

De Heer makes prominent use of fourteen stylized landscape and figurative paintings by Peter Coad, a non-Indigenous painter well known in Australia for blending Aboriginal motifs and vast landscapes. De Heer cuts to framed stills of these paintings in *The Tracker,* interrupting the live action while diegetic voices and sounds continue in the background.

3-4 Gulpilil enchained in *The Tracke*r

The stopped action forces audiences to think about what they have been watching, to create some analysis of their viewing experience. The paintings thus suggest that the film's events are larger than the movie, that they are perhaps emblematic or mythic in some way.

The Tracker reveals some of the changes in Australian cinema that have occurred over the course of Gulpilil's life. Gulpilil's character hangs himself in the 1970s' *Walkabout*, a victim of his encounter with a white girl and white culture. Three decades later, in *The Tracker*, Gulpilil hangs the leading white character, The Fanatic. He administers this justice not because The Fanatic has broken Aboriginal laws, even though the two are by this time in the film deep in tribal lands. Instead Gulpilil invokes western laws of justice as he speaks the same clear Latin to issue The Fanatic's sentence that he has also used earlier in the film when offering a Christian prayer over the grave of The Veteran.

Gulpilil's character is no longer a victim in *The Tracker*, as he was in *Walkabout*. He is a triumphant survivor, as are the Aboriginal peoples who teem across the landscape at the end of the film. No longer are audiences to conclude that Australia's Indigenous peoples are dying out in the face of settler modernity. Rather, *The Tracker* suggests that the deeper one looks into Australia's history and future, the more prominently will the continent's First Peoples appear.

Ten Canoes

Gulpilil had a supporting role in *The Proposition* (2005), but by far the most significant next step in his career came from his continuing work with de Heer. During filming of *The Tracker* and afterward, Gulpilil exhorted de Heer to help make a movie based on an Aboriginal story, in Aboriginal languages, using only Aboriginal actors. At first the two considered telling an Indigenous story that, after ninety minutes or so, would end abruptly with a massacre of the main Aboriginal characters by white invaders. This would have been another version of *The Tracker* but told from an Aboriginal point of view. Gulpilil, though, decided that the film instead should be built around a photograph of ten men in canoes that anthropologist Donald Thomson had taken of Gulpilil's ancestors in the 1930s.[17]

The result was *Ten Canoes*, a film that won lavish praise from the Aboriginal people it represents as well as from international audiences (including a Special Jury Prize at Cannes in 2006). "Everything is changing, everything is going, going, gone now," one resident of Ramingining who acted in the film said. "Maybe they gonna keep this film with them so they can put it in their head."[18] Michael Dawu, another tribal member, explains that *Ten Canoes* "bring me my memory back and my energy."[19]

Ten Canoes works as a cultural artifact in part because its scriptwriting, pre-production, and shooting were guided by the Yolngu people themselves. De Heer explains, "They're telling the story, largely, and I'm the mechanism by which they can."[20] The community decided that the Thomson image of the men in bark canoes and also the activity of hunting for geese and goose eggs must be at the center of the entire film. They also insisted that the era of their ancestors not be in any way criticized or represented as a time of conflict.

Furthermore, the Yolngu people relied on their own culturally appropriate procedures in casting the film. The ten men pictured in the photograph were identified and roles were assigned according to which contemporary people were most closely related to them. Casting was also manipulated so that the relationships of the players on-screen did not contradict current relationships; no lower-ranking contemporary played at being higher ranking than he or she actually was.

The film works as a cultural treasure as well by using languages from the Yolngu Matha group, mostly Ganalbingu but also some Mandalpingu. Each of these languages is the primary tongue of fewer than 1,000 people and so is among the world's most endangered languages. *Ten Canoes* aims to help make speaking Ganalbingu and Mandalpingu seem important, prestigious, and worth learning to the young people in Arnhem Land most tempted to neglect these languages. Gulpilil provides a voice-over in Mandalpingu for some versions and in English for others, but all on-screen characters speak only Indigenous languages. Subtitles are provided, but the community decided that no dubbing would be allowed, to ensure that *Ten Canoes* in all versions celebrates Aboriginal speech. At the *Ten Canoes* showing at the Toronto International Film Festival, the subtitles were inadvertently omitted and yet most of the unknowing audience still found the film immensely enjoyable "just for the imagery and the hypnotic cadence of its [Aborginal] language."[21]

Ten Canoes begins with Gulpilil's voice-over summarizing his tribe's origin story. He speaks about the first fishes, which became humans, and about abandonment, swimming in vaginas, and dying to be reborn and continue life forever. The film that follows this prelude is, among many things, a story about storytelling itself. At the end, Gulpilil summarizes, "Now you've seen my story. It's a good story, not like your story but a good story all the same." In *Ten Canoes*, after thirty-five years of filmmaking, Gulpilil can for the first time claim that he is telling his own story and not just another outsider's story about Aborigines.

In many of his earlier films, Gulpilil's emblematic Aboriginal characters were presented as noble savages, as pre-moderns with little or no future. *Ten Canoes* provides clear evidence that, in fact, the Yolngu inhabitants of Ramingining remain a vibrant community that has not disappeared through assimilation and death.

Integrating the Two Worlds

Ten Canoes marks, one can hope, the end of the divided existence that Gulpilil has led since Roeg abruptly altered his life by casting him in *Walkabout*. *Ten Canoes* also demonstrates both how far Australian filmmaking has progressed during Gulpilil's career and how successfully, with the right circumstances, the medium can be integrated into the lives of Indigenous people.

Of course, hundreds more Aboriginal-controlled films are needed to begin to correct the many misunderstandings and prejudices created, in part, by earlier movies. Happily, at Ramingining at least, more such films are being made. In addition to relearning old skills while creating *Ten Canoes*, some of the participants also learned new filmmaking skills. After the film's release, an ambitious multimedia Many Canoes project continued coaching additional people in the community.[22] Peter Djigirr worked as de Heer's co-director and was trained to begin directing on his own. David Gulpilil's son, Jaime, had prominent dual acting roles in *Ten Canoes* and soon after co-starred with his father in a short film also shot in Arnhem Land, *Crocodile Dreaming* (2007), directed by Aborigine Darlene Johnson. Filmmaking for Gulpilil and his community is becoming an activity not exclusively associated with the white world but rather one that combines ancient storytelling and contemporary filmmaking practices to create new traditions that can be shared with family, tribe, and ancestors. The two worlds that Gulpilil has oscillated between for forty years thus show signs of a fertile integration. "We are the brothers and sisters of the world," Gulpilil says near the end of the documentary about his life. "It doesn't matter if you're bird, snake, fish, or kangaroo. One red blood."[23]

Part Two

Concepts, Challenges, and Confusions

Chapter 4

Some Challenges of Indigenous Films

White is the ultimate condition towards which the grand narrative of evolution, progress, civilisation edges. Everyone else wants to be White, they think.

Marcia Langton, *Blacklines*

Diversity characterizes audiences for Indigenous films as well as the films themselves. It is thus difficult to summarize what any Indigenous film "means" or, sometimes, even to specify with authority what its central plot or conflicts may be. *The Land Has Eyes* (also known as *Pear ta ma 'on Maf*, 2004), made by Indigenous filmmaker Vilsoni Hereniko, provides a useful example of the difficulties. This film has been featured at film festivals across the world, shown on the Public Broadcasting Service network in limited markets in the United States, and released in a few theaters in Hawai'i, Oregon, and Washington, as well as in Australia and New Zealand. In addition, *The Land Has Eyes* was shown on makeshift screens on the Pacific island of Rotuma, where it was shot. The diversity of responses across Rotuman and non-Rotuman audiences has been immense.

Divergent Audiences

At Sundance, Moscow, Montreal, and Shanghai, to name a few of the film's diverse festival venues, audiences typically experienced *The Land Has Eyes* as a coming-of-age story situated among people living in "primitive" conditions on an exotic tropical island. Most have seemed to agree with Duane Byrge, film reviewer for the *Hollywood Reporter*, who writes, "At once an illuminating ethnography of a remarkable people, 'The Land Has Eyes' is most satisfyingly a tale of triumph and assertion."[1] It is "most satisfying," that is, for the sorts of viewers that

Byrge represents, as a story mainstream audiences will recognize as having already seen dozens, if not hundreds, of times. These audiences experience *The Land Has Eyes* through the prism of previously seen feature films and documentaries about "natives" who live in thatched huts near warm oceans.

Rotuman viewers experienced the film differently. In 2004, anthropologist Alan Howard assisted Hereniko and his wife, Jeannette Paulson Hereniko (the film's co-producer), with a week of eight screenings at seven locations on Rotuma.[2] The island has no dedicated movie theaters and no island-wide electricity. Rotuma sits in isolation in the world's largest ocean, 325 miles north of Fiji. Only nine miles long and two miles wide, the island is often left off maps made by continent-based cartographers. The estimated population is about 2,500. Filming on location there in 2001 required that the imported crew of twelve be lodged, fed, and transported to various locations by generous Rotumans, since the island has no hotels, guesthouses, or rental cars. Local chiefs, in fact, pursue an explicit policy of discouraging tourism. Most Rotumans raise the bulk of their own food. Hereniko's sister, Vamarasi, journeyed to Fiji months ahead of production to import and fatten several cows to prepare for feeding the crew and actors during the shoot.

Audiences for *The Land Has Eyes* in Rotuma assembled at diverse improvised sites, including community halls, government buildings, schools, and hospitals. Viewers often had to scramble and strain to find a place where they could see the makeshift screens. The Herenikos and Howard, simultaneously, often had to scramble, too, to locate a generator to power the projector they had flown over from Fiji. Each viewing site also brought its own challenges for finding a suitable spot on which to mount some simulacrum of a movie screen. The first showing, for example, in the village of Salvaka near where much of the film was shot, required borrowing a bedsheet from a nearby hospital. This was stretched and hung on a Ping-Pong table turned on its side. The sound track that night played through an amplifier with two speakers loaned from a private village home.

An unscheduled eighth showing was added when the flight back to Fiji was delayed. Howard reports attempts that night to set up in an open pavilion at the government station were frustrated by the absence of a solid backdrop and by heavy rains. "Prospects looked bleak, but we went across the road to the hospital and checked out the possibility of showing the film on the hospital verandah, which provided more shelter. The

4-1 *The Land Has Eyes* screened on a hospital veranda in Rotuma
(Courtesy of Alan Howard)

doctor was very accommodating and helped us tack up a sheet between two poles at one end of the verandah; he and the nurses then brought out a number of benches and chairs for people to sit on."[3] Many watched while sitting on the ground; others stood outside under umbrellas. A few unlucky others viewed the film through the back side of the sheet.

These physical circumstances for watching *The Land Has Eyes* on Rotuma differ not only from the viewing circumstances of most first world audiences but also from the situations in which many other Indigenous people view feature films made by and for them. The Inuit-made *Atanarjuat: The Fast Runner*, for example, was mostly seen by its primary audience of Inuit as a VHS tape played on generator-fueled televisions.[4] Central and South American Indigenous feature films are frequently screened as parts of fiestas, as a type of performance alongside many other more traditional embodied forms of festival performance. Sometimes, too, these films are traded as videotapes in village markets alongside traditional crafts and foods.[5]

Differences in audience experiences, of course, are grounded in much more than the mere diversity of physical circumstances in which films are shown. The cast of *The Land Has Eyes* was, for example, with two exceptions (the veteran actors Rena Owen and James Davenport) composed entirely of Rotumans selected from auditions on Fiji and on Rotuma itself. Howard reports that seeing familiar people "act" parts different from their everyday roles dominated the viewing experience of many Rotumans more than did the film's narrative. Rotuman audiences also often interrupted the film with raucous laughter, outbursts rarely approximated by festival audiences for the film. *The Land Has Eyes* is in Rotuman, with English subtitles, and Howard speculates that much of the subtlety and humor of the dialogue is lost on non-Rotuman speakers. The film, as well, is built upon an understanding of the pleasures and irritations of daily life in a Rotuman village where privacy is scarce, an understanding few outside Rotuma bring to their viewing experience. Howard observed that most audiences on Rotuma paid as much attention to how accurately mundane details were represented in the film as they did to the film's story. Rotuman audiences did not view the film, then, like the *Hollywood Reporter* writer, as a familiar tale of triumph, to be judged against previously seen films that told related stories. Instead, for Rotuman audiences, *The Land Has Eyes* called forth comparisons to life itself.

Of course, the narrative that structures *The Land Has Eyes* was not entirely neglected by Rotuman viewers, especially by the many who chose to see the film on its island tour a second and even a third time. Here again, however, there seem significant differences between the experiences of Rotuman and of non-Rotuman audiences. Some viewers at cosmopolitan film festivals said they were troubled that *The Land Has Eyes* includes a sympathetic portrayal of a British colonial administrator. So, for example, in Heidelberg, Germany, a professor complained that this white administrator was made to seem "too good." One film festival director on the other side of the world even refused to accept the film for showing because of what he termed "the film's ultimate assertion of faith in the authority of the colonial arbiter." Most Rotuman viewers, on the other hand, remember enough of their history to know that nineteenth-century Rotuman chiefs voluntarily petitioned Queen Victoria to annex Rotuma to England. Most believe Rotuma was generally well treated by subsequent English administrators from 1881 until it became a part of Fiji, in 1970. To have depicted a malign administrator like that which contemporary outsiders expect would have made *The Land Has Eyes* seem unrealistic to Rotuman audiences.

Part of many outsiders' uneasiness with the colonial administrator rests on their perception of the ending of *The Land Has Eyes*. The rejecting film festival director, for example, complained that the white administrator asserted too much power. An anonymous Internet review similarly complains, "The moral of the story seemed to be that native islanders will try and screw each other over, but as long as there is an essentially decent white governor to step in, all problems will be solved."[6] Rotuman audiences, however, do not see the film as suggesting that the white governor has resolved the climactic dispute. For them, final authority in the film and in the island rests with invisible spirits and Rotuman chiefs. The film shows spirits disrupting a meeting where chiefs consult with the white administrator. While Rotumans recognize these invisible forces are using the on-screen administrator to produce their triumph, non-Rotuman audiences do not. Here again, different cultural expectations produce very different experiences of the "same" film.

4-2 Viki questioned by Judge Clarke (Courtesy of Te Maka Productions)

Differences in cultural knowledge have similarly produced different conclusions about the era in which *The Land Has Eyes* takes place. Clothes, houses, roads, trucks, canoes, and many other mundane details, including the very presence of a British administrator, signal to Rotumans that *The Land Has Eyes* depicts not the current island but Rotuma as it was in the 1960s. Howard reports that young people at Rotuma showings sometimes even laughed at the old-fashioned appearance of some of the people and places presented on-screen. Film festival audiences, however, generally assume the film depicts contemporary Rotuma. Based on earlier movies made by outsiders, these audiences expect Pacific Islanders to enact exotic, simple cultures "frozen in time." Just as outsider viewers are not ready to accept that Rotumans and other Indigenous people sometimes had mutually beneficial relations with foreigners, many are unable to view Indigenous people as heirs to histories as complex, long, and varied as those possessed by non-Indigenous people.

Differences like these between non-Indigenous and Indigenous experiences of *The Land Has Eyes* likely occur across screenings of most Indigenous films. For example, screenwriter Sherman Alexie, of Spokane and Coeur d'Alene descent, reports:

> When I first showed *Smoke Signals* in Spokane to a largely Indian audience, we had to reshow it immediately because everyone had been talking so much and laughing so much. But when I showed it at the Nantucket Film Festival [in Massachusetts], it was very quiet during the showing. There was some laughter, but I don't think they saw the humor in it. There was certainly none of the raucous laughter of Indian groups watching the film.[7]

Indigenous films will likely continue to provide very different experiences for their very different audiences. In these pages, and for much time to come, assertions about what any Indigenous film "means" must thus be offered with considerable caution.

Film as Knowledge and Power

Interpretive caution need not mean interpretive silence. Many Indigenous filmmakers actively seek non-Indigenous audiences and their responses, no matter how misinformed. They hope their films will help change perceptions based on earlier outsider misrepresentations. So it was, for example, with *Smoke Signals*, the first major-release film made under the creative control of Native Americans.[8] Directed by Chris Eyre, of the Cheyenne and Arapaho tribes, *Smoke Signals* repeatedly mocks earlier non-Indigenous representations of American Indians. One of its principals, Victor (Adam Beach), blames fellow Indian Thomas's (Evan Adams) awkwardness on too many viewings of *Dances with Wolves* (1990). "Do you think that shit [in *Dances with Wolves*] is real?" Victor complains. "God. Don't you even know how to be a real Indian?"[9]

Smoke Signals aims to change how non-Indian audiences perceive what it means to be an "authentic" native in North America today. *Atanarjuat: The Fast Runner, The Land Has Eyes, Ten Canoes* (2006), and many other films associated with Indigenous people similarly aspire both to engage and educate their audiences.

Nonetheless, a little knowledge is dangerous, and the little that may be acquired from films about what it is to be a "real Indian" or any other type of Indigenous person can be especially dangerous. When films show a canoe being constructed in *Ten Canoes*, preparations for a ritual sweat in *Skins*, ice-house building in *The Journals of Knud Rasmussen*, Indigenous dancing in any of dozens of films, or similar depictions of native customs, audiences generally assume they are seeing the "real" thing. People are accustomed to learning new skills through watching videos, so filmed sequences of native practices are assumed to be opportunities for more learning.

Audiences also treat non-Indigenous commercial films as windows into reality, but the mischief such perceptions can cause is usually far greater in Indigenous than in non-Indigenous films. Consider, for example, how often people throughout the world assume they can learn about the people of the United States through watching Hollywood films. Audiences frequently draw distorted conclusions from these films, but no American film is likely to be the only one that audiences see representing American behaviors. Audiences will generally view many other films that temper and broaden their cultural generalizations. Each Indigenous film, however, is likely to be the only one, or one of a very few, that audiences see showing customs of the Indigenous people represented. The depiction of Inuit ice fishing in *Atanarjuat: The Fast Runner*, or Māori barhopping in *Once Were Warriors*, or Sámi skiing in *Pathfinder* (*Ofelas*, 1987) are likely the only representation of these customs that most audiences will ever witness. Most such representations will thus seem "true" in the absence of alternatives, even though most capture these Indigenous practices no more completely than would, say, a few minutes of a Hollywood film showing a Catholic mass or teenagers cruising a shopping mall.

The negative effects of film representations on non-Indigenous societies are further reduced because most viewers have access to multiple sources of information about dominant societies. Hollywood certainly shapes outsider perceptions of the United States, but most world audiences can also learn about the country through books, magazines, and television. Many viewers, too, are likely to have traveled themselves or to know others who have traveled in North America. Few in the festival or theatrical audiences for *The Land Has Eyes*, however, possess much information about Rotuma beyond the misrepresentations that earlier movies have taught them about the supposed lives of Pacific Islanders. Similarly, few of the millions who watch *Atanarjuat: The Fast Runner*, *Smoke Signals*, or *Whale Rider* will ever encounter other accounts of the Inuit, Coeur d'Alene Indians, or North Island New Zealand Māori. The feature films associated with these peoples will thus likely become many viewers' sole sources of knowledge about the customs and people shown.

There is a final and especially consequential difference between the impact on audiences of Indigenous and non-Indigenous films. The distorted view of American life produced by Hollywood films does relatively little harm because most non-American audiences lack the power to interfere in the internal affairs of the United States through decisions that draw on their filmic knowledge. So, the misunderstandings that Rotumans or reservation-based Native Americans acquire about the United States through watching Hollywood movies seldom impact American lives. The misunderstandings that Americans have about Indigenous peoples, however, have encouraged policies such as nearby nuclear bomb testing, toxic waste dumping, child removal to government-run schools, clear-cutting of forests, mining-based water pollution, and much more. In general, then, non-Indigenous audiences that watch Indigenous films have much more power over the people there represented than Indigenous people have over non-Indigenous audiences.

For multiple reasons non-Indigenous audiences should be wary before concluding they have gained knowledge about any Indigenous people from watching their movies. Even feature films completely controlled by the Indigenous people represented are, after all, but ninety minutes or so of picture-based storytelling. No feature film or collection of feature films can provide the knowledge a person needs before making conclusions, judgments, or decisions about another culture.

The Indigenous to Non-Indigenous Continuum

There is not much agreement about what constitutes an Indigenous feature film, and some of the many obstacles to establishing a firm definition are examined in chapters 5 and 6. For now it is sufficient to explain that this book views Indigenous and non-Indigenous films as labels at the extreme ends of a continuum. Some films, such as *A Bride of the Seventh Heaven* (2001), *The Journals of Knud Rasmussen*, and *Mile Post 398* (2007) with Indigenous writers, directors, actors, and content, clearly belong close to the Indigenous pole of the continuum. Others, films such as *Apocalypto* (2006), *Dances with Wolves* (1990), *Little Big Man* (1970), with few of these elements, can be easily placed at the non-Indigenous end. Many films, however, lie at points between these extremes. So, pioneering Māori filmmaker Barry Barclay's first feature film, *Ngati* (1987), lies near the Indigenous end of the continuum, built as it is on Barclay's direction and on a Māori screenplay with mostly Māori actors. It is not "purely" Indigenous, however, since much of the production crew and many of the principal actors were non-Indigenous. Similarly, a film such as *Dances with Wolves* sits very close to the non-Indigenous end of the continuum. Still, because it features some Native American actors and some use of the Sioux language, *Dances with Wolves* is a little closer to being Indigenous than are many hundreds of other Hollywood films that represent Native Americans. Mel Gibson's *Apocalypto* uses Mayan actors speaking the Mayan language but makes no effort to utilize Mayan storytelling forms. Like *Dances with Wolves*, then, *Apocalypto* is more a Hollywood than an Indigenous film. Still, because *Apocalypto* showcases Mayan actors speaking the Mayan language, it is bit more Indigenous than a feature film that depicts native people using non-Indigenous actors and languages.

The rest of this book focuses on the increasing number of feature films that cluster toward the Indigenous end of this Indigenous to non-Indigenous continuum. I do not try to specify exact degrees of indigeniety nor do I intend to create a definitive list of what should, and should not, be treated as an "authentic" Indigenous film. The diversity of feature films sitting toward the Indigenous end of the continuum is already great, and this diversity seems likely to accelerate as even more of the world's thousands of Indigenous peoples begin making feature films. We can no more foresee the future shape of these films than anyone could have foreseen the future shape of Hollywood's movies in the first decades of their production. It seems both foolish and counterproductive to attempt to define or categorize this diversity. It is enough, I think, to acknowledge that, however defined, for many years to come an increasingly rich assortment of feature films associated with Indigenous people will be appearing to challenge, and sometimes rebuke, the cinemas of colonial and imperial nations.

The Value of Diversity

Though not adequate as sources of knowledge, Indigenous feature films provide powerful evidence of the cultural diversity that Indigenous peoples offer to the contemporary world. Census taking among Indigenous peoples is more guesswork than science, of course, so estimates of the total worldwide Indigenous population range widely, from as few as 250 to as many as 600 million. Though less than 5 percent of the total world population, Indigenous people nonetheless speak approximately 95 percent of the earth's remaining languages and, probably as well, nourish a comparable percentage of the earth's remaining cultural diversity. With many forces currently working to make societies more alike, the plentiful variety found among Indigenous peoples on all continents and across many thousands of islands is becoming increasingly valuable. This rich range of cultural diversity is likely as essential to a healthy human future as biosphere diversity is to a healthy Earth.

Films such as *Atanarjuat: The Fast Runner, Pathfinder, The Māori Merchant of Venice, The Land Has Eyes,* and *Ten Canoes* that rely on native speakers of Indigenous languages promote the vitality of these languages and also the cultures in which they arose. Even the many Indigenous feature films that speak colonizer-introduced languages promote cultural diversity by encouraging new generations of Indigenous youth to value their Indigenous identities. Non-Indigenous audiences need not treat these films as sources of knowledge, then, to find in them demonstrations of the wonder and value of human differences.

There is, however, a danger in emphasizing differences too much, for this can lead to expectations that all Indigenous films will spotlight exotic peoples, places, and practices. Such expectations can lead to disappointment when Indigenous films present characters and situations much like those found in non-Indigenous films. Since, however, many Indigenous people are much like non-Indigenous people, an expectation of difference denies the right of some Indigenous people to make films about who they truly are. Films such as *Jindalee Lady* (1992), *Samoan Wedding* (2006), and *Smoke Signals*, for example, have been criticized on just these grounds, arousing complaints that they present their Indigenous characters as being too much like non-Indigenous people. Being Indigenous, however, in some places and situations is so much like being non-Indigenous that few differences will be found.

A second and opposite danger also stalks discussions of Indigenous features, the danger of denying difference. Sometimes observers include Indigenous peoples and their productions within Anglo-European notions of a presumed universal "family of man." All people everywhere are claimed to possess similar desires and pleasures. Cultural differences, in this view, are but variations on common human themes, and so may be deemphasized, altered, or even eliminated without diminishing the humanity of the Indigenous peoples thus transformed. Long a staple assumption of anthropologists and other social scientists, as Edmund Carpenter explains, in this perspective, "The message is clear: we should love them because they are like us." And, indeed, viewers of Indigenous films do need to see the characters on-screen as enough like themselves to make the story seem to be about people rather than about animals or aliens. Still, thinking of Indigenous people as "like us" represses the question, "What if they aren't like us?"[10] If some group of others is fundamentally different, should they then be hated? Eliminated? Encouraged to change to make them more like us?

It seems to me that some cultural differences are deep, unbridgeable, and incommensurate. In watching many Indigenous films then, non-Indigenous viewers are probably better off accepting that the film's Indigenous characters differ fundamentally from their foreign audiences. Even though radically different, however, Indigenous people should nonetheless be, if not loved or even liked, at least encouraged to flourish independently from the cultures, economies, and universalizing perspectives of globalizing nations.

Some people doubt Indigenous perspectives can be successfully translated on to the screen. Traditional oral storytelling is too unlike a cinematic narrative, they fear, and so once Indigenous stories are translated to film they become mostly western and no longer "authentically" Indigenous.[11] Similar fears were once voiced about how movies represent Shakespeare, the Bible, and other classic western written texts. Now, though, it is generally accepted that film adaptations can reinvigorate older European traditions for new generations. The Shakespearean tradition did not disappear in the film adaptations of Olivier, Branagh, and Luhrmann. Instead, centuries-old texts and staging were transformed for new times. There seems no a priori reason why feature films cannot similarly translate Indigenous stories into new forms that help keep traditional Indigenous cultures alive.

I try in this book to avoid the risk of expecting all Indigenous peoples and films to be very different and also to evade the danger of expecting these films to show people like myself. When I fail to walk this tightrope, as I sometimes do, I hope it reflects the difficulty of the task of intercultural communication more than my lack of effort. If engaging with Indigenous feature films were as uncomplicated as engaging with non-Indigenous features, the potential benefits would be much less.

Chapter 5

Uses and Abuses of Indigenous Films

Filming is like being speared.

Lofty Bardayal Nadjamerrek

Most people today who are labeled Indigenous would in earlier decades have been called savages, pagans, primitives, or uncivilized. The peoples so labeled, then and now, live on diverse continents, inhabit diverse ecosystems, have developed diverse approaches to living, and sometimes even have flourished for many hundreds and even thousands of years separated from most other cultures. Indigenous people are as unlike one another, then, as it is possible for humans to be.

Naming these diverse peoples with a single name was not the work of Indigenous people themselves, of course, but rather part of the imperial practices of explorers, settlers, administrators, and social scientists who invaded their diverse lands seeking profits, conquest, and, occasionally, scientific and social knowledge. Since the practice of applying a universalizing label is associated with histories of misrepresentations and imperialism, it might seem best to shun the label *Indigenous* entirely, especially in a fraught formulation such as *Indigenous films*. Surprisingly, however, the term *Indigenous* is becoming increasingly used by Indigenous peoples themselves as they find that this label can serve their interests, for example, at the United Nations and at other international non-governmental organizations (NGOs). Lumping together diverse films under the label *Indigenous* can have similar positive effects, although, as we shall discuss below, dangers come with this label as well.

Indigenous Uses for Indigenous Films

Rotuman director Vilsoni Hereniko says that Pacific Islanders are "used to being the consumers of images of themselves, so it's important to turn that around and produce their own images."[1] Most other Indigenous people confront a similar need. Some may, like non-Indigenous media artists, wish mostly to create their own images for entertainment, in hopes of making a profit, or out of an artistic desire to produce something new. In addition, however, Indigenous filmmakers frequently share at least two additional desires that distinguish them from other filmmakers. First, many hope their films will help correct the misrepresentations that have been produced by non-Indigenous films and other media. Second, many Indigenous filmmakers want their films to support the survival of the people depicted.

Countering outsider misrepresentations

Though Indigenous people are often on display in non-Indigenous films, these representations commonly present what Ward Churchill describes as "fantasies of the master race."[2] Native American characters in Hollywood westerns provide one of the best-known examples, but colonialist fantasies abound as well in many other genres and national cinemas. Diverse Indigenous people across Africa, the Americas, the Arctic, Asia, Australia, and Oceania have commonly played similar functions for one hundred years in feature films made by outsiders. Each has been depicted as "primitives," as possessors of outdated cultures left over from humankind's pre-modern past. In outsider movies, Indigenous peoples are generally presented as "a simple people lacking in complexity, intellect, or ambition," in short, as less fully human than the non-Indigenous audiences the films entertain.[3]

Outsider-made films have frequently encouraged Indigenous peoples to be embarrassed by their ancestors and inherited cultures. These films have worked as one among many of what Larry Gross calls the "shaming weapons" used by dominant cultures "to convey to the members of ethnic minorities a deep sense of cultural inferiority and inadequacy."[4] Indigenous feature filmmakers frequently aim to reverse the shame that outsider representations have and continue to produce.

Many outsider-made films also depict Indigenous peoples as stubbornly standing in the way of progress, or as threatening invading settlers, or as possessing an animalistic sexuality. Some combinations of these misrepresentations are commonly found even in outsider-made films that intend to praise Indigenous peoples. In those films, for example in *Walkabout, Little Big Man,* and *Dances with Wolves,* outsiders use representations of native cultures to criticize their own industrialized societies as being, for example, too repressed, too unspiritual, or too environmentally insensitive. Even the most affirmative representations of native peoples in such films typically present native peoples as being "close to nature," a concept more often reflecting the perspective of outsider filmmakers than that of Indigenous peoples themselves. Though Indigenous people play prominent roles in these films, neither they nor their cultures are important for themselves. They serve instead mostly to deliver messages from the non-Indigenous filmmaker about the need for his or her own culture to change.

What Comanche writer Paul Chaat Smith says about America's Indigenous people is often true for Indigenous people worldwide: "The movies loom so large for Indians because they have defined our self-image as well as told the entire planet how we live, look, scream, and kill."[5] Some Indigenous people have seen dozens, occasionally even hundreds of films, presenting their culture through the distorting perspectives of outsiders. Many Native filmmakers thus make films that explicitly aim at countering the effect that these earlier misrepresentations have had on their own Indigenous, as well as on non-Indigenous, audiences.

Transmitting cultures

Storytelling has long been fundamental to how most Indigenous peoples articulate and transmit their cultures. As Paula Gunn Allen explains, "The oral tradition is more than a record of a people's culture. It is the creative source of their collective and individual selves. . . . The oral tradition is a living body. It is in continuous flux, which enables it to accommodate itself to the real circumstances of people's lives."[6] Storytellers transmit this body of culture and, as Tewa and Diné filmmaker Beverly R. Singer argues, "Native filmmakers are 'transmitters,' too!"[7]

Speaking was once the primary medium for maintaining the living body of tradition, but now films can contribute to this, too. In many cases, filmmakers aim not to replace oral traditions with cinematic ones but, rather, to revitalize the old in the new. "I think it is a mistake to cast aside whatever has served us so well in the past," Māori filmmaker Merata Mita has explained, "to think that, because we are writing scripts for film, that this is something totally different, that we don't need the lessons of the arts of storytelling that we got from our oral tradition."[8]

Finding ways to use film to perpetuate older traditions may be a necessity for many Indigenous people. So Inuit director Zacharias Kunuk explains, "For four thousand years we have been passing stories to our youth" through speaking. However, Kunuk goes on, "When TV came to Igloolik in 1983 (in time for the hockey series), everyone stopped listening, visiting one another and telling stories. The only way was to put these stories in the box: it was time to tell these stories through TV."[9]

Indigenous feature films that both correct past misrepresentations and also use the screen to reinvigorate older traditions are becoming increasingly important to peoples aspiring to maintain their distinct Indigenous identities. Indigenous peoples all over the world are also discovering that the very process of film production can be turned into an important vehicle for transmitting traditional Indigenous practices. Kunuk's Inuit community in northern Canada offers an especially good example of this.

Inuit Community-based Filmmaking

While residing in one of the most challenging environments on Earth, with a total population of only about 2,500, the Inuit of the village of Igloolik have produced three feature films, *Atanarjuat: The Fast Runner*, *The Journals of Knud Rasmussen*, and *Before Tomorrow*. This community's ways of working may prove inspirational to other Indigenous communities seeking to make feature films while using their own traditional cultural practices.

Zacharias Kunuk, the Inuit director of both *Atanarjuat: The Fast Runner* and *The Journals of Knud Rasmussen*, first became interested in making videos out of a desire to record his father's hunting stories. He began moving away from his successful work as a soapstone carver to become an employee and eventually a manager of the Canadian-government-operated Inuit Broadcasting Corporation (IBC) station in his home village of Igloolik.

5-1 Zacharias Kunuk, Inuit filmmaker

The IBC was charged with providing Inuit programming across the Nunavut Territory, a vast area that makes up about 20 percent of all Canadian land while containing a population of about 30,000 mostly Indigenous people. Kunuk discovered this government-controlled organization had little interest in producing and broadcasting the sorts of visual versions of traditional stories that had drawn Kunuk to video production in the first place. On his own time, then, Kunuk began making such videos, and one of his first works, *Qaggiq/Gathering Place* (1989), earned considerable critical praise. Kunuk also sensed that the IBC's organizational structures were harmful to Inuit community life. "I saw IBC as a dogteam," Kunuk later recalled, with "Inuit producers as dogs, the sled as the Ottawa office and the people who sit in the sled as the board of governors."[10] Kunuk concluded that this hierarchical bureaucracy, managed by people living almost 2,000 miles away, would likely never support productions useful to Inuit communities living by very different rules.

So, in 1990, Kunuk left his job at IBC to form Igloolik Isuma Productions with two other Inuit, Pauloosie Qulitalik and Paul Apak Angilirq, as well as with the non-Indigenous filmmaker Norman Cohn, with whom Kunuk had been working since the mid-1980s. These four provided the company with most of the necessary technical knowledge, but, from the outset, Igloolik Isuma simultaneously relied on Inuit traditions of how people should work together. As Cohn explains, "For four millennia Inuit have refined co-operation as a medium of production and survival, valuing consensus and continuity over individuality and conflict."[11] This collective process guides Igloolik Isuma Productions, which uses as its motto, "Young and old work together to keep our ancestors' knowledge alive." Collaboration takes much longer than traditional film production methods, Cohn says, "but people feel more natural and relaxed and the result is visible on the screen."[12]

Igloolik Isuma determined to find ways to adapt Inuit oral traditions and cultural practices for film. "We started to recreate the past," Kunuk explains; that "was our goal."[13] In 1994, only four years after they began, Igloolik Isuma produced the ambitious *Nunavut: Our Land* (1999), a six-and-one-half-hour documentary broken up into thirteen separate narratives. *Nunavut: Our Land* "dramatizes true stories of today's Elders," the film's official Web site explains, to reenact "a nomadic lifestyle that no longer exists today."[14] *Nunavut: Our Land* focuses on Inuit life stretching across twelve months in 1945–1946, allowing the filmmakers to recreate many of the different activities that occurred in each Arctic season. The mid-1940s was a crucial time, as soon after the Canadian government initiated policies of forced settlement that seriously undermined the Inuit's millennium-old nomadic lifestyle. Kunuk explains, "A lot of our cultural ways that survived for thousands of years have been interrupted and completely changed in the last fifty years. Doesn't make sense, it doesn't make sense. So, just trying to prove that it doesn't make sense. That's my job."[15]

While making *Nunavut: Our Land,* Igloolik Isuma initiated a practice it would increasingly emphasize: using each new production as an opportunity to bring in experienced non-Indigenous crew members to act as teachers of Inuit apprentices. In this way, Igloolik Isuma has created such a large and proficient pool of local talent that its need to import technical expertise is becoming less and less. Indeed, the small community of Igloolik has even become home to other video makers and companies, some with, and some without, connections to Igloolik Isuma.[16]

Despite the clear artistic and cultural success of *Nunavut: Our Land,* Igloolik Isuma struggled for five years to accumulate the relatively modest 1.7 million dollars (U.S.) it took to produce *Atanarjuat: The Fast Runner.* Though Canadian authorities were at first unimpressed with the film, once *Atanarjuat: The Fast Runner* wowed international audiences and won prestigious film festival awards (e.g., the Caméra d'Or Award at Cannes), Igloolik Isuma found it much easier to raise new production funds. *The Journals of Knud Rasmussen,* released five years after *Atanarjuat: The Fast Runner,* was supported by combined Canadian and Danish funds and a robust six-million-dollar budget. A third feature, *Before Tomorrow,* with a mostly female Inuit production crew and a three-million-dollar budget, began shooting even as *The Journals of Knud Rasmussen* was being released.

5-2 Rehearsal for *The Journals of Knud Rasmussen* (Courtesy of Oana Spinu)

Much of the costs for these productions have been spent in Igloolik, producing a major economic boost for the cash-poor region. While encouraging a reinvigoration of Inuit history, culture, and language, then, Igloolik Isuma has simultaneously created a new, relatively clean, community-enhancing business in one of the world's most remote areas. Though its precise strategies may not be applicable for all native peoples, Igloolik Isuma's success demonstrates that feature filmmaking can enhance the lives of contemporary Indigenous peoples while simultaneously reinvigorating older, traditional cultural practices. True to Igloolik Isuma's motto, both their final films and the company's ways of working produce films that show young and old can "work together to keep our ancestors' knowledge alive."

White Shamanism and the Abuse of Indigenous Films

Though, as I have tried to show, there are multiple reasons why non-Indigenous audiences should support Indigenous feature films, there are, as well, dangers that non-Indigenous audiences should avoid. These dangers prominently include what Cherokee writer Geary Hobson and Hopi poet and anthropologist Wendy Rose have separately analyzed under the name of "white shamanism."[17] White shamans are not always white, of course, nor are they particularly interested in authentic shamanism. White shamans are cultural imperialists who appropriate names, concepts, styles, tools, dress, adornment, or practices from Indigenous people without either community permission or training in their proper use.

Viewers of feature films cannot learn enough about the cultural practices they see on-screen to understand the proper contexts in which these practices should be enacted. And no culture's practices can be rightly understood without participation in processes of community acceptance and training. Appropriating activities seen in movies without knowledge of that culture's rules is like adopting the gestures of an on-screen Catholic priest without understanding it is not gestures and vestments but much else that gives the wine and bread its meaning.

Throughout history, of course, people have frequently borrowed ideas, tools, and practices from other cultures without permission, training, or much understanding. In general, these borrowings cause few problems. Troubles do arise, however, when those who appropriate are members of groups with a disproportionate degree of power over those from whom they borrow. So it is when most non-Indigenous audience members adopt ideas shaped by Indigenous feature films. These viewers commonly belong to dominant groups who have earlier, or who may even presently, occupy native lands and claim rights to Indigenous natural resources. When members of these dominant groups also claim the right to appropriate the tools, clothes, music, arts, and spiritual practices of Indigenous cultures, Indigenous people understandably feel attacked. As Margo Thunderbird laments, "They came for our land, for what grew or could be grown on it, for the resources in it, and for our clean air and pure water. . . . And now, after all that, they've come for the very last of our possessions; now they want our pride, our history, our spiritual traditions. They want to . . . claim them for themselves. The lies and thefts just never end."[18]

Because they control most media, dominant peoples can shape how both Indigenous and non-Indigenous audiences perceive Indigenous peoples and practices. So, for example, as Hobson explains, a radically incorrect representation of the North American Indian "medicine man" has often been featured in Hollywood movies, such as in *A Man Called Horse* (1970), *Dances with Wolves*, and *Little Big Man*. As a result, millions of non-Indigenous people now have a similar false understanding of the role of healers in North American Indian cultures. "In reality," Hobson points out, "there was no medicine man. Rather there was—and is—an entire network of medicine people of various categories throughout any given community."[19] Despite this, partly because of movies, across North America there are hundreds if not thousands of fake white shamans currently practicing "healing" ceremonies. These practitioners, generally without Indigenous community support, claim to be perpetuating Indian traditions.

Similar appropriations are common whenever feature films offer representations of Indigenous practices. Hula, for example, is best known throughout the contemporary world to audience members under twenty-five as it is represented in the several Disney films and television shows based on the characters of Lilo and Stich. Disney's animated screen depictions of Hawaiian dancing continue a tradition of film appropriation that began with some pioneering documentaries shot in Oceania at the beginning of the twentieth century. Clara Bow subsequently bowdlerized this native dance in *Hula* (1927), while later Hollywood stars such as Dolores del Rio in *Bird of Paradise* (1932), Eleanor Powell in *Honolulu* (1939), Jane Russell in *The Revolt of Mamie Stover* (1956), and Deborah Walley in *Gidget Goes Hawaiian* (1961), as well as others, established an influential tradition of movie hula. As a result today, at the beginning of the twenty-first century, there are more non-Indigenous people dancing hula in Japan and in the United States than there are Hawaiians dancing hula in Hawai'i. Hula outside Hawai'i has developed different protocols and performance traditions, ones that as often imitate movie hula as much as pre-cinematic hula traditions. Asian and North American hula is, in turn, exerting pressure on hula practitioners in Hawai'i to perform like the images of hula displayed in *Lilo and Stich* (2002) and other films and television programs. These screen-based dances are also what most of the seven million visitors who come to Hawai'i each year expect to see.[20]

5-3 Lilo and Stitch in the world's most often seen hula performance (© Disney)

Though dominant cultures assert much influence over how Indigenous cultures are represented, dominant cultures are themselves seldom threatened with change when Indigenous peoples appropriate their tools and cultural practices. The unique way that Tongans practice Christianity, for example, has not noticeably impacted mainstream Methodism; Inuit use of violins has not altered how Europeans play Mozart. Appropriations of Indigenous practices by any group living in a dominant nation can, however, prove devastating. So, for example, just as the growing number of non-Hawaiian hula dancers worldwide exert pressures on this Indigenous dance form in the islands where hula originated, the small but influential population of white shamans in North America threatens to alter what it means to be a Native American healer.

The dangers of cultural imperialism may not be much diminished even when films are written, directed, produced, and acted by Indigenous people. After all, no films or set of films even by knowledgeable practitioners can enable outsiders to become competent Hawaiian hula dancers or Indian healers. Still, the magic of film is such that audiences tend to believe they are seeing the "real thing" in the cultural practices represented on-screen, especially when they have been told the film's production has been controlled by Indigenous people. No filmed cultural practices, however, can work like those practices do when enacted in embodied contexts.

Film viewers are non-participants, after all, and cannot ask questions or have their impressions corrected. Film viewers also cannot see the entire practice; their vision is limited to the bits of a culture that have been framed on a two-dimensional screen and edited into the final cut. The reality of cultures on-screen is much like the reality of family and friends seen on home videos. Knowledgeable viewers may project strong resemblances onto the cultures and people shown but no one would be long satisfied with mere media representations when they could instead stand alongside the real thing.

Those who know a culture mostly through the power of films should then vigorously resist believing that they understand like those who live that culture. This warning is especially needed for the many non-Indigenous people who believe Indigenous people possess a wisdom non-Indigenous cultures lack. Some western viewers are drawn to In-digenous films and other supposed sites of knowledge about Indigenous people precisely because they are seeking to fill a void they perceive exists in their own cultures and lives. Much that is wrong with modernity, they hope, may be cured by integrating elements from Indigenous perspec-tives into modern life.

Perhaps there is some merit to this view. Perhaps many Indigenous people do live in "harmony" with nature; many may experience deep spiritual connections with the creatures and physical features of their ancestral homelands. Maybe, in fact, much of the psychological malaise of urban dwellers rises from their lack of knowledge and intimacy with the places where they work and live. Still, it seems unlikely that each of the 3,000 or so Indigenous peoples in the world today possesses the wis-dom westerners seek. Some may, but surely not all do. And assimilating potentially useful cultural practices from any Indigenous to any cos-mopolitan context will always be very difficult. It is a mistake, then, to value Indigenous people on the basis of how useful their knowledge or ways of living may be to outsiders. Calculating the use value of Indigenous people, in fact, continues the tradition of colonialism wherein native peoples are engaged with mostly for the benefits they offer to the nations and companies that invade them. The earth's diversity of cultures is best valued for its own sake, I believe, and not because it is hoped this diversity contains answers to the dominant culture's problems.

Even if an Indigenous culture does possess cultural practices much needed by non-Indigenous people, seekers will not find reliable knowledge about these practices in feature films. Films at best offer hints and suggest possibilities. People who sincerely wish to learn about Indigenous peoples should first earn permission to enter those communities and, then, commit the time necessary for difficult learning. Indigenous feature films can be for seekers of wisdom at best but a prefatory moment in a much longer and more arduous process.

Does Media Swallow Culture?

Another form of white shamanism manifests itself in claims that it is impossible for Indigenous people to produce feature films that fairly represent their unique cultures. Media swallows culture, Edmund Carpenter famously explained, after he and his associates gave movie cameras to isolated Indigenous peoples in the 1960s and encouraged them to film themselves. Carpenter hoped each group would manipulate the camera in different ways and that the resulting footage would display each culture as its members saw themselves. The results, however, disappointed Carpenter, and he concluded that in the resulting films "the old culture was there all right, but no more than residue at the bottom of a barrel."[21]

Carpenter's mistake was not in thinking that Indigenous people can produce films uniquely displaying their culture's differences but in greatly underestimating the substantial time required to master cinematic technologies. Carpenter's thrusting cameras on isolated peoples and expecting them immediately to produce unique films was rather like introducing a new musical instrument—a piano or gourd drum, say— with expectations that novice players will immediately produce new music forms. In fact, with sufficient time, different cultures do repeatedly develop novel uses for tools, instruments, and media introduced from other cultures.

Feature filmmaking is one of the most recently introduced and also one of the most complicated tools to be adopted by Indigenous people. Given time, as the diverse films described in this book show, Indigenous peoples can integrate this new technology within their own older, diverse storytelling traditions. Carpenter's dream of Indigenous people creating unique, culturally appropriate cinematic representations

seems in the process of being fulfilled. Indeed, it appears likely that translating Indigenous storytelling traditions to film is often easier than
translating them to other introduced forms, especially to the print form,
which requires reducing the richness of speech to one-dimensional,
linear writing.

Still, skeptics remain, especially among those sometimes known as
media determinists, successors to Marshall McLuhan, Harold Innis, and
others, who maintain that the content and form of Indigenous films matter little since the very act of watching screens transforms all audiences
similarly. These analysts believe that who directs or how cultures are
represented is secondary since, they argue, viewing a television or film
screen in itself alters human consciousnesses more profoundly than do
the specific images displayed. If true, films such as *Atanarjuat: The Fast
Runner, The Land Has Eyes,* and *A Bride of the Seventh Heaven* will always
provide audiences with experiences tied more to the act of movie viewing
itself than to experiences connected, respectively, to Inuit, Rotuman, and
Nenets cultures. For media determinists, Indigenous films are films
first and primarily, so Indigenous films necessarily celebrate western-
technological ways of seeing more than Indigenous ones.

Though provocative, this view seems mistaken in several ways. There
is, first, little evidence that people around the globe are being transformed
into a single homogenous audience through sitting in front of theater,
television, and computer screens. The example of differences in Rotuman
and non-Rotuman viewers of *The Land Has Eyes* described in chapter 4
is likely typical. McLuhan argues in *The Gutenberg Galaxy* that new com-
municative technologies create "new ratios among all of our senses" like
"what happens when a new note is added to a melody."[22] Any new sense
ratios and notes that media may produce, however, depend as much upon
their auditors' and viewers' previous experiences as upon properties "inside" the media itself. A new note will not seem "new" to auditors
unfamiliar with the culture-specific music being played. All "music"
sounds alike to outsiders who lack the training necessary to detect differences. So, to the untrained, the music/noise of Bach and Bartók, of 50
Cent and Eminem, of a Hawaiian oli and a pule, sound the same. The
"same" film shown to differently acculturated audiences thus likely im-
pacts their consciousnesses differently.

It is crucial to note, too, that most Indigenous filmmakers whole-
heartedly reject media determinism. Most make films of and for their
people precisely because they believe this medium helps transmit cultural

practices that pre-date the introduction of western technologies. As Zacharias Kunuk, director of *Atanarjuat: The Fast Runner* and *The Journals of Knud Rasmussen,* explains, Indigenous filmmakers like himself see their films as translations of the ancient arts of "storytelling into the new millennium." There is urgency in many such projects, as Kunuk further states, for some Indigenous peoples need to "unlock the silence of our elders before they pass away."[23]

Since most media determinists are non-Indigenous, perhaps their warnings should be understood as yet another manifestation of white shamanism. Here, once again, outsiders are telling Indigenous peoples how they should live, just as earlier colonialists sometimes warned about the need to "save" Indigenous peoples from innovations such as literacy, electricity, cars, and paved roads by claiming these would "spoil" the indigenes' imagined pre-contact purity.

In general, I think, outsiders err when they advise Indigenous peoples about what is, and is not, authentic and useful to Indigenous cultures. The truth seems to be, as one of Māori novelist Patricia Grace's characters says of the contemporary Māori, "Everything that is new is ours too."[24]

Four Characteristics of Indigenous Films

As I have tried to explain, it is best to avoid embracing strict rules for what is, and is not, an "Indigenous film." Even Indigenous people themselves at the United Nations and at allied NGO forums have avoided creating lists of characteristics that would allow for sorting out who is, and is not, Indigenous. This reluctance in part reflects their recognition that definitions and, in fact, legal thinking itself, are often used by non-Indigenous people to camouflage injustices. So, for example, Erica Irene Daes, chair of the working group that drafted the *Universal Declaration on the Rights of the Indigenous Peoples,* explains that the Declaration avoids specifying who is Indigenous since "historically, Indigenous peoples have suffered, from definitions imposed by others."[25]

As explained in chapter 4, just as one might say that Indigenous people is the name for one end of a continuum, so, too, is Indigenous film best thought of as a name for one end of a continuum. There are people and films that unequivocally cluster at the Indigenous end, as well as people and films that unequivocally do not. Many people and films, also, fit ambiguously at points between the two extremes.

There are four characteristics common to the people and films that cluster at the Indigenous end of the continuum. A film need not possess all four characteristics to be considered Indigenous, but few if any films are likely to be thought Indigenous if they exhibit but one of these four. Possessing some combination of two or more of these characteristics is probably necessary to position most films as Indigenous.

1) Indigenous people who make films generally belong to groups that lack self-governance. They commonly have limited participation and influence over the territorial, economic, and cultural decisions that affect them. Indigenous people thus face multiple threats from external groups and, often as well, from the armies, police, laws, bureaucrats, corporations, and media associated with the nation-states that assert sovereignty over them. In some places, even though Indigenous people form a majority within a territory or nation-state, they are still marginalized by a dominant minority. Indigenous films frequently reflect these asymmetries of power.

2) Indigenous films are made by groups that identify themselves as Indigenous and are accepted as Indigenous by others. This characteristic, rooted in self-labeling, was formalized by the UN Working Group on Indigenous Populations (WGIP) in 1986 to ensure that no people would be excluded from the WGIP due to the vagaries of any formally written, legalistic definition. In practice, as Ronald Niezen points in *The Origins of Indigenism,* this acceptance of self-identification has generally worked well. All peoples who come to the WGIP are allowed to participate. Generally, then, any group who persistently identifies itself as Indigenous becomes so accepted by other Indigenous people, even if it does not clearly possess any of the other three characteristics discussed here. Ambiguities are thus explicitly associated with the term, and these ambiguities naturally can also be found in discussions of what constitutes an Indigenous film.

3) Indigenous films are based in cultures that differ *to a recognizable degree* from the cultures in close proximity to them. These differences may be immense. They may include different languages, economies, and daily activities, as are found, for example, among many of the Indigenous people living in the highlands of New Guinea. On the other hand, these differences may be small, as, for example, with some Native American peoples who have lived for generations in U.S. cities. There are usually recognizable differences, however, that

distinguish Indigenous cultures and films from other cultures and films. Presenting cinematic representations that explore these differences is a frequent goal of Indigenous films.

4) Indigenous films are made by people that currently have or once had a homeland. These traditional Indigenous territories may have been settled, as in agricultural communities, or have been composed of lands and waters to migrate across, as with nomadic communities. Some Indigenous people may have left their homelands, recently or long ago, through migration, relocation, forced resettlement, or through having been supplanted by other cultural groups. Still, the memory, if not the current occupation, of a homeland is a characteristic of most Indigenous people, and homelands often figure prominently in Indigenous films.

Though it is not possible to specify precisely what is, and what is not, an Indigenous film, most will be associated with several and, often, all four of these characteristics. The films also will frequently be made for the two purposes explained earlier in this chapter, made to correct earlier misrepresentations and also to transmit languages and cultures. Despite their commonalities, however, feature films associated with Indigenous peoples are most noteworthy for their dissimilarities, from mainstream cinema certainly, but also in their differences from one another. Chapter 6 explores several of the dimensions of diversity so prominent in Indigenous films.

Chapter Six

Dimensions of Difference in Indigenous Films

Just because I hold a white man's camera, that doesn't mean I am not a Kayapo.... [I]f you were to hold one our head-dresses, would that make you an Indian?

Mokuka

Indigenous feature films exhibit so much diversity that it is impossible to generalize about them. Thinking about the collection of Indigenous films as a whole, then, calls for a focus on their dimensions of difference rather than on their similarities. Many, for example, employ mostly Indigenous people as cast and crew while many do not. Some adapt traditional cultural practices to filmmaking, but others follow western production schedules. Many emphasize distinctively Indigenous content, and yet an increasing number do not. The editing and narrative structure of some Indigenous films mimics older oral traditions; many native features, however, are plotted like mainstream commercial films. Production values are high in some Indigenous features and low in others.

This chapter explores the most significant dimensions of difference found in Indigenous films while drawing on examples from films made by dozens of peoples spread around the world. A concluding section then explores how this diversity disturbs attempts to use non-Indigenous ideas to understand Indigenous films.

Indigenous Personnel

Great variation exists not only in the indigeniety of directors, writers, cinematographers, editors, and other members of production crews, but even among the actors who work on films labeled Indigenous. Toa

Fraser's *Naming Number Two* (aka *No. 2* [2006]) is a particularly interesting example of the complexities associated with personnel issues. Fraser, a Fijian partly raised in New Zealand, wrote and directed this film, which focuses on a the character of a Fijian matriarch. *Naming Number Two* covers a single day as this matriarch attempts to supervise a traditional feast where she hopes to pass on the legal title to her house while simultaneously keeping important secrets from her children and grandchildren. Ruby Dee, an African-American actor, plays the Fijian matriarch, while the roles of her children and grandchildren are taken mostly by Māori actors. International film festival audiences found few problems with this casting, but, when the film was shown in Fiji, the largely Indigenous Fijian audience hissed and booed. It was evident to them that an African-American woman and Polynesian actors were not Fijian.

6-1   Ruby Dee as a Fijian matriarch in *Naming Number Two*

Most audiences outside Fiji, of course, will neither notice nor much care about the differences among Polynesian and Melanesian actors. Outsider audiences, too, are little concerned when an origin story like that of Paikea, the Whale Rider, closely connected with one Māori tribe, is acted by people from other Māori tribes who have no genealogical connections to the whale story. In North America, similarly, Indigenous films often rely on actors with various tribal affiliations to tell stories rooted in specific places and tribes. Still, it is good to keep in mind that Indigenous peoples in Fiji, New Zealand, North America, and elsewhere will have different expectations about who may, and may not, pretend on-screen to be one of them.

Different peoples, too, have different expectations about how much of a production crew must be Indigenous in order for the film to seem to belong more to their community than to the commercial circuits of feature films. In many places, first and early Indigenous productions have required substantial assistance from outsiders while, simultaneously, local communities have asked for and, sometimes, even required that they be provided training so that subsequent work can be done by the Indigenous people themselves. One impressive example of this occurred with the production of *Ten Canoes*. Though the film was made with substantial contributions and funding from outsiders, the production process was used as an opportunity to teach Indigenous Ramingining community youth technical skills so that future productions would be less dependent on non-Indigenous crews. Planned spin-offs from this training include projects 1) to teach older teens how to shoot, record, and edit video, 2) to rehabilitate a moribund closed-circuit television station previously abandoned in Ramingining, and 3) to record as many as possible of the traditional Ganalbingu songs that remain.[1] Similar apprenticing strategies have been used as well during film shoots in Bolivia, Canada, Mexico, and New Zealand.

Though this book views Indigenous and non-Indigenous films as labels at the extreme ends of a single continuum, pioneering Māori filmmaker Barry Barclay recommends an alternative approach, one that is at once simpler and stricter. Barclay argues that only the dimension of creative control should be used in choosing whether or not to label a film Indigenous. So Barclay maintains, for example, that *Whale Rider* is not an Indigenous film since Niki Caro, its director and screenwriter, is not Indigenous. Barclay's criteria would also lead to the exclusion of *Ten Canoes* from the list of Indigenous films, since Rolf de Heer, a non-Indigenous man, is *Ten Canoes'* credited screenwriter and its co-director. Barclay would also have problems labeling *Before Tomorrow* as an Indigenous film since this Igloolik Isuma co-production has a non-Inuit, Marie-Hélène Cousineau, as its co-director and co-screenwriter.

Barclay is surely correct that creative control of the final cut is very important in determining whether a film should be called Indigenous. Important, too, however, are factors associated with production methods, film content, and story structure. Māori director Lee Tamahora had creative control of both *Once Were Warriors* and the James Bond vehicle *Die Another Day* (2002) but, because of their very different actors, content, and story structure, only the former is widely considered to be an

Indigenous film. Similarly, Māori director Taika Waititi's (*née* Cohen) Academy Award–nominated short film, *Two Cars, One Night* (2003), features Māori actors and so seems clearly to be an Indigenous film, while Waititi's later feature film, *Eagle vs Shark* (2007), is likely to seem Indigenous only to those few who know much about this film that does not appear on-screen. (See chapters 10 and 11 for discussions of *Once Were Warriors, Eagle vs Shark*, and other films from Oceania.)

When there are disputes over whether a film should be labeled Indigenous, it seems best to allow the community being represented to decide. So, as reported in chapter 12, though directed by a non-Indigenous director (Stephen Johnson) and produced by the Australian Children's Television Foundation, *Yolngu Boy* (2001) tells an Indigenous story using Indigenous actors. It has been widely embraced by the Yolngu people of Australia's northeast Arnhem Land and can then, it seems to me, rightfully be labeled an Indigenous film. Similarly, if the Māori of the Ngati Porou tribe accept *Whale Rider* as their own, then it, too, is Indigenous. If the Aborigine community at Jigalong agrees that *Rabbit-Proof Fence* tells the "wrong story," as its real-life protagonist, Molly Craig, maintains, then it is probably a mistake to label the film Indigenous. (See chapter 1 for further discussion of *Whale Rider* and *Rabbit-Proof Fence*.)

Indigenous Productions

Indigenous filmmakers frequently rely on their people's distinctive ways of working. Many Indigenous approaches to film production are thus, not surprisingly, quite different from the ways of working associated with commercial cinema.

Differences often manifest themselves even in pre-production. So, for example, Hereniko reports that as he developed ideas for *The Land Has Eyes*, he went back to the island of Rotuma where he had grown up "and I would stand up in the kava circle and tell them the story, act by act. Then I'd ask the people for their reactions and I'd incorporate some of their suggestions into the script."[2]

A similar pre-production process was used on the other side of the world by the makers of *Atanarjuat: The Fast Runner*. The film's official Web site explains, "First we recorded eight elders telling versions of the legend as it had been passed down to them orally by their ancestors. Isuma's team [the production company] of five writers then combined these into a single detailed treatment in Inuktitut and English, consulting with elders for cultural accuracy and with our Toronto-based story consultant, Anne Frank. This same bi-cultural, bilingual process continued through the first and final draft scripts."[3]

Once production begins, working with Indigenous actors also often requires working in culturally appropriate ways. Some Rotumans, for example, were reluctant to perform in *The Land Has Eyes*, as to do so violated the island-value of humility. Hereniko overcame these objections by appealing to another Rotuman value, one emphasizing the importance of personal connections and mutual obligations. Rotuman Voi Fesaitu explained, "Vili [Hereniko] came and asked me to try out for the part of Hapati, but I rejected it, refused it. Then we started to discuss it and I found out it's something I had to handle because it's between me and him, so I took the part."[4] As Hereniko's neighbor and cousin, Fesaitu decided personal obligations outweighed the value of humility.

Alan Howard reports that during the shooting of *The Land Has Eyes*, Rotumans sometimes confused pretense with reality. People wanted to continue with their lives, to talk or make other noises and distracting movements while cameras were rolling. Such disturbances sometimes had to be accepted as parts of the shots. In addition, though many of his non-Rotuman crew did not understand the necessity, for one scene Hereniko produced a real feast, as he knew that for most Rotumans "there was no clear separation between acting and being at a wedding, and at a wedding you are fed, and fed well."[5] Trying to film the wedding without food could have led to an end to further production.

Large- as well as smaller-budget Indigenous films can be shaped by the customs of the people for and about whom they are made. *Atanarjuat: The Fast Runner* cost nearly two million dollars (Canadian) and, as mentioned earlier, relied on the Inuit community even in its pre-production phase. The shoot itself employed mostly Igloolik Inuit as cast and crew, in part because only natives of the region could be expected to care for themselves and to survive in the frequently extreme subarctic conditions. As filming proceeded, director Kunuk reports,

All the heads come together, we talk about what it's going to be like and understand each other at length; if we're going to do a scene where tents are—we ask each other "Are they right?" It's everybody's job to get it right, and so we all talk about it: "Should that be there?" "No—I think it should be there. Oh, let's get Anele to tell us where it is." (Chuckle.) We just work like that.

And of course, all the actors come from our own little community, and you just tell them when they have to get into their characters and they do. I have very little directing to do. Because the script is already written and people know what to do. I just tell them "start" and "stop" and "wrap" and that's about it.[6]

Indigenous productions often require different sorts of performances from actors from what is common in non-Indigenous cinematic productions. The Aboriginal actors and crew who made *Ten Canoes*, for example, labored to recreate on-screen an entire way of life that more knew through stories and photographs than through direct experience. The photographs had been made in the mid-1930s by the white anthropologist Donald Thomson. Prints of a few of his several thousand plates had found their way back to the Yolngu at Ramingining and been reappropriated as a legacy from the ancestors who lived in what some now call the "Thomson Time." Much of *Ten Canoes* is in black and white precisely because it is widely understood that life in Thomson Time unfolded in black and white.

6-2 Paddling a bark canoe in *Ten Canoes*

Freya Schiwy describes how production practices like those used in Australia and Canada's Northwest Territories were developed independently among Indigenous video makers in Bolivia associated with CEFREC (Center for Cinematographic Training) and CAIB (Organization of Indigenous Audiovisual Communicators of Bolivia).[7] Schiwy explains that media productions in Indigenous Bolivia are also commonly organized around principles of reciprocity rather than through wage-labor.

Even non-Indigenous people who assist or who, like Schiwy, wish to research these media productions must first be woven into the community's webs of reciprocity. Outsiders may be required to assist, for example, in aiding in the distribution of the finished videos. These strategies help maintain what Schiwy describes as the continuing co-presence of both capitalist and reciprocal economies across the rural Andean highland region.

The CEFREC-CAIB community illustrates how Indigenous practices can shape even post-production and also the distribution of Indigenous films. Most of their documentary and fiction videos are distributed to villages throughout the region through existing systems of trade exchange. Some are also sold in existing markets and to foreign NGOs, scholars, festivals, and academic institutions. Increasingly, however, Schiwy reports, Indigenous Bolivian video makers have become wary of allowing their work to circulate as commodities in the global marketplace. There are concerns about who should receive the payments—the video makers or the communities shown? Disagreements arise as well about whether the stories and images in these videos should be allowed to leave the villages in which they are rooted. In 2006, the CEFREC-CAIB video makers decided they would no longer sell their films, at any price.

Few other Indigenous filmmakers have made this choice to restrict sales and distribution, but most do share the Andean filmmakers' desire to provide easy and first access to the communities represented in their films. So, for example, Chris Eyre brought his film, *Skins*, described in chapter 2, to eleven Indigenous communities across North America by creating the "Rolling Rez Tour 2002." Eyre offered the film for free viewing inside of a large mobile cinema trailer transported from place to place by a semitruck. Audiences sat in luxury seats to watch this film made especially for them.[8]

Most Indigenous filmmakers, of course, lack the resources to create special tours and traveling theaters for their films. Most, especially in Anglo-American settler nations, have to trust that Indigenous people will find their way to watching through the usual distribution channels of film festivals, theaters, rentals, and television. The continuing growth of DVD rentals via mail and of film downloading via broadband Internet connections may one day make it easier to distribute Indigenous films to specialized audiences.

From pre- through post-production and distribution, then, there is tremendous variation in how Indigenous peoples make and share their films. This is yet another area where it seems fruitless to try to generalize about the archive of Indigenous films.

Screening Indigenous Content

Indigenous filmmakers have made hundreds more documentaries than feature films, in part because producing a documentary is generally cheaper and easier, but also because many filmmakers want most to carefully record the unique cultural practices of their people. Feature films can also represent these practices, of course, but documentaries can do it while less encumbered with the requirements associated with offering a unifying story. Some Indigenous features, nonetheless, emphasize carefully photographed sequences that seem ethnographic. Films like *Atanarjuat: The Fast Runner*, *Seven Songs from the Tundra*, and *Ten Canoes*, for example, seem aimed at helping strengthen and perpetuate precontact traditions. The effect of recording these details can be like that described by an Igloolik elder upon viewing *Atanarjuat: The Fast Runner*. He commented, "We strongly believe this film has helped in keeping our traditional way of life alive and to our future generations it will make them see how our ancestors used to live."[9]

Some Indigenous feature films work at the other extreme. They seem determined to avoid showing behaviors that might emphasize differences between Indigenous and non-Indigenous peoples. *Beneath Clouds*, *Samoan Wedding*, and *Smoke Signals*, from Australia, New Zealand and North America, respectively, are geographically diverse examples of this approach. Most Indigenous feature films lie somewhere between these extremes. Films such as *Radiance* (1998), *Skins*, and *Whale Rider* linger on a few sequences of distinctive practices but seldom so long that outsider audiences become aware they are witnessing an unfamiliar practice.

Indigenous feature films can include significant Indigenous content merely by casting Indigenous people in prominent roles. Non-Indigenous filmmakers have historically avoided placing native peoples in these roles, even when the characters on-screen were supposed to be Indigenous. So Dolores del Rio and Debra Paget famously played Polynesian women in, respectively, the original (1932) and the remake (1951) of *Bird of Paradise*. Even decades later, Trevor Howard in *Windwalker* (1980) and various Disney animators in *Pocahontas* (1995) were still assuming they could represent Native Americans better than these Indigenous peoples could represent themselves. The favorable reception of such

Indigenous features as *Ngati*, *Pathfinder*, and even *Once Were Warriors* rested to some extent on their pioneering casting of Indigenous actors to play leading roles in films telling Indigenous stories.

In addition to cultural practices and actors, Indigenous films may include a third content element, an Indigenous language, one that has seldom, if ever, been heard before on-screen. *Ten Canoes* relies on several Aboriginal languages; *The Fortunate One* (*Sonam*, 2006) uses the Monpa dialect of India's Himalayas; *The Land Has Eyes* puts Rotuman on-screen for the first time. Māori, the language of *The Māori Merchant of Venice*, had been spoken occasionally in several earlier films, but Don Selwyn's version of Shakespeare's play was the first feature entirely in this Indigenous language. Pei Te Hurinui Jones had translated the play into Māori in 1945. Selwyn worked for ten years to get a film version made. "When I was going to school they brought Shakespeare in to colonise [*sic*] me," Selwyn explains; "now I've put it into Māori language I've colonised Shakespeare."[10]

6-3 Shylock with a knife in *The Māori Merchant of Venice*

Filming in an Indigenous language may discourage wide distribution in English-speaking countries, where audiences avoid movies with subtitles. Still, as mentioned, many Indigenous filmmakers make their films primarily for their own people, foregrounding their Indigenous language in hopes the film will assist in that language's preservation. Sometimes, of course, Non-Indigenous filmmakers also use Indigenous languages, too, generally in efforts to make their films seem more authentic. So, *Windwalker*, for example, uses an English language voice-over and non-Indigenous actors, but the characters all speak either Cheyenne or Crow. Mel Gibson uses Mayan for similar purposes in *Apocalypto*, hoping to coax audiences into mistakenly believing that they are witnessing a Mayan story.

Non-Indigenous languages are now the first language of many Indigenous peoples. The Māori in *Once Were Warriors* or in *Whale Rider* are no less Māori for speaking English, just as the actors in *Smoke Signals* represent authentic Coeur d'Alene people while speaking English quite as much as if they spoke an Indigenous tongue. Still, it is likely that bilingual Indigenous people will increasingly emphasize their Indigenous languages in the feature films they create. Since many Indigenous languages are currently under threat, in part from the dominance of non-Indigenous media, spotlighting Indigenous languages in feature films can help new generations honor and speak the languages of their ancestors. I do not think anyone, however, would want to claim that a film is less Indigenous because its actors do not speak an Indigenous language. On the other hand, *Windwalker* or *Apocalypto* do not become Indigenous films merely because they rely on Indigenous languages. Degree of Indigenous-language use will just have to be one more of the many dimensions of difference displayed by both Indigenous and non-Indigenous films.

In addition to content differences across cultural practices, actors, and languages, Indigenous films also differ in the degree to which they dwell on Indigenous landscapes, seascapes, symbols, and other related iconography. In many instances, outsiders will not even recognize when significant Indigenous scenes are being shown. Panning across a particular landscape in an Indigenous feature film, for instance, may seem to mainstream audiences as yet another stereotypical establishment shot or an attempt to show the beauties or harshness of nature. These same shots may be seen by Indigenous people as images of their ancestors, or as invocations of spirits or gods, or as a wordless retelling of historical events.

So, for example, while most audiences think it is about two contemporary Indigenous youths, *Beneath Clouds* may also be viewed as a story about Australia's Aboriginal landscape, particularly as connected to a particular cliff that the film describes as where white "farmers chased all the blackfellas up there a long time ago. They just shot them and pushed them off. Now, no one gives a shit. I suppose they've got their own shit to worry about." Later, beneath this cliff, the two Aborigine protagonists, Lena (Dannielle Hall) and Vaughan (Damian Pitt), confront police officers, contemporary manifestations of those earlier murdering farmers. Lena's surprising subsequent actions are motivated in part by her new understanding of the powers inherent in that site, but audiences who do not recognize that the Aboriginal past persists in places may find her choices unbelievable or, perhaps, "out of character."

Many Indigenous people beyond Australia similarly experience their own places as living stories that contain themselves, families, ancestors, and clans. So, for example, Navajo Blackhorse Lowe lingers on the western United States' plains landscape in *5th World* in ways much like director Ivan Sen does in *Beneath Clouds*. Non-Indigenous viewers of *5th World* may share the experience of the reviewer who complained, "Rather than introducing anything as revolutionary as, say, a plot, Lowe gives us endless shots of desert landscapes and blue skies . . . . Something does eventually happen in *5th World*, but it's more than an hour into the film—and the film's only an hour and 15 minutes long. By then it's too late."[11] For viewers who cannot recognize that "the land has eyes and teeth, and knows the truth," as Vilsoni Hereniko's Rotuman characters say in *The Land Has Eyes*, the content of some Indigenous films may, indeed, seem "tiresome." Indigenous filmmakers and viewers, however, likely expect to see their narratives "inscribed on the landscape," as Tongan writer Epeli Hau'ofa explains is common in Oceania. Hau'ofa argues that preservation and study of these landscapes are important to the Indigenous people of the Pacific much as books, libraries, museums, and monuments are important to Oceania's continental colonizers.[12]

Feature films that emphasize Indigenous places are often foregrounding a type of content that only the initiated see. Yet it is clear there are Indigenous feature films, too, at the other end of the continuum, which place their Indigenous characters firmly within non-Indigenous landscapes. *Grand Avenue* (1996) and *Naturally Native* (1998), for example, similarly emphasize that Native Americans continue to be Indians even when living entirely within urban landscapes. An ocean away, two recent New Zealand–made films, *Naming Number Two* and *Samoan Wedding*, correspondingly examine diasporic Pacific Islanders, respectively from Fiji and Samoa. The loss of connection to homelands is part of the stories that all four films tell, but none of them suggests that new generations should try to return to or reclaim their ancestors' land- and island-rooted lives. In their treatment of Indigenous landscapes, symbols, and related content, then, Indigenous features once again exhibit more differences than commonalities.

Screening Indigenous Storytelling Forms

Content and form are notoriously interconnected and confusing concepts; still, it seems useful briefly to consider form separately from content, especially since Indigenous films sometimes mystify audiences accustomed to western film forms. An emphasis on places, discussed above, is one striking form found in many Indigenous films. These films may, in addition, exhibit Indigenous storytelling forms 1) through translating culture-specific oral tales, 2) by focusing more on groups and communities than on individuals, 3) in presenting time as multi-directional rather than as linear, and 4) through relying on styles of shot selection and editing that differ from dominant film preferences. In each of these four manifestations of form, however, as we shall see, there is so much variation among Indigenous films that it does not seem accurate to claim that even one of these forms characterizes most Indigenous films.

Oral storytelling on-screen

Māori filmmaker Merata Mita maintains that "Film is very close to an oral tradition."[13] Film invites speech and gesture, so, Mita suggests, translating indigenous storytelling traditions to film is much easier than translating them to other introduced forms, especially to forms such as print that reduce the richness of speech to one-dimensional, linear writing. Some Indigenous peoples thus may be able to move their storytelling traditions directly from speech to film, without intermediary steps involving writing and reading.

Freya Schiwy describes this process in the many on-screen fictions produced by Indigenous Andean video makers associated with CEFREC/CAIB in Bolivia. Schiwy maintains these videos adapt western filmmaking conventions in the service of Andean oral-visual traditions that predate colonialism.[14] Similarly, on the other side of the world, Pacific Islanders Sean Mallon and Pandora Fulimalo Pereira point to the many ways that an older pre-literate, pictorial iconography based in tattooing, in jewelry, mat, and quilt making, as well as in indigenous architecture and dance, can guide Pacific Islander filmmakers adapting older visual storytelling traditions to the new screen media.[15]

Atanarjuat: The Fast Runner provides a well-known example of an attempt to translate an oral tale to the screen. Zacharias Kunuk and his collaborators began with an existing allegorical tale, a story Kunuk says "has been passed down from generation to generation. . . . It was taught to me as a little child and I never forgot it."[16] Most of *Atanarjuat* comes directly from the older tale; even the changes made in the ending have been explained as a continuation of the common practice of maintaining multiple versions of oral tales.

Other Indigenous filmmakers have also adapted older stories but revised them for situations associated with more recent times. The opening of *The Land Has Eyes* retells an oral tale then moves on to near contemporary times, the 1960s, to establish the relevance of this story for a modern Rotuman girl. Marcelina Cárdenas, in her Quechua-language *Loving Each Other in the Shadows* (2001), uses a similar mixing of the oral and the modern in an attempt, as she says, to present "the myths and legends of our Quechua existence in a new form of storytelling."[17]

On the other end of this continuum of difference, there are also many Indigenous filmmakers who make little or no use of pre-cinematic oral or visual traditions. Both those who use new media to revitalize older storytelling traditions and those who make films with no traces of culture-specific traditions contribute to the body of Indigenous films.

Collective stories

At least since Fredric Jameson's well-known introduction of the concept of third-world allegory in "Third-World Literature in the Era of Multinational Capitalism," there has been a tendency to interpret non-western films as if they illustrate stories about entire peoples.[18] While Euro-American protagonists represent individuals, it is said, most third-world and Indigenous films should be understood allegorically; their characters represent not autonomous individuals but whole nations and peoples.

Allegorical films generally do not develop characters or plots with the complexity common to non-allegorical films. Audiences, then, who do not recognize the allegory in an Indigenous film may judge them to be simplistic or underdeveloped. These same films, however, may resonate deeply for viewers who recognize that the history of an entire Indigenous people is being shown.

One can interpret any film allegorically by seeing any one actor as representing not a particular character but, say, for example, the proletariat, as in Sergei M. Eisenstein's *Battleship Potemkin* (1925), a self-consciously allegorical film. Darrell Varga has produced just such a thoroughly allegorical reading of *Atanarjuat*. The film is not what it seems on the surface to many, a tale about individuals involved in a revenge adventure, Varga claims, but rather should be understood as offering a moral lesson about the importance of community over individuals.[19]

Even a film such as Chris Eyre's *Skins* can be interpreted allegorically. Non-allegorically inclined audiences would view *Skins* simply as the story of two very different brothers, Rudy and Mogie, living sharply divergent lives on the modern Pine Ridge Reservation. Interpreted as allegory, however, the story is less about two individuals than about one native people. In the spectacularly cinematic ending, when Rudy throws paint across the Mount Rushmore image of George Washington, the resulting long red tear marks no particular pain, not for Mogie's recent death, nor for Rudy's culpability in that death. Rather, the tear, like the film itself, speaks a collective story, a collective grief.

We should be very careful with such allegorical interpretations, however. As critics of Jameson have pointed out, there is something reductive and even condescending about expecting third-world and Indigenous films to work allegorically. Some Indigenous films may be allegorical, but surely many others are not. Here we have yet one more dimension of difference across the archive of Indigenous films.

Temporality

Just as western modernity helped produce a decline in allegorical narratives so, too, has modernity encouraged an exclusively linear conception of time. Western films may sometimes toy with alternative temporalities, but most generally fall back on stories of what Catherine Gallagher labels as a linear "undoing."[20] Films such as *Back to the Future* (1985), *The Terminator* (1984), and the TV series *Star Trek: Deep Space Nine* (1993) show characters going backward in time to try to undo the past in order to alter the future. These films assume that time only flows one way; a change in the past will thus lead along a single path to determinate consequences. Even a film such as *The Matrix* (1999), while alluding to alternative temporalities, ultimately ties its narrative together by positing a single linear temporality. A more recent spate of commercial and independent films, beginning perhaps with *Pulp Fiction* (1994) and including later releases such as *Memento* (2000), *Eternal Sunshine of the Spotless Mind* (2004), and *Babel* (2006), experiment with temporalities while not attempting any fundamental assertions about the possibly fundamental illusion of linearity.

Indigenous storytelling traditions, however, frequently embrace alternative temporalities, sometimes by offering circular or spiral views, and sometimes by suggesting that, as Lilikalā Kameʻelehiwa says of Hawaiian time, the past is out in front leading the present into the future. "It is as if the Hawaiian stands firmly in the present, with his back to the future, and his eyes fixed upon the past, seeking historical answers for present-day dilemmas."[21]

Before there were Indigenous films made by Indigenous peoples, Jorge Sanjinés tried to develop techniques for representing an Indigenous Aymaran sense of time in his films. As, for example, John Mowitt notes, while it principally tells the story of a 1967 massacre, Sanjinés's *The Courage of the People* (*El coraje del pueblo*, 1971) is framed by a sequence drawn from an earlier 1942 massacre.[22] Showing the earlier massacre first at the beginning of *The Courage of the People* serves to introduce the later massacre; at the end of *The Courage of the People*, showing this earlier massacre a second time points to the circularity of time while, as Schiwy points out, emphasizing that the community has and will survive by offering continuing resistance to such attacks.[23]

Some North American Indigenous feature films have also explored multidirectional temporal perspectives. As detailed in chapter 7, *Smoke Signals* weaves together parallel events on Fourths of July that are decades apart. The film integrates these multiple time periods so thoroughly that it seems to end simultaneously in 1976, 1988, and 1998, while also suggesting there are no endings—or beginnings—in Coeur d'Alene Indigenous time. *Ten Canoes* uses very different editing and narrating strategies to also mingle three time periods, one contemporaneous with the film audience and narrator, another associated with the Thomson Time frame tale, and yet another with the first Aboriginal ancestors who emerged as time itself began. As with *Smoke Signals*, the effect in *Ten Canoes* is to suggest that Indigenous time is not linear.

And yet, once again, we should not expect all Indigenous films to avoid linear narratives. Alternative temporalities may be more common among Indigenous peoples than among contemporary non-Indigenous peoples, but this does not imply that Indigenous filmmakers can or should only make films rooted in their ancestors' senses of time.

Shot selection and editing

Probably more has been written about the shot selection and editing of Indigenous films than about any other element of Indigenous cinematic form. Here again, some claim that a desire to present a specifically Indigenous sense of time and place leads filmmakers to adopt styles of cinematography and editing seldom seen in commercial cinema.

Some analysts claim, for instance, that Indigenous filmmakers show a preference for medium-to-long shots. Close-up views are rejected, it is said, because they force an unnatural intimacy on people that is very different from what is common in their daily lives. Close-ups, too, some claim, tend to emphasize individuals rather than the communities and groups that are the real subjects of Indigenous feature films.

An absence of close-ups, however, is not characteristic of the majority of Indigenous films. Also, an increasing proportion of films is being shot for viewing on smaller screens, such as for television and home viewing. This means that preferences for long and medium shots will likely increasingly fade even for Indigenous filmmakers who have preferred them in the past. Close-ups generally work better for smaller-screen viewing than do medium and, especially, long shots.

Long takes, uninterrupted shots from a single camera, are another form that has frequently been associated with Indigenous films. As the anthropological filmmaker David MacDougall points out, any editing of shots, of whatever scale, cuts into fragments what participants themselves experience as continuous.[24] Long takes are thus sometimes claimed to replicate the experience of cultural insiders better than shots edited to compress and otherwise alter filmed events. *Atanarjuat: The Fast Runner, The Journals of Knud Rasmussen*, as well as other work by Igloolik Isuma Productions, are often cited as examples of an Indigenous embrace of the long take. Such diverse films as Navajo director Blackhorse Lowe's *5th World* and the Aborigine *Ten Canoes* also lend some support to the view that Indigenous filmmakers find long takes especially effective.

Just as many or more Indigenous filmmakers, however, use long takes no more frequently than do non-Indigenous filmmakers. Indeed, according to Schiwy, the very Andean Indigenous people Sanjinés aspired to represent more accurately through developing his long-take "integral sequence shots" now control the cameras themselves and rely on editing and other techniques that Sanjinés explicitly denounced.[25] Correspondingly, the pioneering Indian political action film *Tushka* (1996) exerts much of its power through frequent and sometimes frenetically edited short takes.

There is yet one further element of form that deserves special mention. Just as some mistakenly claim that frequent depictions of landscapes and emphases on long takes characterize Indigenous films, so others say these films typically manifest on-screen the power of ancestral, spiritual, and other unseen beings. The much-respected and pioneering Hopi filmmaker Victor Masayesva Jr. has said, for example, "There is such a thing as an Indian aesthetic, and it begins in the sacred."[26] Support for this view can be found in many Indigenous feature films. So, for example, as detailed in chapters 10 and 11, all Indigenous films made in Oceania for almost two decades engaged with the sacred. The three most recent films from the region, however, all break with this tradition. *Naming Number Two*, *Samoan Wedding*, and *Eagle vs Shark* may presage a type of secular film that Indigenous filmmakers in settler communities will increasingly make if the integration of Indigenous and non-Indigenous peoples becomes more common. Even in their engagement with the spiritual, then, Indigenous feature films may be becoming too diverse to support any single characterization.

Varied Production Values

Production values are a fifth dimension of difference found in Indigenous films. Some Indigenous films cost millions of dollars, employ experienced crews and actors, rely on elaborate sound and lighting apparatuses, and often shoot scenes on custom-built sets. The result is polished screen images like those shown in Hollywood films. *Once Were Warriors*, *Rabbit-Proof Fence*, *Whale Rider*, and *Ten Canoes* are examples of Indigenous films with high production values. Films such as *Atanarjuat: The Fast Runner*, *The Journals of Knud Rasmussen*, *Pathfinder*, *The Land Has Eyes*, and *Smoke Signals* also offer fairly polished scenes, though they do not show off their expensiveness on-screen in the manner of high-end Hollywood films. Farther down the continuum of production values are films such as *Beneath Clouds*, *The Business of Fancydancing*, and Barry Barclay's two features *Ngati* and *Te Rua*.

Many Indigenous features exhibit even less of the polish that a small budget and some professional crewmembers provide. Films such as the Navajo *5th World*, the Quechua *Loving Each Other in the Shadows* and *Angels of the Earth*, and the Nenets *A Bride of the Seventh Heaven* were shot with little more equipment than that which thousands of amateurs around the world today rely on in shooting and editing their own home movies.

Production values in themselves are not, of course, the sole predictor of audience engagement. Low production values can, in fact, sometimes work in a filmmaker's favor, as uneven lighting, audio, editing, and similarly inexpensive effects are sometimes associated with "realism," with films that supposedly present the world more as it is actually experienced by its participants than do more expensive films. This sense of realism in inexpensive techniques has been exploited by some Indigenous filmmakers who wish to present perspectives that are different from Hollywood's versions of human experience.

The absence of high production values often makes little or no difference to Indigenous audiences hungry to see their own stories onscreen. Many of the short and feature films made by Indigenous people in Latin America have had a strong impact on their local audiences even though, as Schiwy observes, their "visual aesthetic is closer to home video and television" than to commercial films.[27] The pleasure in at last seeing people that look, speak, and act like themselves on-screen can dwarf concerns about the sophistication of the representations being shown. The fact that such a feature film exists at all, after so many decades in which non-Indigenous outsiders controlled most media, can make even the "crudest" Indigenous feature film into an exhilarating viewing experience.

Some films by Indigenous people probably will continue to follow commercial trends toward increasingly expensive productions. And many, likely, will not. Important, effective Indigenous films have been and doubtless will continue to be made along all points of the continuum of production values.

Eurocentric Aesthetics

Reviewing these five dimensions of difference underscores the extraordinary diversity to be found in Indigenous films. Even more diversity may well emerge as more Indigenous peoples turn to filmmaking. The range of differences makes it impractical to seek a single perspective for thinking about all Indigenous films. At the least, no such pan-Indigenous perspective should be constructed from ideas rooted mostly in Anglo-European traditions. To do so would be to once again deny Indigenous people the right to interpret and represent themselves.

The peculiarity of using outsider ideas to guide thinking about Indigenous film becomes evident if one considers how this method would work in reverse. Suppose, for example, that the Māori wrote books and sponsored film festivals that evaluated contemporary Anglo-European movies on the basis of how well they fit into Māori traditions of visual representation; or, similarly, suppose that the Hopi produced articles and reviews judging the worth of Hollywood blockbusters from a perspective grounded in centuries of Hopi storytelling. Most audiences would probably declare that Māori and Hopi traditions do not provide sensible criteria for understanding and evaluating European-based cinema. Nonetheless, as Native American poet and anthropologist Wendy Rose explains, just such an ethnocentric perspective grounds most Euro-American thinking about Indigenous art. Euro-American audiences assume that their culture has provided them with a universal viewpoint that makes them "uniquely qualified to explain the rest of humanity, not only to Euroamerica, but to everyone else as well." Rose connects this universalizing way of understanding Indigenous art, including films, within a broader "matrix of contemporary Eurocentric domination."[28] Such an ethnocentric perspective suppresses the probability that much Indigenous art and film rest within cultural traditions that may be incomprehensible to outsiders.

Indigenous films might, at first glance, seem to represent a possible exception to the dangers of conceptual Eurocentrism. Filmmaking, after all, depends on western technologies, and so all films, wherever produced, might seem amenable to analysis using western ideas. I suspect not, however, for technologies do not enter new cultures bearing restrictions on their use. Quite the opposite: When new technologies are adapted, new cultures generally forge unique uses that reflect the characteristics of the adopting cultures. So, for example, the colonists' introduction of domesticated horses led to numerous innovative adaptations by different Indigenous peoples across North America. And, similarly, after World War II, the introduction to California of the Hawaiian technology of *he'e nalu* produced, within a few decades, a massive global sport and industry, surfing, that exhibits far more characteristics of its adapting than its originating culture.

In the same way, Indigenous filmmakers frequently adapt film technologies to reflect their own culture's pre-existing visual and storytelling traditions. Many—though not all—Indigenous films are thus better understood as instances of specific older visual and oral Indigenous arts than as expressions of aesthetic traditions associated with western films. Concepts and experience based on western aesthetics and cinema can thus as often mislead as help. In these pages, while I do frequently rely on Euro-American concepts, I try simultaneously to keep open the possibility that each Indigenous film may be different not only from commercial and national cinemas but also from other Indigenous films. Indigenous feature films commonly work to correct and undermine non-Indigenous cinemas, but they do this work in very different ways.

Part Three

Indigenous Film Regions

Chapter 7

North American Indigenous Films before 2000

The only thing more pathetic than Indians on TV is Indians watching Indians on TV.

Thomas, in Smoke Signals

As mentioned in chapter 1, in 1998 *Smoke Signals* became the first Native American feature to earn a wide theatrical release. Though some have called it the first Indian feature, in fact several lesser-known features had come before. These included two rarely seen early films, *House Made of Dawn*, first released in 1972 and then re-released in 1987, and *Itam Hakim, Hopiit* (1985). In the 1990s, three more Indian films appeared just before *Smoke Signals*, the made-for-television *Grand Avenue*, the Indian casino–funded *Naturally Native*, and the political action thriller *Tushka*. A dozen or so more Indian features have been made in the decade since *Smoke Signals*. Four of these were directed by Chris Eyre and are discussed in chapter 2. The other Indian-made features that came after *Smoke Signals* are the focus of chapter 8. This chapter concentrates only on Indian feature films made before 2000, that is, on *Smoke Signals* and its overlooked predecessors and contemporaries.

Two Early Indian Features

As the media gushed excitedly over the release of *Smoke Signals*, its screenwriter, Sherman Alexie, reminded people that "many other Indian filmmakers, our elders," previously "made wonderful films that have been wrongfully ignored or dismissed."[1] *House Made of Dawn* and *Itam Hakim, Hopiit*, two frequently ignored Indian films made over a decade before *Smoke Signals*, deserve special notice.

N. Scott Momaday's novel *House Made of Dawn* won the Pulitzer Prize for Fiction in 1969. The award came as part of an era of very visible Indian artistic and political action that also produced, among other markers, Vine Deloria's influential book of essays, *Custer Died for Your Sins, An Indian Manifesto* (1969), the occupation of Alcatraz Island (1969–1971), the creation in 1968 and subsequent prominence of the American Indian Movement (AIM), and the AIM-led 1973 siege at Wounded Knee. Upon its release in 1972, the film adaptation of Momaday's novel seemed one more manifestation of this hopeful period sometimes called a "Native American renaissance."

The optimism of those times led many to expect that *House Made of Dawn* would signal the start of a wave of Indian features. No longer would Indians be appropriated by white directors for white purposes. In fact, however, *House Made of Dawn* disappeared from public view and, as its director Richardson Morse laments, "it was quite totally unseen for damn near 30 years."[2] In 2005, the National Museum of the American Indian (NMAI) made a new print for limited use through its NMAI Resource Centers. Still, however, neither this version nor an earlier re-edit made in 1988 is widely available.[3]

As Joanna Hearne explains, *House Made of Dawn* was likely too radical even for most audiences in the supposedly radical times in which it first appeared. Abel (Larry Littlebird), the center of the novel and the film, seldom speaks; his feelings and actions reflect his Pueblo culture and generally confuse non-Indian audiences. Abel is an urban-based Indian, a Vietnam veteran in the film though a World War II veteran in the book. Abel's traditional beliefs help him recognize that multiple evils are manifesting in his life. In Los Angeles, he works mostly on his own and with episodic turns to violence in futile attempts to restore harmony. Finally, Abel embraces ceremonial practices, including a return to the country and to the Pueblo practice of running at dawn.

House Made of Dawn and Abel's choices are very different from the types of films and resolutions for Indians that 1970s' audiences expected. *Billy Jack* (1971), for example, became a multimillion-dollar smash hit at about the same time by glorifying an Indian character who uses his karate skills in repeated acts of vigilantism.

House Made of Dawn anticipates many elements of Indian features that would appear decades later. The film's use of editing to integrate multiple times, for example, pioneers a similar cinematic interweaving of pasts and presents like that in *Smoke Signals,* discussed later in this chapter. The film's exploration of tensions between urban and reservation Indian perspectives is central to *The Business of Fancydancing*. The debilitating effects on Indians who serve the United States in foreign wars is treated again in *Skins*. Ceremonial running is a motif in *The Doe Boy*. Healing ceremonies play prominent roles in *Skins*, *Skinwalkers*, and *A Thief of Time*. It seems clear, then, that *House Made of Dawn* is the most important Native American feature film that few people have seen.

At fifty-eight minutes, Victor Masayesva Jr.'s *Itam Hakim, Hopiit* (*We Someone, The Hopi*) is shorter than the other films described in this book. Still, like *House Made of Dawn*, *Itam Hakim, Hopiit* deserves wider notice for its pioneering attempt at translating an Indian perspective to the screen.

Itam Hakim, Hopiit begins with the creation story of the Hopi, traces their history to the present, then ends with prophecies for their future. Throughout, however, past and present are intertwined. The contemporary landscape, daily activities, and ceremonies are used to illustrate how it was in the past. Masayesva Jr. suggests that as it was, so it is now and shall be.

Images and music dominate the film, but viewers are also guided by elder Ross Macaya. He sometimes appears on-screen but mostly speaks Hopi in a voice-over. A sparse translation in English subtitles provides non-Hopi speakers with hints at what is being said. Though sometimes miscataloged as a documentary, *Itam Hakim, Hopiit* seems better understood as an historical fiction film. Masayesva Jr. does illustrate Hopi history and cultural practices, but *Itam Hakim, Hopiit* aims not to "document" Hopi cosmological traditions as much as to recreate a Hopi sensibility, a Hopi feeling, in a new medium. As Leslie Marmon Silko explains, in *Itam Hakim, Hopiit* as well as in his later eighteen-minute *Ritual Clowns* (1988), Masayesva Jr. demonstrates that "the subtle but pervasive power of communal consciousness, perfected over thousands of years by Hopi, is undiminished. In Victor Masayesva's hands, video is made to serve Hopi consciousness and to see with Hopi eyes."[4]

Itam Hakim, Hopiit concludes with a prophecy that, in part, announces what Indian filmmakers like Masayesva Jr. and those who came later wish their work to do. "These stories are going to be put down so the children will remember them," narrator Macaya declares. "The children will be seeing this and improving on it. That is what will happen. This will not end anywhere."

Lost in *Smoke Signals'* Blaze

Though there had been very few before, four Indian feature films appeared in rapid succession over a three-year period in the 1990s. *Smoke Signals* attracted wide attention, while its three contemporaries—*Grand Avenue, Naturally Native,* and *Tushka*—received, and still receive, little notice. Like *Smoke Signals,* however, these three neglected films offer representations of Indians unlike any that had appeared before.

Grand Avenue (1996) was based on a screenplay by Greg Sarris, sometime chair of the Federated Indians of Graton Rancheria, formerly known as the Federated Coast Miwok. Sarris adapted his own book, *Grand Avenue: A Novel in Stories,* into an HBO made-for-television miniseries that is almost three hours long.[5] *Grand Avenue* was the first Indian-made film to focus mostly on women and is noteworthy, too, for its fulsome and convincing examination of teenagers. Two teen sisters, Justine (Deeny Dakota) and Alice (Diane Debassige), struggle with their much-flawed mother, a seriously ill cousin, threats from armed gangs, boyfriends, absent fathers, and their separately and very differently emerging Indian identities. This richness of conflict is presented with a naturalness seldom achieved in filmic representations of teenagers.

Like *House Made of Dawn, Grand Avenue* emphasizes urban lives, drawing attention to the fact that most contemporary Indians in the United States live in cities. The film concentrates on the Pomo, one of the many California tribes that have been vastly underrepresented in the hundreds of films with Indians made by Hollywood-based producers. *Grand Avenue* differs from most Indian and non-Indigenous films as well in its casual acknowledgment of how frequently urban Indian lives intertwine with the lives of non-Indians. *Grand Avenue*'s principal characters are Indian, but they are shown to also engage in frequent exchanges with Hispanics and African Americans.

Grand Avenue is like *House Made of Dawn,* too, in foregrounding a tortured and sometimes violent Indian protagonist. Mollie (Sheila Tousey), the mother of three in *Grand Avenue,* struggles to show love to her children, each fathered by a different man. "I'm hateful all the time," Mollie explains at one point, and it often does not seem she exaggerates. Mollie's habitual response to trouble is to run away, to leave cities or houses, or to escape through drinking or sullen denial. During one crisis when the children offer Mollie a birthday cake, she refuses to eat and storms out to go to a bar. The oldest daughter, Justine, has a nearby, relatively prosperous father who could help her in many ways, but Mollie is bitter the man abandoned her and so keeps Justine ignorant of his paternity. Despite Mollie's many flaws, however, *Grand Avenue* slowly makes audiences aware that she loves her children and will fight fiercely to keep the family together. Though the children seem candidates for foster homes and detention facilities, *Grand Avenue* leaves viewers rooting for Mollie to hold it together enough to ward off various intruding white agencies accustomed to intervening in Indian lives.

Naturally Native (1998) appeared two years after *Grand Avenue* and continued the earlier film's emphases both on urban California Indians and on women. *Naturally Native* follows three sisters (of Morongo and Viejas parents, according to the film) struggling to launch a business that will enable them to continue living together in an unnamed California city.

We learn at the beginning of *Naturally Native* that the three sisters were placed at an early age with white foster parents, as part of a pre-1978 U.S. government policy that encouraged removing Indian children from reservations. The horrific consequences of this policy on the sisters' sometimes confused senses of identity, as well as other issues such as alcoholism, racism, and date rape, provide texture to the story of the sisters' search for financial and familial security. *Naturally Native* is notable, too, for foregrounding an Indian-inflicted Christianity, a type of Christianity that seems to worship a god associated with no specific terrestrial homeland. The sisters pray together in moments of crisis in ways that combine traditional Indian beliefs with what they have learned from their foster parents' Presbyterianism, the Protestant denomination to which one sister says they still belong. *Naturally Native* suggests that spirits and gods connected to specific tribal places may not have much relevance for some urban Indians.

The middle sister, Karen (Kimberly Norris Guerrero), has just earned an MBA and prepares an impressive business plan through which the three will market cosmetics and salves based on traditional formulae taught to one sister by their now-deceased father. The sisters use this plan to shop for a loan but are repeatedly rebuffed. They are refused first by a small business agency for minorities since, they are told, they are not "Indian enough," because they are not officially enrolled in any government-certified tribe. A second chance at a loan falls apart when the sisters refuse to act as the authenticating Indian faces for a scheming white spiritualist who claims to have been an Indian "in a previous life."

Next they are refused by a foundation that opposes Indian gambling and even Indians, like the sisters, with familial connections to tribes that sponsor gambling. Rejections come first because they are not Indian enough, then because they are too Indian and, finally, because they are the wrong kind of Indian.

In desperation, the sisters turn to their father's casino-owning Viejas tribe, a place and people they have not visited for years. The tribal elders welcome the three as returning family. "It's good to see you come home." The loan is granted and the sisters held up as a model of the entrepreneurial spirit that the Viejas elders wish to encourage. This on-screen fictional tribal funding is significant since *Naturally Native* was, in fact, entirely funded (at $700,000) by the Connecticut-based Mashantucket Pequot Tribal Nation, which operates Foxwoods Resort and Casino, the world's largest casino. *Naturally Native* contains some explicit praise for the benefits of Indian-controlled gambling and, before the credits roll, an on-screen title explains that Indian reservations with casinos generally no longer require government welfare grants.

Naturally Native was written, co-directed, and co-produced by Valerie Red-Horse, who also plays the oldest sister, Vickie. The film is thus not only about Indian women but is also the first Indian feature to be creatively controlled by women. (Red-Horse's co-director, Jennifer Wynne Farmer, proved especially important when Red-Horse discovered during shooting that she was pregnant and no longer had the stamina to fulfill multiple production roles.) The quest for funding that the sisters undertake in the film parallels the quest for funding that Red-Horse followed to secure funding for the movie. Only Indian sources understood the fictional sisters' on-screen plan just as, in reality, only Indian financial sources were willing to fund an Indian film by and about Indian women.

Ian Skorodin's *Tushka*, shot and first screened in 1996, announces at its beginning that it is based on a true story. That story—the murder through arson of a family of five—is told so vividly that viewers of *Tushka* will likely wish they could believe it is fiction. Skorodin wrote, directed, and produced *Tushka* at the age of twenty-one, while home on summer vacation from college.[6] Skorodin's youth seems to have allowed him to embrace an ambition well beyond that commonly exhibited by more experienced filmmakers. *Tushka* not only focuses on the horrific fact that federal agents of the United States in the 1960s and 1970s frequently tortured, framed, and killed innocent people that they casually labeled "subversive," it does this while trying to sympathetically represent the government murderers' own stories. *Tushka* carefully examines why FBI officers might find it reasonable to burn to death innocent, sleeping Indian women and children.

Tushka's narrative core is drawn from an arson attack on the Duck Valley Reservation in northern Nevada on February 12, 1979. This assault killed the pregnant Tina Manning Trudell as well as her three children and mother. These murders occurred fewer than twelve hours after Tina's husband, John Trudell, delivered a speech at a rally in front of FBI head-quarters in Washington, D.C. Trudell burned a United States flag as part of his speech, and this flag burning and speech are reenacted in *Tushka*. In reality, no suspects have ever been charged, but, in *Tushka*, the killers are shown to be FBI officers who have seen the flag burning on television and who have, as a result, resolved, one says, to teach "that red nigger a lesson."[7]

Tushka begins with black-and-white footage, in documentary style, reminding viewers, as a title explains, that "In the 1960s, the FBI created COINTELPRO, a counter-intelligence program designed to infiltrate, subdue and neutralize 'subversive' movements in the United States. COINTELPRO targeted Native American organizations from that era for behavior considered anti-American." Tushka is the film's fictional name for organizations like the American Indian Movement (AIM), which endured years of unprovoked U.S. government agency attacks. Trudell, a Sante Sioux and onetime chairman of the AIM, becomes Choctaw (as is Skorodin) and is named Marcus Beams (Robert Eades) in *Tushka*. "They don't send soldiers now," Beams explains, "they send the FBI." Beams leaves Oklahoma with members of Tushka to make his speech in Washington despite pleas from his wife and mother-in-law. He makes this choice not in defiance of their wishes but because he believes open resistance is best for his children's future. Submission to federal rule, Beams declares, is no better than death since it is not really life, "at least not the life of a Choctaw."

Tushka's emphasis on family ties the film together. Skorodin repeat-edly cuts from scenes of Choctaw families to focus on Jack Raines (Tim Johnson), an FBI agent who has spent three years harassing, attacking, and trying to silence the Tushka Indian movement. Raines is mentored by Paul Williams (Orvel Baldridge), a senior agent who convinces him that Beams's love of family is a weakness that good agents should exploit. Raines is haunted by memories of his father, a legend in the FBI known particularly for his clever, cold-blooded, and successfully hidden killing of "nigger" subversives such as Fred Hampton. *Tushka* offers five flash-backs to agent Raines's memories of the elder Raines, preparing audiences to understand why, at the film's end, this son feels driven to murder when he is reminded yet again about the greatness of his legendary father. His mentor Williams warns Raines, "Don't you disgrace his memory." And the murdering fire is lit.

Tushka's ambition extends to its cinematography. Every shot shows care and is jammed with information. Even the music, sometimes including Choctaw chants, exceeds expectations for a low-budget ($45,000) independent feature. There are youthful weaknesses in the film, too, of course, including dialogue that is sometimes stiff, repetitive, or too on-the-nose. There are weaknesses as well in the acting and repetitiveness of sets. Still, *Tushka* looms increasingly large in the archive of Indian-directed feature films since few films made since have attempted either to depict Indian historical events or to focus on organized Indian political and martial resistance.

Skorodin later produced a stop-motion animated short, *Crazy Ind'n* (2006/2007), which also combines history and politics. The narrative borrows from the life of Prescott Bush, father and grandfather to presidents, who describes in his journals his pleasure at digging up and stealing Geronimo's skull. Skorodin is currently in production with a much-expanded version, *Crazy Ind'n the Movie*, which follows the animated action figure Crazy Ind'n as he battles to reclaim the stolen skull and to right this and other injustices.[8]

Smoke Signals

Though already discussed in chapter 1, *Smoke Signals* deserves further comment not only because it remains the most widely seen Indian-made feature film ever produced but also because it continues to attract much more critical attention than any other Indigenous feature. Much of this continuing interest seems to stem from *Smoke Signals'* humor, disruption of stereotypes, impressive acting, and deft interweaving of times. Each of these deserves examination.

Smoke Signals contains more comedy than any other North American Indigenous film; its many laughs may alone account for much of its commercial and critical success. In voice-over, Thomas (Evan Adams) begins and ends the film telling serious stories; however, in between, he mostly offers riddles and tales he considers serious but which seem to be jokes to his audiences, on-screen and off. The screenplay describes Thomas as "very much an Indian nerd," and Adams plays him with prominent buckteeth, ridiculous glasses, and clothes better suited for a costume party than for a contemporary American Indian man.[9]

Thomas and Victor (Adam Beach) dominate the film, but additional surprising, quirky characters come and go. Lester Fallsapart (Chief Leonard George) offers laconic traffic and weather reports "from atop the KREZ traffic van, broken down at the crossroads since 1973." Velma (Michelle St. John) and Lucy (Elaine Miles), in homage to Thelma and Louise, cruise the reservation and the film inside a junk car that drives only in reverse. When confronted by cowboy rednecks who steal their bus seats, Thomas and Victor do not fight but belt out an impromptu chant, with a powwow rhythm, speculating about the nature of John Wayne's teeth. "Are they false, are they real? Are they plastic, are they steel?"

Watching these two young Indian males burst into song rather than into battle creates humor and, simultaneously, undercuts earlier movie-Indian stereotypes. The ample comedy in *Smoke Signals* enabled writer Sherman Alexie and director Chris Eyre to present multiple alternatives to most representations of Indians audiences had previously seen. Viewers learn as they laugh that one of this pair of twenty-two-year-old Indians is a colossal nerd and that the other mostly looks sullen and watchful when he is imitating how television and movies have told him that young Indians should behave. The rez itself in *Smokes Signals* becomes not a stereotypical home of despair and resentment but a place full of loving families, struggling against social trends—as do many non-Indigenous North Americans—in a quest to find ways to nurture children into healthy adults.

Both the humor and successful shattering of stereotypes in *Smoke Signals* is due to the skills of its two principal actors. Adam Beach has since played several prominent roles, for example, in Eyre's two made-for-television mysteries, *Skinwalkers* and *A Thief of Time* (both discussed in chapter 2), as well as in Clint Eastwood's *Flags of Our Fathers* (2006), episodes of the television series *Law & Order: Special Victims Unit* in 2007, and in Georgina Lightning's debut directing venture, *Older Than America* (2008). However, Evan Adams's performance as Thomas in *Smoke Signals* is probably even more impressive than Beach's Victor, especially if one compares Adams's nerdy Thomas with his role in Alexie's second feature, *The Business of Fancydancing* (discussed in chapter 8). In this second film, Adams plays a cosmopolitan, successful poet, a sophisticated and tormented man about as far from the character of naïve Thomas in *Smoke Signals* as an actor could get.

7-1 Victor and Thomas on the road in *Smoke Signals*

Irene Bedard, who provided Pocahontas's voice-over as well as the face for the animators of *Pocahontas*, uses her role as Suzy Song in *Smoke Signals* to construct a rich and complex alternative to the one-dimensional representation of Indian women that Disney and other whites typically construct. It is, however, Gary Farmer who probably best illustrates the impressive contributions that the cast of professional actors brought to this film. Farmer had already had challenging principal roles, in *Powwow Highway* (1989) and *Dead Man* (1995), among others. As Victor's father in *Smoke Signals*, Farmer had to make audiences feel sympathy for a man often shown staggering drunk, who punches his son for accidentally spilling a can of beer, and who abruptly abandons his wife and ten-year-old son to move a thousand miles away. Farmer's performance enables the audience to maintain enough sympathy through the first hour to be ready to accept the film's late revelation of the unintended sin that drove Farmer's character both to alcoholism and to flee.

These three elements—the comedy, the shattering of stereotypes, and the strong acting—reflect well both on Alexie's screenplay and

Eyre's direction. Alexie and Eyre's successful collaboration manifests itself as well in the deft interweaving of time that allows *Smoke Signals* to
tell a single story unfolding on-screen in 1976, 1988, and 1998. *Smoke
Signals* transitions between scenes in ways that suggest what is past
is never completely past. So, for example, in one scene, the twenty-
two-year-old Victor walks through a door, which slams to reveal his
twelve-year-old self walking out the other side. In another scene, the
adolescent Victor runs beside a bus. The older Victor gazes out as the bus
gathers speed and leaves his younger self behind. A basketball thrown out
of the frame in one flashback rolls into the following scene taking place
years "later" on the same desert court, connecting scenes and generations
in timelessness.

Smoke Signals also offers seamless flashbacks within flashbacks and
stories told about stories being told. Voices in one scene linger in succeeding ones. Victor's father, now dead, helps him to his feet on a desert
highway; those hands then belong to a road construction worker, at once
the father and not-the-father, at once past and present. The film ends
in 1998 but so thoroughly integrates its multiple time periods that it
seems to end in 1976 and 1988 as well, suggesting perhaps there are no
endings—or beginnings—in Coeur d'Alene time.

This discussion does not exhaust *Smoke Signals'* aesthetic accomplishments, but should indicate why the film continues to attract viewers
and critical attention years after its initial release. *Smoke Signals* launched
director Eyre's prolific career, discussed in chapter 2. The other Indian
films that followed *Smoke Signals*, including Alexie's second film, *The
Business of Fancydancing*, are examined in chapter 8.

Chapter 8

North American Indigenous Films after 2000

You're making fiction in spite of reality. Reality is a powerful thing and you have to shut it out.

Randy Redroad

As noted in chapter 2, Chris Eyre went on after *Smoke Signals* to direct one more theatrically released feature, three made-for-television movies, as well as the museum-commissioned *A Thousand Roads*. Writer Sherman Alexie, meanwhile, used the success of *Smoke Signals* to help him finance, produce, write, and direct *The Business of Fancydancing* (discussed below). Nine additional Indian-directed features appeared in North America between 2004 and 2008, creating an archive large enough to prove that contemporary Indians now have the skills to produce their own features, independently from the dominant Hollywood industry. This archive includes films in diverse established genres as well as films that reflect Indian-specific cinematic forms.

The Business of Fancydancing

Skins can be understood, in part, as Eyre's attempt to direct a second feature that avoided the formulaic elements included in *Smoke Signals* to make it more attractive to mass audiences. Alexie's own second feature, *The Business of Fancydancing* (2002), similarly aimed to step away from the commercial elements that made *Smoke Signals* so successful toward a film that more accurately reflected the vision embodied by Alexie's short stories and poetry. Alexie says he wanted *The Business of Fancydancing* to "be as strange or irritating as I want it to be," without having "someone with a checkbook telling me I can't do it that way."[1]

Smoke Signals was generally lighthearted with occasional dark under-tones. Alexie's writing, however, commonly works in the opposite way; it is usually dark with light undertones. It is this later sensibility that guides *The Business of Fancydancing*, as it guided Alexie when he pub-lished his first book using the same title.[2] That book adopts the uncom-mon strategy of including both stories and poems; the film *The Business of Fancydancing* is best understood, too, as a cinematic amalgam of poetry and prose.

The Business of Fancydancing explores friendship, sorrow, and loss among a group of thirty-something Spokane Indians and a few of their non-Spokane acquaintances. Seymour Polatkin (Evan Adams), the cen-tral character, is an internationally famous poet who no longer maintains close ties to his childhood reservation friends. He returns to the rez after many years' absence for the funeral of Mouse (Swil Kanim), dead of an overdose. The film emphasizes the similarities between the Spokane poet character Seymour and Spokane poet and writer-director Alexie through scenes where Seymour reads poetry or tells stories that appear in Alexie's published books. Few films about writers foreground writing as promi-nently as does *The Business of Fancydancing*. And few, too, expose how completely poems and stories emerge from the experiences of entire communities and not simply from individual "genius."

Seymour's life on the poetry-reading circuit draws from Alexie's life, as does much of the portrayal of the Spokane reservation where both the Seymour character and Alexie were born. And yet, in important ways, Seymour is not Alexie. *The Business of Fancydancing*, both film and book, are fiction, not autobiography. And, unlike writer-director Alexie, the Alexie-character Seymour is gay. One long scene shows Seymour coming out to his much-disappointed female lover Agnes (Michelle St. John); another scene presents Seymour telling an audience a humorous story about his grandmother's response to his confession about his sexual ori-entation. There are several scenes, too, that emphasize the physical intimacy between Seymour and his white lover, Steven (Kevin Phillip). These elements have led some to label *The Business of Fancydancing* as a "gay film," and it has been screened at several queer film festivals.

The film is not, however, much about Seymour's homosexuality. His choice of a white lover is consequential, as it propels him farther away from the reservation and Indians. Seymour's preference for male over female partners, however, is treated as mundane. Seymour's sexual orientation thus works as just one more of the multiple ways Alexie thwarts audience expectations.

The film features many touching moments but only one likable character, Agnes Roth. She is mixed race, raised by her Jewish mother, knowing nothing of her Spokane Indian father. Seymour is perhaps the least sympathetic character, though he seems to not entirely deserve all the vitriol that his childhood friend, Aristotle Joseph (Gene Tagaban), and others repeatedly unleash toward him. The deceased friend Mouse, a long-time "gas-huffer" and alcoholic, is shown in several beautiful, haunting sequences playing a poignant violin, but he also verbally attacks not only Seymour but also a white newcomer to the reservation. Alexie's determination to make the film his own way also leads him to show Aristotle and Mouse assaulting an unarmed white motorist; the stranded driver has the bad luck to appear before them on the side of the road a moment after they wonder what would have happened if Indians had battered Columbus when he first landed.

Alexie further disrupts expectations by deemphasizing the narrative to foreground visual and verbal imagery instead. Overall, *The Business of Fancydancing* reflects Alexie's lyric poetry more than his fiction, though even the latter is often as driven by imagery as by plot. The story of Mouse's suicide and Seymour's return to the reservation is repeatedly interrupted by scenes from the friends' earlier, sometimes idyllic, sometimes abusive, childhoods, by poetic intertitles, and by mock-video footage shot by Mouse on a low-quality handheld camera. There are, as well, multiple inserts of scenes showing different characters performing both ceremonial and secular dances, sequences of Seymour reading to rapt, predominantly white audiences, and clips from a faux-television show where an aggressive interviewer (Rebecca Carroll) asks confrontational questions.

8-1 Mouse and Aristotle videotape their savaging of Seymour's book
(Courtesy of Larry Estes)

Seymour begins the film performing a shawl dance, traditionally a woman's dance, and so offers a visual image that is suggestive both of Seymour's homosexuality and his Indian identity. *The Business of Fancydancing* concludes with Seymour dancing once again, this time in an elaborate male ceremonial costume that he slowly begins to remove. The painful visit to Mouse's funeral has left Seymour ready to shed even more of his Spokane identity. He has become a widely praised spokesman in the white world for a people that now mostly despise him. (Some of the cruelest accusations against Seymour spoken at Mouse's funeral are uttered by Alexie himself, in an uncredited role that allows him to speak taunts he has heard savaging the impropriety of his literary career beyond the rez.) "They're not your tribe anymore," Seymour's lover, Steven, has told him earlier. "I'm your tribe." With the film's final disrobing, dancing image, however, viewers are left suspecting that Seymour has no tribe at all. He is not a hero but a tragic figure, like Hamlet, whom he quotes and paraphrases throughout the film. "The whole world is a prison," Seymour-Hamlet laments. Alexie says that he wanted *The Business of Fancydancing* to participate in the traditions of storytelling that reject Hollywood endings, to offer a story on film where questions of whether to be or not to be linger even at the end.[3]

The contrast between the characters that Evan Adams plays in *Smoke Signals* and in *The Business of Fancydancing* succinctly highlights Alexie's very different visions. As Thomas Builds-the-Fire in *Smoke Signals*, Adams is rez-born and bound; his lighthearted, naïve, and optimistic character delighted audiences in 1998 and continues to delight. Adams's Seymour Polatkin, on the other hand, is rez-born and, at film's end, unequivocally rez-fled. He is somber, hyper-self-aware, and deeply conflicted. The diversity of these two characters, and their creation and embodiment by single people, by Alexie as author and Adams as actor, illustrate again the extraordinary diversity exhibited across the archive of Indigenous feature films.

Shirley Cheechoo's Films

Shirley Cheechoo, a James Bay Cree, has directed two feature films, *Bearwalker* (2000) and *Johnny Tootall* (2005). *Bearwalker* was the first feature to be directed by an Aboriginal Canadian and only the second to be directed by a North American Indian woman. (Valerie Red-Horse's *Naturally Native*, discussed in chapter 7, was the first.) Cheechoo's accomplishments, however, stretch far beyond her two feature films. She first attracted wide attention in 1992 as a writer and actor with her one-woman play, *Path with No Moccasins*, examining Cheechoo's painful experiences at an Indian residential school. In 1997, she produced, wrote, directed, and acted in *Silent Tears*, the first of her several well-received short films. Cheechoo is also a successful painter and the founder of a touring youth drama company, the Debahjehmujig Theatre Group, which often performs in the Ojibwe language.

Bearwalker was shot entirely on the Manitoulin Island Indian Reserve, in Lake Huron on Manitoulin Island, the largest freshwater lake island in the world, now a community composed mostly of people from the Odawa, Ojibwe, and Potawatomi tribes. *Bearwalker's* Aboriginal characters switch back and forth between Cree and English, while several white Canadian characters speak both English and French. Through flashbacks and flashforwards, *Bearwalker* spirals around a single act in 1976, Ella Lee Thomspon's (Renae Morriseau) brutal murder of her long-time husband, Eric (Tim Sampson). The jumps in time enable Cheechoo to establish a context for the murder that stretches well beyond the married life of Ella Lee and Eric to include, among others, the lives of her three sisters, Grace (Sheila Tousey), Ruby (played by Cheechoo herself), and Tammy (Greta Cheechoo, the filmmaker's real-life sister).

By *Bearwalker's* end, Ella Lee's violent act is revealed to have emerged not from Ella Lee herself so much as from the entire history of white-Cree relations and from the influence of a bearwalker. *Bearwalker's* opening titles explain that a bearwalker is a "powerful spiritual phenomenon that employs the darkside." Later, a voice-over adds, "Christians call it the devil. My people call it bearwalker." This malign, shape-shifing spirit appears in *Bearwalker* sometimes as a black vintage car and sometimes as a swirling greenish light. Ella Lee's three sisters occasionally speculate on the role it may be playing in their lives. "I think our mother was bearwalked," one concludes as calamities crash upon them, one after the other.

Amid the horrors, *Bearwalker* maintains a surprisingly whimsical and often comic tone. So, Ella Lee's shock at her impulsive slaughter of her husband sometimes manifests itself as catatonia and sometimes in the production of a peanut butter-and-jelly sandwich. Later, the sisters pause in cleaning up Ella Lee's blood-smeared hardwood floor to watch, and analyze, a favorite television soap opera. Even as two sisters are being led off to jail, the old sibling rivalries and resentments continue, as does the familiar teasing and impertinent bantering the four sisters have been sharing for thirty years.

Bearwalker was made with some assistance from the Sundance Institute and shown at the Sundance Festival under the title *Backroads* the year after *Smoke Signals'* triumphant debut there. When no theatrical release materialized for this cut, Cheechoo re-edited, rescored, added a narrative voice-over, and changed the title to *Bearwalker*. In this form, in 2002 and 2003, *Bearwalker* played on two Canadian cable-television networks, including the Aboriginal Peoples Television Network.

Johnny Tootall, Cheechoo's second feature, also played on Canadian television, but with it Cheechoo's focus shifted from women to men and from sisters to brothers. Adam Beach plays Johnny, the honored eldest child of a now-deceased tribal chief. Johnny joined the military as a youth to escape his Vancouver Island family and tribal responsibilities. Later experiences fighting for Canada in Bosnia leave him in despair. His wolf spirit guides Johnny to return home where he finds himself thrust into another war, this time over land and the preservation of his ancestors' way of life.

Johnny finds out that his old girlfriend, Serena (Alex Rice), has married his brother, RT (Nathaniel Arcand). Johnny and RT have long been at odds, and now RT is heading a political campaign to save tribal lands. RT wants Johnny to help, but Johnny is struggling with so many demons that he seems unable even to help himself. Tensions and familial connections are at the center of *Johnny Tootall*, just as they were in Cheechoo's *Bearwalker*. And, once again, family members are situated in particular historical contexts as well as being people whose lives are intertwined with spirits.

8-2 Johhny Tootall returns home

Adam Beach is probably North America's best-known Indian actor. He had already appeared in many television shows before starring in *Smoke Signals*. His varied film work since has included featured roles in *Flags of Our Fathers* (2006) and *Windtalkers* (2002), as well as in the two Eyre-directed Hillerman mysteries discussed in chapter 2. Beach has also been a regular on the Canadian television comedy series *Moose TV,* and in the United States on the crime series *Law & Order: Special Victims Unit.* (He co-stars, too, with Georgina Lightning in a film Lightning directs, *Older Than America,* in production as *Native Features* goes to press.) Among his many roles, however, it is probably as Johnny Tootall that Beach best exhibits his acting range. Beach's Johnny is convincingly conflicted, confused, and complex, very different from the macho, commanding, simpler characters that Beach usually plays. Cheechoo's long experience in the theater seems to have helped her prepare to be an especially effective director of actors.

Two Oklahoma Films

Randy Redroad's *The Doe Boy* (2001) and Sterlin Harjo's *Four Sheets to the Wind* (2007) return to settings pioneered in *Tushka,* to rural and small-town Oklahoma, to offer stories about Indians living side by side with white people. Both the later films feature Jeri Arredondo in a central role as a mother. Both, too, were written and directed by young Indian men who choose debut stories focusing on a young Indian man's struggles with a distant father.

Cherokee writer-director Redroad won much attention and awards with several fiction short films, beginning with the ten-minute *Haircuts Hurt* (1992), about racial prejudice in a barbershop. Two years later, Redroad made the more ambitious, forty-minute *High Horse* (1994), presenting urban Indians who find help from tribal spirits as they traverse the crowded streets of contemporary Manhattan. Redroad's first feature, *The Doe Boy,* continues his practice of mingling contemporary and older traditions. The setting, however, shifts from the city to the small town of Tahlequah, Oklahoma, the current capital of the Cherokee nation.

The Doe Boy is a coming-of-age film that puts special attention on an uneasy father-son relationship within a hunting culture where killing game is equated with maturity. The protagonist, Hunter (Andrew J. Ferchland as a boy, James Duval as a late teen), grows up with a Cherokee mother and a white father, just as Redroad did. Hunter is a hemophiliac, who can be seriously debilitated by bruises and cuts and so must get a shot of a coagulant whenever he is injured. Hunter continually disappoints his father, Hank (Kevin Anderson), since he cannot participate in most of the outdoorsy activities expected of rural Oklahoma males. Redroad, similarly, had such severe asthma as a child that he remembers "asthma basically formed my personality."[4] Early in the film, Hunter earns his nickname, the Doe Boy, while on his first hunt. After his father neglectfully falls asleep, Hunter shoots a doe, though only bucks are considered fair game.

The doe incident, too, is drawn from Redroad's life. Redroad recalls when it happened to him, "To make it even worse, the doe's almond shaped brown eyes looked like my mother's and like all the Indian girls' I knew. . . . On the way home, we ran into one of dad's friends and I saw a hint of embarrassment in my father's eyes that I never forgot."[5] This event came to take on a "mythic significance" in his life, Redroad says, and he later came to feel it "would only fit on the big screen. It became the moment through which I would attempt to resolve many of the emotional phrases of my youth and reintroduce myself to a long lost cowboy."

The autobiographic roots of *The Doe Boy* seem to have helped Redroad create a richness of character and events beyond that often found in debut feature films. Hunter's Cherokee mother, Maggie, for example, is a nurse at a nearby hospital who demonstrates a complex love for both her hemophiliac son and her sometimes drunken, abusive husband. Hunter's white father, Hank, treats Hunter with disdain for most of the film, even smashing him in the face after his son complains, "Why are you always blaming me for everything? It's not my fault you couldn't make it as a pilot." Still, neither Hunter nor filmmaker Redroad finally condemn the man. He is a redneck, cowboy father, facing his own demons, doing the best he can. Geri (Judy Herrera), a love interest for Hunter, emerges in the last half of the film. Yet their relationship, too, does not follow an expected route but rather further illustrates *The Doe Boy*'s interest in evoking something deeper than is found in most commercial movie lives.

Hunter's search for a world beyond his father's is abetted by his Cherokee grandfather, Marvin (Gordon Tootoosis), who provides an intermittent voice-over narrating a story about an unnamed boy who is clearly Hunter. "There was a boy who was part deer, part bird, part science and four-leaf clovers," Marvin's voice intones toward the film's end. "There was a boy who dreamed of becoming a good story." Marvin carves a flute for Hunter and, later, a bow, while Hunter makes a single arrow. When in the film's climax a buck offers himself as a sacrifice to be killed by Hunter's sanctified arrow, Hunter's choices simultaneously disprove his father's earlier remark that "there ain't no magic around here" while proving Hunter has grown into a man his father can accept and love.

A second recent Oklahoma-based Indian film, *Four Sheets to the Wind*, premiered six years after *The Doe Boy*. The film began in Seminole and Creek writer-director Harjo's mind with an image of a body being laboriously dragged across the screen. This image now stands as the opening shot of the film, after which the audience learns, through a voice-over in Creek with English titles, that the body belongs to a father whose death will precipitate great changes in the life of his son. The voice-over returns intermittently throughout the film until, as it speaks again to narrate the concluding scenes, viewers learn that this is the voice of the dead father. The surprise is great, for most events in *Four Sheets to the Wind* are driven by the pain created by the living father's lack of communication. In death, he waxes loquaciously, though during his life he practiced an extraordinary silence.

After the funeral, mother Cora (Jeri Arredondo) recalls for her twenty-something son, Cufe (Cody Lightning), that when she first met his father he was hiding in the shadows at a dance. She forced herself on him and asked him his name. "Four-sheets-to-the-wind," he answered, charming her and providing the film with its title, which suggests a state of inebriation beyond ordinary drunkenness. The father's and family's dominant problem is not alcohol, however, but an inability to give or receive love.

8-3 Cufe, Miri, and Cora briefly together again

Lightning here tackles his first starring role after a prominent career as a child actor, including supporting appearances in both *Grand Avenue* (as Sheldon) and *Smoke Signals* (as the young Victor Joseph), as well as an adolescent in *Edge of America*. Cufe learned to be almost as taciturn as his father, so Lightning must show his emotions on-screen more with looks and gestures than with words. Cufe spends the movie mostly grieving silently, as do his mother and older sister, Miri (Tamara Podemski). Miri had run away from her family and small town years before, rarely to return. Cufe visits her in Tulsa where he and the audience see that Miri is a petty thief with few resources to keep her from living in the streets. By film's end, Cufe's grief seems to be lifting enough to allow him to venture away from the familiar but restrictive nest his mother provides. Sister Miri, on the other hand, after a perhaps-not-accidental overdose, is preparing to take the opposite journey, to return to stay with her mother after years of self-destructive flight.

After the film's premiere at Sundance in 2007, Harjo was nominated for a Grand Jury Prize and Podemski was awarded a Special Jury Prize "for a fully realized physical and emotional turn."

Two Navajo Films

For a century the Navajo have been misrepresented in films made by outsiders. Finally, with Chris Eyre's two films *A Thief of Time* and *Skinwalkers*, an Indian director for the first time directed Navajo-based stories. Eyre himself is not Navajo, however, and his two films are based on mystery stories by a white novelist, Tony Hillerman. Though both films employed many Indian actors, most were not Navajo. It was only with the release of *5th World* in 2005 and of *Mile Post 398* in 2007 that the Navajo were able to see feature films that used predominantly Navajo crews and actors and told Navajo-created stories.

Blackhorse Lowe's *5th World* derives its title from the central creation story of the Navajo, which tells of a time when Insect People created the First World. These people angered the gods of that world and were cast out into a Second World, occupied by the Swallow People, a race of flying creatures. Once more the Insect People misbehaved and were cast out into a Third and then into a Fourth World. Eventually, they had to flee again and ended up in the current world, the Fifth World, where they are obliged to continue ceremonies they learned in the Fourth World.[6] Lowe's film focuses on two couples, a generation apart, to explore how Fourth World traditions are holding up under the pressures to change exerted on them in contemporary America.

On-screen, affection and, ultimately, passion slowly grows between Aria Clyde (Livandrea Knoki) and Andrei Bedonie (Sheldon Silentwalker). They are twenty-something Navajo college students hitchhiking across the 27,000-square-mile Navajo reservation, the largest area controlled by Native Americans within the United States. (This land includes much of northeastern Arizona and extends into Utah and New Mexico.) Aria and Andrei tease, mock, shove, and flirt in often awkward and childish ways, walking and standing in the foreground of many striking desert landscapes filmed mostly in the Four Corners region between Tuba City and Kayenta, Arizona.

As viewers watch Aria and Andrei's relationship develop, they often hear other voices off-screen: a second, older couple recounting their courtship in an earlier era. Eventually, these voices are attached to a couple represented on-screen as Andrei's aunt and uncle, who are, in fact, filmmaker Lowe's own parents. This long-married pair takes turns telling how they met, grew interested in each other, and decided to wed. Aunt and uncle, mother and father, speak mostly Navajo as they describe the slow development of their relationship, the need in earlier years for parental supervision and permissions, the requirement of negotiating a bride price. "I wanted to offer a horse," the uncle/father says, "but they asked for money. Now, though, I have my Blackhorse [i.e., his son]."

Aria and Andrei's romance seems at first to be developing much differently. The two mostly speak English, only rarely Navajo; they are traveling unsupervised, without either parental approval or knowledge. And, Lowe's script emphasizes, Aria and Andrei's common understandings are strongly rooted in contemporary American music, television, and movies. In many ways these two young Navajo of today's Fifth World thus seem to have abandoned what their ancestors brought over from the Fourth World. Then, suddenly, in the film's last fifteen minutes, the power of older traditions erupt to reshape Aria and Andrei's lives as deeply as they did earlier generations.

Mile Post 398 appeared soon after *5th World*. Both films were made with small budgets, were shot at overlapping reservation locations, and even used two of the same actors, James Junes and Ernest David Tsosie III, known also as the comedy duo James and Ernie. Overall, however, it is difficult to imagine two more different films. *5th World* concentrates on the mood and atmosphere surrounding its two main characters while *Mile Post 398* is not only plot driven but relies on that plot to deliver an unmistakable lesson. *5th World* aims to work as a light entertainment; *Mile Post 398* unfolds with a gravity reminiscent of Greek tragedy or of *King Lear*.

Shonie and Andee De La Rosa, the husband-and-wife team who wrote, produced and directed *Mile Post 398*, had previously made *G: Methamphetamines on the Navajo Reservation* (2004), a documentary about this drug's devastating effects. *Mile Post 398* retains some of the De La Rosas' earlier documentary style as well as their desire to present a message. In *Mile Post 398* the dangerous drug has shifted from meth to alcohol.

The film opens with a flashback showing one alcohol-fueled night that shaped the childhood of Cloyd (Beau Benally), the protagonist. Soon we jump forward to see Cloyd as an adult with a wife (Kim White) and a son. The boy is about the same age as Cloyd in the flashback and is played by the same actor (K. J. White). We see Cloyd's very old friends (Junes and Gerald Vandever) frequently coax him away from his family for late-night carousing. Cloyd finally drinks so much that he loses his low-wage job. His wife pleads with him to sober up and find new work. Cloyd does, succeeds for a time, then goes off with his two drinking buddies once again. Another cycle of recriminations and forgiveness follows before a shakily sober Cloyd makes yet another effort to resist his friends' influence. They proclaim that they are part of Cloyd's family, too, and that he owes at least as much allegiance to them as he does to his more recently acquired wife and son.

Mile Post 398 was made by a volunteer Navajo cast and crew, Shonie Da La Rosa says, as a "collaboration of talent from all over the Navajo Nation."[7] All shooting took place on the reservation, frequently around the actual mile post 398 near Kayenta Township referred to in the title. The screenplay borrows from Shonie De La Rosa's own experiences with alcohol addiction. Many of the cast and crew had had similar personal experiences. *Mile Post 398* was, then, a community effort to try to create a fiction film that would help people within the Navajo community change or, at least, begin a discussion about the dangers of alcoholism. The film debuted at a community high school auditorium in Kayenta, then had a limited release in similar venues across the reservations. The DVD has since been sold in local stores along the reservation highways it pictures, as well as online. *Bearwalker* had similar aims to spotlight social problems, but *Mile Post 398* is perhaps the only Indian-made feature whose dominant purpose is to provide its community, as Carol Quattro Levine says, with "a kick-in-the-gut." Levine concludes, *Mile Post 398* is "painful to watch, yet you do. Like a train wreck."[8]

Two Films by Rodrick Pocowatchit

Rodrick Pocowatchit has made two feature films, *Dancing on the Moon* (2003) and *Sleepdancer* (2005), in which he served as writer, director, producer, and one of the principal actors. Neither film is directly auto-biographical, but both draw from Pocowatchit's own Kansas roots, relationships, and experiences to create what is probably the most intimately personal cinema created by any Indigenous filmmaker anywhere in the world. While *The Doe Boy*, for example, drew from writer-director Randy Redroad's own childhood, the producers and most of the crew and actors were outsider professionals. Pocowatchit not only acts in, directs, and produces his own scripts, he even draws his crew and actors exclusively from family and friends. So, for example, Pocowatchit's brother, Guy Ray Pocowatchit, plays roles as Pocowatchit's fictional brother in each of the films.

Pocowatchit is a member of the Pawnee, Shawnee, and Comanche tribes, and his films aim to represent the everyday life of Indians like himself in Kansas today. These people, Pocowatchit says, are "just like everybody else. They just happened to have this other thing about them. They're Native American and they go to dances, go to powwows."[9] Powwow dancing has long been one of Pocowatchit's passions, and each film reflects the importance of dancing, although in very different ways.

Dancing on the Moon is a road movie. Three men are driving together to attend a powwow, and they encounter multiple physical and psychological obstacles along the way. There are occasional references to the most famous of all Kansas-based road movies, *The Wizard of Oz* (1939), and Pocowatchit's three men could very roughly be lined up as a Lion (Guy Ray Pocowatchit), a Scarecrow (Rodrick Pocowatchit), and a Tin Man (Mark Wells). They even meet and are sometimes led by a Dorothy (Jill Jarsulic), who steals their car before she steals their hearts. This Dorothy also helps the three, metaphorically, find their way home.

Dancing on the Moon takes every opportunity to exploit the cinematic possibilities of rural Kansas. Pocowatchit's second film, *Sleepdancer*, however, stays rooted in residential Wichita. *Sleepdancer* is a psychological mystery where, as in *Dancing on the Moon*, resolution is found through dancing. As mentioned, Pocowatchit plays the faux scarecrow in *Dancing on the Moon*; there, as Joey, a slow-witted character with much heart and not much brain, he requires much looking after. In

8-4 *Dancing on the Moon* pays homage to *The Wizard of Oz* (Courtesy of Harmy Films)

Sleepdancer, Pocowatchit's character, Tommy, is a traumatized, mute recluse who also must be cared for. Tommy clutches a small stuffed bear in several scenes and this bear is a replica of "Harmy," Pocowatchit's own childhood bear and the model for both the name and the logo of Pocowatchit's film production company, Harmy Films.[10]

Sleepdancer is an expanded version of an earlier short film. Both short and feature are based on a dream Pocowatchit had about the power to be found in nocturnal dancing. *Sleepdancer* does not aim to create the trancelike experiences of dreams or dancing, but instead follows a formal structure with three distinct acts, each announced on title cards. Act One takes the point of view of Derek (Mark Wells), a coroner's assistant, as he develops an interest in Tommy, the thirty-something son of a recently deceased Native American man. Act One is shot with much handheld, shaky camera work, reflecting Derek's own uncertain psychic state. Act Two focuses on Tommy's brother, Ben, and is in black and white, with close-ups and interior shots imitating film noir to reflect Ben's hard-boiled point of view. The final act, Act Three, shifts back to color but uses mostly an unmoving camera to give viewers a sense of the extreme stillness in Tommy's traumatized mind.

Pocowatchit's willingness to cast himself as the most vulnerable character in each of his films mirrors the persona that emerges on his blog, "Harmyland, The Useless Ramblings of a Clueless Filmmaker." Here, since 2004, Pocowatchit has chronicled the sometimes exciting and often discouraging details of his attempts to conceive, produce, and then try to find an audience for both his features and for his several short films. "So, a tally sheet," Pocowatchit blogged on May 16, 2006, "Total rejections so far, including tomorrow's: 10. Total rejections including festivals we've submitted to but still waiting for our rejection letter: 16. Total amount spent on submission fees thus far: $460.00. Yeah, it's time to really, really catch a clue. Time for Plan B." Some months later, Pocowatchit posts, "Me and my mom head to Chicago for some great screenings of 'Sleep-dancer' at the First Nations Film & Video Festival. Some screenings had a very small turnout, but I'd go door to door to show my film if I could."[11] The blog amplifies the sensibility of the films, sharing Pocow-atchit's belief that he and other contemporary Indians "have these other beliefs, but really they're just like everybody else."[12]

Future Indian Films

Except for *Skins*, which received a limited release, none of the new century's sixteen Indian-made features has been shown in commercial theaters.[13] A few have appeared on television (*Bearwalker*, *Johnny Tootall*, *Skinwalkers*, and *A Thief of Time*), but most have circulated at film festivals where they have been viewed by a few hundred or, at best, a few thousand people. Some Indian films (e.g., *The Business of Fancy-dancing*, *The Doe Boy*, *Mile Post 398*) reached additional viewers as DVD releases. Compared to the impact and distribution of commercial the-atrical releases, however, Indian-made self-representations remain today almost as absent from movie and television screens in North America as they were throughout the twentieth century.

Simultaneously, the non-Indigenous filmmakers who dominate the media world continue providing large audiences worldwide with fan-tasies of the master race, powerful images of what white filmmakers imagine are Indian stories. So Mel Gibson's *Apocalypto* (2006) or, even, a high-end art-house movie like Terrence Malick's *The New World* (2005) has been viewed by audiences larger than all who have seen the new cen-tury's entire archive of Indian-directed films. In terms of altering the mass audience's understanding of Indians, then, Sherman Alexie seems correct in his lament that "absolutely nothing" was changed by *Smoke Signals'* commercial success.[14]

Of course, audience size and profits do not determine the value of an Indian-made film. Their absence can, however, make it very difficult for an Indian filmmaker to create a new film. As Redroad explains, even if a film has pan-tribal appeal, the Indian audience alone is not large enough to support most productions, "even if every Indian saw the movie twice. . . . It's the cold mathematical reality of genocide."[15] Indian films with even modest budgets, then, often need to appeal to non-Indian as well as Indian audiences if their makers hope to secure funds to make additional films.

All filmmakers face intensely unforgiving commercial pressures, but contemporary Indian filmmakers encounter additional challenges. The long tradition of North American filmmaking has provided millions of people with the false belief that they already know much about America's Indigenous peoples. Indian-made features that seek a broad audience must somehow counter these decades of influential stereotypes while simultaneously convincing viewers that Native peoples are a topic not already done to exhaustion, that there is something fresh to be found in feature films focused on Indians.

Appealing too much to mainstream audiences can, however, lead to the loss of cultural specificity, to films that might as well have been made by non-Indian filmmakers. So, for example, several reviewers agreed with Phil Hall that *The Doe Boy* was not "Indian enough," that it "often seems as if its Cherokee story angle was tacked on to provide an exotic accessory."[16] On the other hand, Indian films may emphasize cultural differences so much that non-Indigenous audiences do not understand what is going on. The penalties for failing to find the right balance were explained by Jonathan Saturen, art director for *The Business of Fancydancing.* Saturen warned Alexie during production, "This movie's going to be too white for Indians, too Indian for whites, and too gay for everybody."[17]

Despite these many challenges, the archive of Indian features is rapidly growing. The number of experienced Indian filmmakers is now far greater than ever before. This expanding community of directors, producers, cinematographers, actors, and others is increasingly working together to complete more and larger projects. Indians in the movie business may already, or will soon, constitute a community of talent large enough to sustain itself independently from North American commercial cinema.

Aiding this emerging community are new possibilities for funding created by the gaming wealth that a few tribes have accumulated. The Pequot were the executive producer for *Naturally Native*; tribes in California, Minnesota, and Oklahoma joined together to finance writer-director-actor Rick Schroder's *Black Cloud* (2004). Neither of these films were commercial successes, but their productions did demonstrate it is possible for Indian people to finance their own features. Chris Eyre's company, Seven Arrows Signature, described in chapter two, explicitly aims to help tribes produce media that reflect their specific cultural goals.

Still, as in other regions of the world, it is probably the rich, as yet mostly unfilmed, traditions of Indigenous North American storytelling that provides the single most promising resource for Indian filmmakers. Successful feature films require powerful stories and, though the hundreds of Indian tribes across North America lost much to white colonialism, most retain elements of oral traditions much older than the Greek and Roman storytelling traditions that ground Anglo-American films. Adapting Indian stories for a visual medium should prove at least as fruitful as adapting Eurocentric stories for the screen.

In concert with these adaptations, or independently, the future also seems likely to see more Indian movies that borrow from familiar Anglo-American movie genres. There are likely to be more Indian action movies like *Tushka*, more coming-of-age Indian movies like *The Doe Boy*, more Indian romances like *5th World*, more Indian sisterhood films like *Naturally Native*, more Indian crime dramas like *Skinwalkers*, more Indian teen sports movies like *The Edge of America*, more Indian ghost stories like *Imprint*, more Indian adult dramas like *Skins*, more Indian family dramas like *Bearwalker*, more Indian road movies like *Smoke Signals*, as well as Indian experimental, art-house movies like *The Business of Fancydancing* and *Sleepdancer*. The combination of ancient storytelling traditions and western film genres seems likely to produce an increasingly rich archive of Indian feature films.

Chapter 9

Indigenous Films of the Arctic

Seventy years ago, we didn't know about the existence of paper, and in such a short time, we learned how to read, write, how to work with paper, and we started making films collectively with all the 35,000 Nenets people.

Anastasia Lapsui

Despite many obstacles, the sparsely populated Arctic region has proven to be a rich land for producing feature films. Stretching across the northern border of many countries and three continents (Asia, Europe, and North America), the Arctic is today home to about ten different Indigenous peoples with a total population of approximately 400,000. The Indigenous peoples of this region have already produced eight Indigenous feature films and more are in the pre-production phase.

The Sámi of Finland have made three features, *Pathfinder* (1987), *The Minister of State* (1997), and *The Kautokeino Rebellion* (2007). Yet another feature, *Bázo* (2003), used a mostly Sámi crew and actors, who spoke Sámi throughout the film. The Nenets of Russia have produced two features, *Seven Songs from the Tundra* (1999) and *A Bride of the Seventh Heaven* (2004). And the Inuit of the Nunavut Territory of Canada have made three features, *Atanarjuat: The Fast Runner* (2001), *The Journals of Knud Rasmussen* (2006), and *Before Tomorrow* (2007).[1]

Little unites these Arctic peoples or their films beyond the challenging climate they share. Still, it may be that the very rigors and isolation of this region make it a particularly fertile location for cinema. Robert J. Flaherty's much-praised *Nanook of the North* at the very beginning of commercial cinema demonstrated the potential for influential filmmaking in the Arctic. Thirty-four years later, the Danish-made *Qivitoq* (1956) was nominated for an Academy Award for Best Foreign Language Film (won that year by *La Strada*) in large measure precisely because of the impressive way it utilized the remote Greenland setting where it was shot. *Qivitoq* told paralleling stories of Danish and Sámi events without actually using any Sámi actors. Films exploiting the snowy scenery while rejecting Indigenous actors were still appearing as late as 1992, when *Shadow of the Wolf* (*Agaguk* [1992]) offered Japanese and part-Chinese performers (Toshirô Mifune, Lou Diamond Phillips, and Jennifer Tilly) as supposed Inuit characters even though Sámi writer-director Nils Gaup had already demonstrated in *Pathfinder* five years before that Indigenous Arctic actors could perform well in feature films. It was not until 2001, however, with the appearance of *Atanarjuat: The Fast Runner*, that worldwide audiences finally became aware that the Flaherty-pioneered tradition of innovative Arctic cinema would continue even once the region's Indigenous people controlled the camera.

Pathfinder

Pathfinder, the Arctic's first Indigenous-made feature, won an Amanda Award for Best Norwegian Cinema Release and became the first and, so far, the only Indigenous film to be nominated for an Academy Award (in the Best Foreign Film category).

An epigraph at the beginning of *Pathfinder* proclaims, "Among the Lapp people, this history has been passed on for almost 1,000 years." The history that follows, in Sámi with English subtitles, is both brutal and beautiful. It begins with Aigin, a young man (Mikkel Gaup, no relation to director Gaup) watching from a hiding place as his family is slaughtered by the Tchudes, a band of marauders. Aigin escapes, though wounded, and inadvertently leaves a trail of blood guiding the Tchudes to a nearby small settlement. The people there quickly head off toward a more populous village near the seashore while Aigin and four others stay behind to fight.

Pathfinder was shot in Finnmarksvidda, the northernmost part of Norway, and Gaup effectively exploits this snowy vastness both to enhance the film's grandeur and to add surprises to its several action sequences. There is relatively little dialogue, as emotions are more often conveyed through faces, eye movements, and gestures. Many scenes show Aigin or others racing to get from one place to another, often through stunning shots of skiing. Gaup and his director of photography, Erling Thurmann-Andersen, used a 70 mm lens to better capture the snowy enormity and relative size of the humans who roam across it. The wide film gauge is particularly effective in emphasizing contrasts between the bright blue Arctic sky and the equally bright white mountains arching to meet it.

There are sufficient shots of daily life to provide a glimpse of how the Sámi may have lived a millennium ago. Overall, however, *Pathfinder* emphasizes action and adventure more than ethnography. The resulting narrative constructs a morality tale. The barbarous Tchudes are dressed in black, while Aigin and the settlers wear shades of white and brown. Though viewers see the implements and practices the settlers use, the Tchudes seem to require no earthly possessions. All men, they travel without tools or packs, roaming like some force of pure evil, existing but to pillage and murder. The Tchudes do not understand that all beings are bound together, the Sámi shaman, Raste (Nils Utsi), explains to Aigin. To help Aigin recognize the reality of this invisible connection, Raste chokes Aigin until he becomes frantic for breath. As it is by air, Raste explains, "everything is tied together with invisible bonds."

Before he dies, Raste passes on his shaman's drum to Aigin, who, in the film's climax, proves his worthiness to become his people's next pathfinder. The last shot of the film is on that drum, as the film's epigraph announces this succession tale has been passed down among the Sámi for endless generations. (*The Journals of Knud Rasmussen*, discussed below, offers a tragic, post-contact Arctic shaman succession story, told by the Inuit rooted in another part of the Arctic.)

Willow G. Mullins and Holly Hobbes point out that *Pathfinder* spoke directly to the political situation of the Sámi during the decade of its release.[2] Though the Tchudes are identified as Norwegian or Russian in some oral versions of the tale, in *Pathfinder* they become simply generic outsiders, stand-ins for any of the many invaders who have come to pillage Sámi lands. The Sámi in the film, by contrast, are presented as thoroughly integrated with one another and with the land and animals surrounding them. Their language in *Pathfinder* also sets them apart from the Tchudes, whose strange speech, invented for the film, is generally left unsubtitled. So, Mullins and Hobbes maintain, *Pathfinder* sent a message of support in the 1980s to both Sámi and non-Sámi who were struggling to establish Indigenous language rights and separate Indigenous parliaments across Scandinavia. The people in *Pathfinder* find food and escape dangers because they are able to move freely across the Arctic. So in this, too, the film spoke to the threat posed by Scandinavian nation-states trying to restrict cross-border Indigenous movements.

Still, it was not its ancient story or its contemporary political impli-cations that created so much attention when *Pathfinder* was released. Rather, critics marveled mostly at Gaup's direction, at how tightly and effectively each scene was staged. *Pathfinder* was not compared to the slow pacing of Flaherty's *Nanook* but rather to Hollywood's classic west-erns, transported to snow. Stanley Kauffmann wrote, for example, that *Pathfinder* "tells its story cleanly with a keen sense of theater-in-space. I'd guess that Gaup knows his John Ford."[3] The reputation of Gaup's *Pathfinder* is so great that Marcus Nispel directed a remake twenty years later. This mass-market *Pathfinder* (2007) retains little of Gaup's vision, beyond his joy in imagining snowy chases. Still, the original *Pathfinder* remains the only Indigenous feature so far to have provoked a commer-cial remake. *Pathfinder* also remains, probably not coincidentally, one of the few Indigenous features made so far to fit firmly within the genre of action and adventure.

The Kautokeino Rebellion

Pathfinder's success created multiple opportunities for Gaup, its first-time feature director and writer. Gaup had previously been best known as the co-founder of the Beaivváś Sámi Theatre, now known as the Sámi National Theatre Company. He used many actors from this theater as principals in *Pathfinder*. Kauffmann had concluded his review of *Pathfinder* by declaring, "with this film Gaup obligates himself to con-tinue, in Lapland or elsewhere," and mostly "elsewhere" it has turned out to be. Gaup's second film became the partly Disney-financed *Ship-wrecked* (*Haakon Haakonsen*, 1990), released in an English-language version. Gaup's third film, *Hodet over vannet* (*Head Above Water*, 1993), won another Norwegian Amanda award for Best Film and was remade for American audiences in 1996 with Cameron Diaz and Harvey Keitel in the leads. Gaup's next films were *Tashunga* (also known as *North Star*, 1996) and *Misery Harbour* (1999). None of these offered Sámi sto-ries, but then, twenty years after *Pathfinder*, Gaup returned to his roots to co-write and direct *The Kautokeino Rebellion*, based on a true story about events in 1852 in the area of Norway where Gaup grew up.

Gaup once again uses the actor Mikkel Gaup, who made his debut in *Pathfinder*. He plays Aslak Hætta, a Sámi who runs a business selling goods to rural Sámi communities. His success threatens Ruth (Mikael Persbrandt), an outsider who runs a store in the village of Kautokeino.

Aslak and Ruth repeatedly clash, especially over who will dominate the lucrative liquor sales that are turning an increasing number of Sámi into alcoholics. Aslak's brother, Mathis (Aslat Mahtte Gaup), and wife, Elen (Anni-Kristiina Juuso), have become teetotalers and rabid exponents of a local revivalist church. Their expanding temperance movement further threatens Ruth's liquor sales, and Ruth persuades the church authorities to ban all village revival meetings. Ruth also convinces the legal authorities to imprison Aslak, Mathis, and several others. The group is eventually released, but Ruth and his supporters claim that Elen's extensive herd of reindeer must now be butchered to pay fines and legal costs.

Much of this narrative is speculative, but the film's climax tries to remain true to the historical record of what is sometimes called the Sámi rebellion of 1852. Then, a group of thirty-five Sámis joined together in Kautokeino to kill a merchant and the sheriff. In reality and in the film, Aslak and his closest ally were later captured, charged, convicted, decapitated, and buried without their heads. A century later their skulls were located in the Anatomical Institute in Oslo. After much struggle by the Sámi against official resistance, these skulls were reunited with their skeletons. Elements of the Kautokeino uprising had already been used in five novels and two operas prior to the production of *The Kautokeino Rebellion*. Gaup is a descendent of Aslak Hætta, however, and so had a familial reason for wanting to bring this story to the screen.

Other Sámi Films

Sámi filmmaker Paul-Anders Simma has made several documentaries, including *Give Us Our Skeletons!* (1999), depicting the long campaign that Niillas Somby led to force the Anatomical Institute of Oslo to return to their families the Sámi skulls taken after the events at Kautokeino. Simma had previously written and directed *The Legacy of the Tundra* (1995), a film that exists in both feature-length (eighty-two-minute) and edited-for-television (fifty-minute) versions. *The Legacy of the Tundra* has sometimes been labeled a documentary and sometimes a feature film as it contains elements of both genres.

The Legacy of the Tundra draws from Simma's experiences as a child raised by reindeer herders in a village of thirty families and 15,000 reindeer. The film explores dilemmas like those the young Simma once faced over whether to follow the occupations of his father and ancestors.

In the film, seventeen-year-old John Andreas feels rising pressures to choose his path after his father dies. The government offers a substantial cash payment if John will slaughter his small reindeer herd and then abandon his family's herding license forever. Simultaneously, owners of neighboring larger reindeer herds are trying to force John to keep his reindeer out of the communal pastures. Further complications arise from an opportunity for John to earn a lot of money by delivering thirty reindeer bulls for the opening ceremony of the 1994 Winter Olympics in Lillehammer, Norway. The future of John's widowed mother and his younger siblings depend on his decisions.

Two years after the drama *The Legacy of the Tundra*, Simma wrote and directed a comedy, *The Minister of State*. This film grew out of a story that Simma heard as a youth about a charlatan who took advantage of the chaos that engulfed the border region of Finland, Sweden, and Norway at the end of World War II. Simma explains, "He came to Sagojokk [Norway] from the south, cheated the villagers, took their money and left. But the people still considered him a big hero."[4]

The Minister of State transforms this incident into a burlesque tragicomedy. Seppo Rävmark (Erik Kiviniemi) is the larger-than-life faux minister who begins the film wanting only to escape from the Nazis. The Sagojokk villagers mistake him for a representative of the government, who they hope will institute postwar land reforms. Seppo acquiesces and is soon giving land to the landless, while taking modest fees for himself. Not everyone is convinced of Seppo's authenticity, however, and the large landowner Antti Neja (Björn Sundquist) eventually plots murder to end Seppo's generous schemes. A second stranger arrives and recognizes the fraud. He attempts to blackmail Seppo who, by now, has acquired not only a sense of morality but also the love of the beautiful Marit Jaha (Sara Margrethe Oskal). From this lighthearted comedy of errors, the expected final pleasures arise.

The comic tone of *The Minister of State* makes it a rarity among Indigenous feature films. Indeed, it is another Sámi-based film, *Bázo*, whose mood may come closest to that of *The Minister of State*. Though written and directed by Lars-Göran Pettersson, not himself Sámi, most of *Bázo*'s actors are Sámi and are veterans of the Kautokeino's Beaivvás Sámi Theatre founded by Nils Gaup. Most of the often hilarious, always deadpan dialogue in *Bázo* is in Sámi. Several members of the production crew were Sámi and Pettersson himself, like most of the cast and crew, resides north of the Arctic Circle, near or in areas where the Sámi retain their dominance. Similarities of attitude in *Bázo* and *The Minister of State* suggest these films reflect portions of the same straight-faced Sámi comic view.

Emil (Sverre Porsanger) is *Bázo*'s somewhat obtuse but implacable protagonist. ("Bázo" is Sámi slang for slow-witted.) The thirty-something Emil lives contentedly at home with his father, and the first third of the film carefully establishes the dull routines of their rural life on a reindeer farm. Then, abruptly, Emil and the film's rhythms change. Emil's father mishandles a power saw, leaving his arm a shockingly bloody mess. Soon after, Emil learns that his brother, Kenneth, has been crushed and killed in a supposed industrial accident. Emil must leave the farm to claim his various inheritances, including, he discovers, an almost-new shotgun, an illegally impounded, costly rock-excavating machine, a Mercedes, a seven-year-old boy (a previously unknown nephew) and, even, if he wants, Kenneth's old girlfriend. Finding and learning about each of these forces Emil to crisscross national borders and explore settlements and cities much different from what he has known. Emil discovers, too, that he must confront the motley crew of small-time criminals and crooked politicians who had filled Kenneth's life.

Of course, Emil doggedly defies first appearances and proves himself clever enough in all necessary ways. He charms some people and tricks others. He even finds a way to orchestrate a spectacular concluding explosion that destroys the business of the villains who will not yield either to his charm or tricks.

Humor generally translates less easily across cultures than do more sober cinematic tones. This may help explain why neither *The Minister of State* nor *Bázo* has been much seen outside film festivals based in northern Europe. This may also partially explain the rarity of Indigenous film comedies across all regions. *Smoke Signals* from North America and *Ten Canoes* from Australia do offer frequent lighthearted moments, but seem, in their different ways, aimed at offering dramatic narratives more often than comedy. Only *Eagle vs Shark* and *Samoan Wedding*, both made in New Zealand, seem as thoroughly committed to humor as are *The Minister of State* and *Bázo*. The recent appearance of these two Pacific Islander comedies, coupled with *Bázo*, also recently made, may signal that the pace of production of Indigenous comedies is accelerating.

Two Nenets Films

Two remarkable films by Nenets filmmaker Anastasia Lapsui and her non-Indigenous partner, Markku Lehmuskallio, have received awards and praise at dozens of film festivals across Europe though, so far, neither film has been widely exhibited in North America. Both films feature Nenets actors speaking Nenets in stories set in their vast Arctic homeland stretching across the northern coast of Russia. With a total population of about 40,000, the Nenets are among the smallest groups of Indigenous peoples to have thus far produced multiple feature films.

Finnish filmmaker Lehmuskallio had made both documentary and feature films about Arctic life before beginning his collaborations with Lapsui. Their collaboratively made features *Seven Songs from the Tundra* and *A Bride of the Seventh Heaven,* as well as a documentary, *Mothers of Life (Ehaman Aidit,* 2002), demonstrate how fruitful it can be for outsiders to make films with, instead of about, Indigenous peoples.

Seven Songs from the Tundra is one of the most directly political Indigenous films ever made. Probably only the Māori-directed *Te Rua* and the Choctaw-directed *Tushka* match its political focus. *Seven Songs from the Tundra* links seven tangentially related stories through the incantation of seven Nenets songs. The first story presents the ritual sacrifice of a reindeer to the gods; the seventh shows a woman singing to her child. The five middle episodes provide different views of the harsh treatment the Nenets received because of the mid-twentieth-century Soviet policies of forced relocation and assimilation.

One middle episode, for example, shows a Nenets man with a large reindeer herd being told by a Soviet official that he must abandon his stock and become poor like most of the rest of his people. The Soviet official speaks no Nenets; the herder speaks no Russian. A translator's misinterpretations increase tensions between the two. In another episode, Nenets are praising a statue of Lenin, calling him a god, when they are chased away as vagrants by Soviet officials.

Each of the middle five episodes seems drawn from a different historical period, but the exact dates remain unclear. The beginning and ending episodes showing traditional Nenets practices signal that the old ways persist, despite the traumas of the decades of Soviet interventions.

The actors are Nenets who themselves experienced many events like those they here reenact. Their performances, combined with the cinematographic and editing style, encourage the sense that the film is not fiction but ethnographic documentary. The print is even in a grainy black and white, suggesting older, historical photographs.

The screenplay for *Seven Songs from the Tundra* was based in part on Lapsui's own experiences as well as on those of her family. Lapsui then drew on her life again in scripting a second feature, *A Bride of the Seventh Heaven*. She had been forced by the Soviets to leave her reindeer-herding family and attend school. The shock was so great that, for a few years, Lapsui became blind. Seeking comfort, she often visited a neighbor, an old woman living by herself who told her stories about her life as a Nenets bride of God. *A Bride of the Seventh Heaven* recreates many of these stories.[5]

9-1 Bride of Seventh Heaven

Syarda, an old woman in *A Bride of the Seventh Heaven*, tells a young blind girl, Ilne, how she was chosen before birth to become a bride of God. Syarda describes and the audience sees various shamanistic rituals that consecrate Syarda and that, as one consequence, mark her as unsuitable for marriage with Nenets men. Viewers then see the traditional Nenets world in the Yamal peninsula from the perspective of a woman excluded from most activities prescribed for Nenets women.

Being chosen to be a bride of God is thought a great honor among most Nenets, but *A Bride of the Seventh Heaven* emphasizes the loneliness this honor brings. Syarda is left friendless when her parents die and so decides to live with a childless older couple, who want her to bear a child for them. She proves to be infertile and eventually runs off with a younger man with whom she is also unable to conceive. He rejects her, and Syarda is left alone once again, a bride of God with no human relationships, until the blind girl befriends her. Filmmaker Lapsui was herself selected in her youth to serve for a few years as a bride of God. Lapsui's film suggests the honor of being so selected requires an emotional price that some Nenets women may no longer be willing to pay.

Atanarjuat: The Fast Runner

Atanarjuat: The Fast Runner won the prestigious Cannes Caméra d'Or (Best First Film) at Cannes in 2001, the first Canadian-based film to do so. It subsequently received more awards at film festivals around the world than any other Indigenous feature made before or since. Much of this acclaim grew from the film's innovative visual style, a style that Jerry White shows had slowly evolved for over a decade in numerous videos produced in Canada's Northwest Territories settlement of Igloolik.[6] Many aspects of this style were created by *Atanarjuat*'s director Zacharias Kunuk and others associated with *Atanarjuat,* but, White makes clear, even videos made by others in this small community of about 1,200 people frequently display a similar innovative aesthetic.

The on-screen look of *Atanarjuat: The Fast Runner* was self-consciously crafted to present a visual equivalent of the oral tale upon which it is based. "When we were growing up it was a bedtime story for us," Kunuk remembers.[7] The choice to film this particular bedtime story sprang from Kunuk's recognition that the tale contained, at heart, an especially arresting visual image. As Kunuk explains, "Once you get that picture into your head of that naked man running for his life across the sea ice, his hair flying, you never forget it. It had everything for a fantastic movie—love, jealousy, murder and revenge, and at the same time, buried in this ancient Inuit 'action thriller' were all these lessons we kids were supposed to learn about how if you break these taboos that kept our ancestors alive, you could be out there running for your life, just like him."[8] (The Australian Aborigine film *Ten Canoes*, discussed in chapter 12, was similarly sparked by a single image, albeit not from a legend but from an anthropologist's seventy-year-old photograph.)

Some of Kunuk's earlier videos had similarly borrowed from the melodramas common to North American media. Kunuk's *Qaggiq/Gathering Place*, for instance, was inspired by the filmmaker's onetime enthusiasm for the television soap opera *All My Children*. "It's great," Kunuk explained, as the characters in these television shows "never leave the house and it's never boring. I wanted to make something like that."[9] Part of *Atanarjuat: The Fast Runner*'s success with non-Indigenous audiences no doubt arises from its embrace of familiar themes such as romance, jealousy, betrayal, and revenge.

The chase sequence, and the murder that precedes and precipitates it, as Kunuk says, forms the film's narrative core, but this core is more deeply rooted in a pre-modern Inuit epic than in commercial cinema. The chase abruptly and surprisingly transforms the pace of the film, which until that moment likely seems to most non-Inuit audiences to be moving forward very slowly, more like an ethnography or a documentary than a feature film. The violence and terror surrounding the chase sequence abruptly infuses new meanings into the long, meditative scenes that have come before.

9-2 Atanarjuat escapes across the snow

The chase is divided into two parts. Initially, for about a minute, the audience sees Atanarjuat escaping from the tent and leading his pursuers out onto the ice. After an interlude that focuses on the returning wives as they discover and grieve for the dead brother, the chase continues for about five minutes in a dozen shots that are at once dramatically effective and technically simple. Drums, breathy flutes, and, toward the end, singing voices form a background to the prominent blasts of Atanarjuat's heavy breathing and, occasionally, the sound of racing bare feet slapping shallow water. The camera remains still or slowly pans, only once moving beside Atanarjuat in a dogsled-enabled tracking shot.

Using these simple techniques, Kunuk and crew reinvigorated the clichéd movie chase scene that has been prominent almost from the first year of film's invention. In addition, Atanarjuat's run concludes in a fundamentally Inuit manner, through guidance from a spirit and then a magical leap over a wide crack in the ice that, White points out, is much like a similar leap across a river that Kunuk also presented in his earlier video *Saputi* (1993).[10]

Creating authentic representations of the ancient Inuit material world required the Igloolik production community to recreate pre-contact Inuit tools, shelters, and clothing that were little known by the end of the twentieth century. Determining how to make many of the needed objects required supplementing current Inuit knowledge with research into nineteenth-century visitor records, including the journals of Admiral William Parry's British naval expedition to Igloolik in 1822–1823. The resulting props shown on-screen include: knives made of bone and stone; sleds constructed from caribou bone, skin, and sinew; clothing made from caribou, wolf, seal, and bird skins and adorned with intricate embroidery; as well as both snow and stone houses reconstructed with traditional materials. Making *Atanarjuat* thus helped revive interest and knowledge in forgotten and neglected cultural practices even before the film was shown. As Kunuk explains, "When the missionaries forced their religion on us, storytelling and drum dancing were almost banned. Our film *Atanarjuat* is one way of bringing back lost traditions. I have never witnessed shamanism. I have only heard about it. One way of making it visible is to film it."[11]

Though he kills his enemies in the oral tale Kunuk was taught as a child, Atanarjuat does not choose this ultimate revenge in the film. "Revenge is not the subject" of the film, Kunuk says, "the subject is sharing. People who are not in the system could be killed or sent away— and we choose to send them away."[12]

The success of *Atanarjuat: The Fast Runner* with international film audiences counted for much less with its makers than did its success among the Inuit themselves. "Children right now are very interested in our movie, because for the first time, it's in their language. It's not Arnold Schwarzenegger, blowing people's heads away. Now it's Atanarjuat. It's a story that kids are even playing, like playing some scenes out. I even get feedback from parents. One time a parent told me that he had been look-ing for his kids and he couldn't find them. When he found them outside, they were playing tent and he could hear they were playing 'Atanarjuat.' That's cool."[13] (Additional discussion of *Atanarjuat: The Fast Runner* is included in chapters 1 and 5.)

The Journals of Knud Rasmussen

The artistic and commercial success of *Atanarjuat* helped Igloolik Isuma Productions find financing to begin developing new features. The first of these, *The Journals of Knud Rasmussen*, appeared in 2006 and a second, *Before Tomorrow*, was scheduled to appear shortly after *Native Features* went to press.

The Journals of Knud Rasmussen provides a glimpse of how Christianity took root among the Inuit by focusing on one family, led by the shaman Avva (Pakak Innuksuk), as its members agonize about the prospect of abandoning traditional customs and spirits. Kunuk said he wanted the film to examine the question of "What happened to us?" Kunuk explains, "For 4,000 years of our history, it is only the last eighty-five years that Christianity came. It doesn't balance. We traded 100 taboos—laws of nature—for Ten Commandments, which now I don't have any trust for after looking at where they came from."[14]

The film draws from two volumes (out of twenty-six) that the Dane Knud Rasmussen wrote based on his observations and conversations with the Inuit of Igloolik in 1922, the same year that Flaherty was filming *Nanook of the North* several hundred miles away. Rasmussen, born in Greenland to Danish parents, was one-quarter Inuit and spoke fluently the language of those he interviewed. Two long monologues in *The Journals of Knud Rasmussen*, one by Avva and the other by his wife, Orulu (Neeve Irngaut), speak the exact words recorded in Rasmussen's journals.

Rasmussen's writing, however, is placed within a larger context provided through incorporating both Inuit oral traditions and also memories shared by contemporary Inuit elders. One of the seven screenwriters, Pauloosie Qulitalik, was even the son of Rachel Uyarusuk, a living witness to Rasmussen's expedition. The screenplay, then, reflects the self-understandings of the contemporary Inuit of Igloolik as much as what Rasmussen's journals record.

The Inuit who composed the indigenous cast and crew were often the great-grandchildren of the people whose story they enact in the film. Choices about how to act in each scene were thus based as much on each actor's own sense of his or her ancestors as on suggestions offered by co-directors Norman Cohn and Kunuk. Getting into the roles required, as well, that these contemporary Inuit put on costumes that had been carefully made to replicate the clothes shown in Rasmussen's photographs. Actors also enacted rituals, spoke ancient words, and sang

traditional songs in ways that invited them to experience the contemporary power of many forgotten and neglected customs. (Similar reenact-
ments of ancestor practices with similar effects occurred with the
Aboriginal film *Ten Canoes*; see chapter 12.)

The effects of reenacting the ways of their ancestors linger for cast and
crew, as well as for Inuit who view *The Journals of Knud Rasmussen* and
the earlier *Atanarjuat: The Fast Runner*. As Kunuk says, "Shamanism was
here, and it's going to be here, that's what my elders tell me. After *Atanarjuat*, the elders started to talk about shamanism more. With this film
[*The Journals*], because their families are in this community, people
learned about their namesakes. We live by namesakes. When I was born,
I was given five names, but the government couldn't pronounce them so
we were given tags and family names."[15]

The Journals of Knud Rasmussen begins and ends with black-and-
white still photographs that reproduce images Rasmussen himself made.
These photographs, like much else in the film, signal that the story is
taking place in a post-contact world that is losing its connections to the
mythic era evoked in the earlier *Atanarjuat*. The Inuit in *The Journals of
Knud Rasmussen* smoke tobacco, use metal thimbles, shake hands, and
are not terribly surprised when three white men show up asking strange
questions and seeking directions.

Just as the onscreen objects mingle pre- and post-contact tools and
customs, the cinematic style of *The Journals of Knud Rasmussen* mingles
pre- and post-contact ways of watching. Elements of ethnographic style
recur; some shots even pay homage to Flaherty as, for example, the several extended igloo-making sequences that correct misrepresentations
included in Flaherty's *Nanook*. There are, as well, the two scenes already
mentioned where Avva and Orulu tell their life stories in the exact words
Rasmussen recorded. Each speaks directly to the camera, recalling many
thousands of films and audio recordings similarly created by anthropologists. Avva's words have especial force, as he converted to Christianity
soon after Rasmussen left, and so his spiritual stories, says Kunuk, were
likely never spoken by an Inuit again until Pakak Innuksuk spoke them
in the film.[16]

Though it employs a familiar documentary approach, *The Journals of
Knud Rasmussen* embeds its ethnographic elements within an Inuit-
based style that emphasizes patience, silence, and watching. As co-
director and cinematographer Cohn explains, while *Atanarjuat: The Fast
Runner* aimed to teach its audiences "how to watch," *The Journals of Knud*

Rasmussen lacks a "propulsive narrative" and so is for viewers "like going to a graduate school."[17] The camera often lingers on faces that are neither speaking nor showing emotion. Audiences are thus invited to wait and watch just as these characters are themselves waiting and watching. Sequences of seemingly unrelated events slowly unfold at—a phrase used by multiple reviewers—"a glacial pace." There are dozens of long takes that by the standards of dominant cinema need cutting, at both the beginning and the end.

The Journals of Knud Rasmussen asks audiences to listen, as well as watch, with great care. The film opens with a gramophone playing a crackling version of Caruso and ends with diegetic juxtapositions of Inuit and Christian songs. For those who can hear properly, these different songs reveal the profound differences between two competing ways of life. Neither Inuit nor Christian lyrics are much translated and so, as Martha Fisher points out, "the songs work on the audience as pure sound and emotion, and affect us on a very fundamental level. They bypass the brain and go straight to another, more basic part of our consciousness, acting with a totally unexpected power."[18]

Attentive viewers listen to the film's long silences and to the many minutes when the only sound is the crunch of boots compressing Arctic snow. So, in the final minutes, viewers are prepared to experience with the characters what the film shows to be the transformative power of singing. "These songs, they're not so hard to learn," the converted Christian shaman tells the doubters. And, later, he adds, "Sing only Jesus songs. Do not drum and sing shaman songs." With the new songs comes the new culture. With the new culture comes banishment for the spirits who shared the Arctic with the Inuit for thousands of years.

9-3 Avva stands with one of his spirit guides (© Igloolik Isuma Productions)

The Journals of Knud Rasmussen does not tell the story of conversion so much as represent a collection of loosely linked memories that, combined, evoke the conditions that led many Inuit to abandon the ways of their ancestors. Spirits are the center of this cinematic project, and *The Journals of Knud Rasmussen* present these important forces without special effects or costuming. Inuit spirits here are simply presences on-screen, human-like participants in the daily life of Avva and his family. Even Rasmussen and his white companions see them. "They're people like us," Rasmussen marvels. "They look like us," Avva corrects him, "but they are shadow people."

At the film's end, Avva walks away from the human settlement with his three guiding spirits. "Now I have to follow the way of Jesus," he tells them. "So leave me. You all have to go away. You have to leave now." The spirits reluctantly obey, trudging slowly off to disappear into the white horizon. Thus Kunuk answers his initial question, "What happened to us?" Such is the power of filmmaking, however, that this final scene, as mournful as it is, simultaneously increases the possibility of sequels, of movies and a reality in which descendents of Avva walk back to that or similar places to invite the old songs and spirits to return. As co-director Norman Cohn says, "The spirits are there, man. The next question is: where'd they go? Just because you kick them out doesn't mean they disappeared."[19]

Innovative Arctic Filmmaking

Before Tomorrow, co-produced by Igloolik Isuma Productions, is likely to much enrich the archive of Arctic Indigenous films in part because it has a substantial production budget and even more because it is the creation of a mostly female creative crew. Marie-Hélène Cousineau and Madeline Ivalu co-directed and, with Susan Avingaq, wrote the screenplay, which is based on a novel, *For Morgendaggen*, by the Danish writer Jørn Riel.

In the Inuktitut language, like earlier Igloolik Isuma features, *Before Tomorrow* is set at a time during the nineteenth century when the Inuit had heard rumors of white people but seen none. A grandmother (Madeline Ivalu) and her young grandson set off together for an isolated island, expecting their extended family to follow. Too many weeks pass, winter approaches, and still the others have not come. Grandmother and grandson go in search and discover all their family lying dead, with their bodies twisted in pain and covered with blisters. Strange objects lie beside the bloated corpses: a steel needle, a tin cup. With no family, the two feel as if they are the last humans on earth. They return to the relative safety of the isolated island, and then, in the darkest days of the winter, the grandmother senses her own death coming on. She must find a way to ensure the survival of her young grandson.[20]

Before Tomorrow was shot on video and, like the several Igloolik Isuma television productions and feature films that preceded it, could not have been made at all before the recent advancements in digital technology. Digital cinematography eases some of the filmmaking difficulties created by the Arctic's often-extreme weather conditions. Digital cameras, for example, are able to shoot the interiors of igloos lit only by traditional lamps; film cameras would have required additional light sources. Digital cameras work, with care, in the 30-below-zero Fahrenheit temperatures Arctic filmmakers sometimes face; film cameras do not.[21]

Despite its advantages, however, digital filming also presents challenges, since it generally creates an on-screen look quite different from that associated with traditional film cinematography. Viewers are usually not able to articulate the elements that make a digital film different, but most can nonetheless sense that there is something distinctive about the visual experience provided by a digital film. Some of the unprecedented excitement generated by *Atanarjuat: The Fast Runner* in 2001 likely derived from its being the first digitally photographed feature film most of its viewers had seen. George Lucas's own first digital film, *Star Wars: Episode II: Attack of the Clones*, appeared the same year, but *Attack of the Clones* showed off so many additional and expensive cinematic tricks that audiences seldom noticed the distinctive elements that signaled Lucas had migrated from film to digital cinematography.

Digitally based films rely entirely on deep focus shots, shots that show background and foreground objects with equal clarity. Film tradition has made shallow focus the norm, and so most movie shots draw the eye toward clearly delimited foreground objects, offering more or less visual fuzziness behind. Traditional films are also somewhat grainy, an effect caused by bits of silver halide residing in film stock. Digital pictures, however, include none of the graininess and vague blurring associated with film. Digital film images thus seem, by comparison, extremely, sometimes even distractingly, sharp. Since all on-screen objects in *Atanarjuat: The Fast Runner*, *The Journals of Knud Rasmussen*, and *Before Tomorrow* are equally in focus and offered in a resolution much sharper than seen in traditionally filmed shots, their distinctive look can seem to be reflecting qualities in Arctic Indigenous cultures rather than choices about filming technologies.

Digital cinematography also differs from film in its superior ability to pull details out of shadows, a handy trait for shooting scenes inside dim Arctic ice and stone houses, and inside tents. Digital cameras, however, are inferior to film in adjusting to bright lights, and so in both *Atanarjuat: The Fast Runner* and *The Journals of Knud Rasmussen*, for example, snowy landscapes sometimes seem to overwhelm or "blow out" with light everything else in the frame. In addition, digital cinematography cannot easily produce the motion blur effect that viewers see when a traditional film camera moves very quickly; digital cameras must generally be turned more slowly to avoid the strobing effects that can arise from too-rapid panning.

Predictions that filmmakers around the world would swiftly abandon film and adopt digital cameras have proven wrong. Digital feature films instead remain the exception. Indeed, the continuing prejudice against digital filmmaking is so large that many digitally shot movies are carefully altered before release to give them a film-grainy look. Because digital feature films remain rare, then, some digital effects in Arctic films may be mistaken for self-conscious elements chosen to reflect an emerging Indigenous film style. How much of this visual style in fact reflects a distinctive Inuit sensibility and how much is a by-product of digital cameras may not be clear for years. It is evident already, however, that filmmaking with digital cameras can enrich the lives of contemporary Arctic peoples in ways that fulfill goals Flaherty set almost one hundred years ago.

Chapter 10

Oceania's Indigenous Films before 2000

I have talked in the past of our films being like a carved meeting house, rich with stories. People like myself are but the carvers.

Barry Barclay

To varying degrees, all Indigenous films made in Oceania offer a perspective like that presented in the opening of *Once Were Warriors*. There audiences first see a frame of the expected New Zealand panorama: Mountains dusted with snow rise out of a rolling landscape that seems expectant of the arrival of flocks of sheep. Round green trees dot the banks of a lake that glassily mirrors the bucolic scene surrounding it. Slowly, the camera pans right to left to reveal that this countryside is but a picture on a billboard planted within a bustling urban neighborhood. In this cityscape, as the opening titles roll, viewers meet the main characters, a contemporary Māori family, whose lives are no more connected to the cliché New Zealand postcard on the billboard than are the lives of most people who view this opening.

10-1 The billboard introducing *Once Were Warriors*

Indigenous films in Oceania both before and after *Once Were Warriors* have similarly attempted to correct the stereotypes created in the hundreds of outsider-made films about the region that audiences have viewed for one hundred years. As importantly, however, the earlier Indigenous filmmakers in Oceania often aimed to produce films with stories rooted in the oral and visual traditions that Pacific Islanders had developed centuries before the invention of moving pictures. These Indigenous traditions may sometimes simply be spoken by characters on-screen; they can as well be integrated into the very styles of acting, cinematography, and editing employed. Sean Mallon and Pandora Fulimalo Pereira[1] describe several ways that an older pictorial vocabulary persists in contemporary Pacific Islander tattooing, in jewelry, mat, and quilt making, as well as in Indigenous architecture and dance. These various visual storytelling traditions also stand ready-at-hand for adaptation by Oceania's filmmakers, enabling them, as Rotuman filmmaker Vilsoni Hereniko writes, to act as "a conduit through which the community tells a story about itself to its present and future generations and to the rest of the world."[2]

Several recurrent themes have emerged in the archive of Pacific Islander–made movies across its more than twenty-year history. This chapter traces these themes in the five earliest films, all made before 2000. Chapter 11 looks at the six films made since.

Tukana

Conflicts between generations are spotlighted in many feature films about Pacific Islanders. These clashes, for example, drive both of the pioneering feature films based on Albert Wendt's novels, *Sons for the Return Home* (1979) and *Flying Fox in a Freedom Tree* (1989), and remain at the center of *Naming Number Two* (2006), made decades later. Still, none of these or other Pacific Islander features explore cross-generational problems with more prescience than does *Tukana*, the first feature film to tell a Papua New Guinean story.

Tukana[3] is based on a story by Papua New Guinean Albert Toro and on a screenplay co-written by Toro with producer and director Chris Owen. Owen is well known for his many documentaries about Papua New Guinea, including *Man Without Pigs* (1990), *Bridewealth for a Goddess* (2000), and *Betelnut Bisnis* (2004). Entirely in Tok Pisin (Papua New Guinea pidgin) with English subtitles, *Tukana* explores challenges faced by villagers on Bougainville and Buka islands in the early 1980s, as western-style schools and a growing money economy increasingly interfered with long-established customs. "Traditionally education was the responsibility of our ancestors," a voice-over explains early in the film. "Today western influences have changed all that. After years away at school, students become strangers." *Tukana* traces how one group of school-made strangers, Tukana (played by Toro) and his friends, adapt—and fail to adapt—to the many changes.

The gigantic copper mine at Panguna on Bougainville Island looms as a major force throughout much of the film. Prospects of earning easy money there help lure Tukana away from his parents, village, and betrothed. *Tukana* includes many shots of this imposing mine, in the early 1980s the largest human-made pit in the world. During the era of the film, this mine was the single largest source of revenue for the central government of Papua New Guinea, headquartered in Port Moresby, 500 miles away across the Solomon Sea. The film exposes the condition of the lives of men like Tukana who share "modern" rooms in newly built workers' dorms far from home. The men work long hours for relatively handsome wages. They have insufficient time to maintain familial connections but enough to drink, gamble, fight, and pursue sexual intrigues.

Tukana rejects Josephine (Regina Talsa), the betrothed that his parents in the village have taken into their home for him. Tukana instead pursues Lucy (Francesca Noruke), another girl from his home village, who, like him, has been sent away to school. Lucy now values money and making herself look like girls in advertisements more than the customs that she derides as "old-fashioned village ways."

Tukana and his age-mates are foregrounded in the film, but the related frustrations of their parents are explored as well. Multiple village government meetings and earnest family discussions expose the anguish and disorientation of elders who have seen their children return from school with educations that seldom seem to do anyone any good. "Now you're a dropout like the other lazy village kids," Tukana's father, Tamasi (Timothy Hamanim), complains. Throughout the film, these many dropouts fiddle with their guitars, drink, play cards, and hitch to bars in nearby towns, while their elders build canoes, tend gardens and cocoa trees, prepare copra, and cook. "Nowadays many people think only of buying tinned fish from the store," one parent laments. And why not? Tukana explains, since canoe building is "old man's work. I'm going to buy a speedboat like my friends."

Tukana's several plot elements converge shortly after Tukana begins to feel affection for Josephine, his parents' choice. Josephine is then struck and killed by a truck, the instrument of a village sorcerer who is taking revenge for Tukana's earlier improper behavior. The immense trucks digging the copper mine at Panguna here metamorphose into a weapon of personal sorcery. The film concludes with a series of intercutting scenes that call attention to the tensions between village and town, between traditional and western ways. One final set of scenes shows Tukana joining his village to dance and sing. Tukana and his age-mate Tohiana (Wenceslas Noruke), in western clothing, move at the rear of many dozens of villagers in traditional dress. All dance and chant to traditional rhythms unlike any seen or heard previously in the film. This scene offers vivid images of the new generation, the school-made strangers, at last reunited with their elders and ancestors.

This optimistic tableau, however, is intercut with scenes from the bar in town that Tukana and Tohiana have recently left to join the village dance. Viewers see this bar, filled with men in western clothing, overflowing with empty beer bottles, much like other collections of empties presented several times throughout the film. A small band plays a cover of the Rolling Stones' "Brown Sugar" and, later, "Jumpin' Jack Flash," rhythms that contrast with what we hear when we see the intercut villagers' dancing scenes. Intoxicated men at the bar gyrate in imitation of Mick Jaggar. The camera lingers on one such man, then freezes. The credits roll, and this drunken dance—not the village ceremony—stands as *Tukana*'s final image.

In May 1989, six years after *Tukana* was released, Bougainville Island was roiled with a civil war that lasted over a decade and caused as many as 20,000 deaths. *Tukana* provided a prescient examination of the conditions that led to this conflict. Current agreements to create an autonomous Bougainville region headquartered in Buka have ended most of the chaos but not the continuing tensions between generations in these and other Pacific Islands. This topic is likely to appear in the Indigenous films of Oceania for many years to come.

Ngati

Tukana emphasizes the gap between traditional and western practices, but some Pacific Islander feature films instead show how to successfully fuse the old and new. *Ngati* (a Māori word for "tribe") represents an early and powerful illustration of this approach. Based on a screenplay by Tama Poata and directed by Barry Barclay, *Ngati* was the first feature film to be made under the creative control of the Māori. Poata and Barclay met this challenge by offering an ambitious exploration of how it is possible to remain fully Māori while living within a modern capitalist society.

Ngati is set in the fictional North Island seaside community of Kapua during one summer week a few years after the end of World War II. A pre-adolescent boy, Ropata (Oliver Jones), is wasting away with what some call "*mate Māori*" (the Māori sickness), suggesting that Ropata to some extent symbolizes the condition of all Māori. Ropata's father, Iwi (Wi Kuki Kaa), like most of the villagers, faces unemployment as the local meatpacking plant ("freezing works," in New Zealand vernacular) is about to be closed by its absentee Pakeha (white) owners. Ropata's adult sister, Sally (played by Connie Pewhairangi), and her Pakeha best friend, Jenny (Judy McIntosh), fret about how they can forge modern lives in such an isolated community. A young, newly trained, Aussie doctor, Greg (Ross Girven) arrives for a visit with Jenny's parents, hoping to understand why his Pakeha father fled Kapua soon after his mother died while giving birth to him.

This stew of troubles provides the film its plot but seems, often, to work mostly as a device for presenting a loving cinematic tribute to the community's everyday life. Viewers are shown kids going to school, running through pastures and down dirt roads, fishing, half listening to parents, breaking rules, and worrying about Ropata. The camera lingers on adults shearing sheep, riding across paddocks, cleaning fish, preparing meals, gossiping, holding meetings, praying and singing, drinking beer, dancing, arguing, and worrying about "the works" closing and about Ropata. Viewers see the local Pakeha doctor, Jenny's father, Paul (Norman Fletcher), lovingly caring for Ropata and other Māori patients; such scenes are juxtaposed with those of village *tohunga* (traditional practitioners) and elders offering Māori medicines as well as both Christian and older prayers and orations to try to cure Ropata. The audience learns that Jenny survived a childhood epidemic that killed many others because she received traditional Māori medicines. Though Pakeha, she, too, is an accepted part of the Kapua community.

When Ropata dies at the film's end, some say it is from the Māori sickness, while others say it is from leukemia. Viewers see, however, that the community Ropata has symbolized will not also soon die. The everyday rhythms that honor the Māori past are absorbing the challenges that

Pakeha (white settler) practices present. Ropata's wake (*tangi*) is as much a celebration of continuity as it is the mourning of a loss. During its lovingly filmed, almost eight-minute sequence, we see that Kapua may have lost a boy, but that it is simultaneously claiming the foreigner Greg as its own—his mother was Māori, he has learned, and so, as one villager says, "He's one of us, then." Greg will return, humbled, with his western education to become a second doctor serving the community. "I thought I was sent out here to teach the natives something about the outside world," he says. "I've been a bit stuckup, eh? I was the pupil." He is answered, "Lot more to teach you, boy."

Ropata's father, Iwi, finds a way for all to pull together, like "in the old days," he says. Jobs are saved by combining communal and capitalist practices. Ropata's best friend, Tione (Michael Tibble), is embraced by several adults eager to help him add to his already impressive spiritual understanding. Tione learns, for example, as audiences of *Ngati* learn, too, that Ropata, Greg's mother, and the village dead remain active in the community. The Māori past persists in the Kapua present, fusing the new and different with the old and same. Director Barclay's very embrace in 1987 of the medium of feature films for telling Pacific Islander stories itself demonstrated the effectiveness of fusing the old with the new.

Mauri

The attention to Tione's education that punctuates *Ngati* anticipates the even greater emphasis on children that appeared the following year with the release of *Mauri* (1988). Later Pacific Islander feature films such as *Once Were Warriors*, *Whale Rider*, and *The Land Has Eyes* have also explored issues surrounding modern Pacific Islander childrearing. Children even provide the central focus of two of the best-known and most widely acclaimed short films by Pacific Islander filmmakers, *Two Cars, One Night* (2003) and *O Tamititi* (1996). It is, however, in *Mauri*, written and directed by Merata Mita, where this topic seems most extensively presented.

Like *Ngati*, *Mauri* is set in a small, rural, mostly Māori community. While *Ngati* offers a view of this life in the 1940s, when director Barry Barclay was a child, *Mauri* is placed in the 1950s, the decade of much of Mita's own childhood. The film has several prominent characters but most often assumes the point of view of Awatea (Rangamarie Delamere), a pre-adolescent girl. Gradually, audiences are invited to judge events by their impact on Awatea and to learn what Awatea learns.

Mauri, which roughly translates as "life force," begins with a birth and ends with a death. (*Whale Rider* begins with a birth scene so similar to the beginning of *Mauri* that it seems likely the screenwriter and director Niki Caro intended thereby to pay homage to Mita's pioneering film.) In between, *Mauri* foregrounds several ill-fated men living out their misfortunes against a background of an enduring and wise community composed, primarily, of women. By film's end, Awatea has learned enough to become another female pillar of this community.

One Māori man, Willie (Willie Raana), possesses many virtues but, finally, proves unable to lead. He lives in the city but returns often with friends in his biker gang to care for village sites and people, including Awatea. Willie's service and virtues are honored midway through the film by the aging matriarch, Kara (Eva Rickard), when she bestows her blessing on Willie, passing to him the authority to lead once she dies. That same night, however, after he leaves his ancestral home to return again to the city, Willie is murdered by one of the men he has befriended.

Mauri also tells the story of Rewi (Anzac Wallace), a man with a secret that keeps him from accepting the love offered by Ramari (Susan D. Ramari Paul). "I'll only hurt you," Rewi warns Ramari. "I'm not the man you think I am. I'm just not good enough." Rewi hides when Willie and his friends visit from the city. Rewi's rejection drives Ramari to marry a local Pakeha farmer, Steve (James Heyward), though Steve is yet another man haunted by demons. Ultimately, the audience learns that Rewi is actually Paki and not the person that he has told the village he is. After a fatal automobile accident seven years earlier, Paki assumed the identity of the newly dead Rewi before returning to the community that the deceased Rewi had left twenty years before. "I've broken more than Pakeha laws," Paki/Rewi tells Ramari. "You carry the weight of a dead man," Kara warns him. "The aura of death is heavy upon you."

Paki/Rewi begins to find some personal peace at the movie's end as he is taken away by two Māori police officers (Don Selwyn and Temuera Morrison). Paki/Rewi has learned, too, that he is the father of Ramari's newborn son; his male line will go on. "One day that boy is going to have to know who his father is," Paki/Rewi tells Ramari's husband, Steve. This newborn has been named Willie, after the murdered Willie. The name and the circumstances of the baby's birth suggest the boy will face troubles growing up much like those *Mauri* implies most Māori males face.

Mauri concludes, however, not with these male troubles but rather with almost a full minute of spectacular aerial shots of Awatea running to the top of the hill where the recently deceased Kara has told her that people leap off to go to Hawaiki and to peace with the ancestors. In these long shots viewers see the village far below, the bright, dark sea, a heron spiraling, sun sparkling, and, centrally, Awatea arriving at the summit where she understands all thing are connected. Awatea now seems ready to assume the place of leadership for which the departed Kara has prepared her.

Similar messages about the importance of educating the young appear in other Pacific Islander films, but none surpass the emphasis on nurturing children found in *Mauri*, the first and so far only Indigenous Oceanic feature made by a Pacific Islander woman.

Te Rua

Tukana, Ngati, and *Mauri* each contain scenes where officials in formal meetings discuss economic and political issues, but it is only in Barry Barclay's second film, *Te Rua* (roughly translated as "the pit"), that these issues are at the center of the plot. Questions of what is correct and effective political action hold this ambitious feature together as characters and events frequently switch back and forth between Berlin, Germany, and the Wairarapa coast on the southern tip of the North Island of New Zealand.

At the center of the struggles in *Te Rua* are three wooden carvings that were stolen from a Māori community decades before the film begins. Each carving contains the spirit of a different ancestor and yet all now reside in a German museum on the other side of the world. The film begins with a village matriarch, Nanny Matai (Nissie Herewini), weeping in the rain on the beach, grieving for her people's lost ancestors. Nanny's knowledge and persistence shame and embolden younger generations in the community to attempt to bring the carvings home. Eventually, there are dozens at home and in Germany working together to force the museum to repatriate the ancestors. However, though Nanny's wishes are pure, many of those who embrace her cause have more complicated and, sometimes, more selfish desires.

One such allied group is composed of German activists, who wish to manipulate the issue of the stolen carvings to create publicity for their group. They seek to achieve their own ends—to increase their notoriety and power—more than they want to actually repatriate the ancestors. Other allies in Germany include two white women, Fiona

(Donna Akersten) and Hanna (Maria Fitzi), who sometimes wish more to impress their Māori men than to advance the Māori cause. Political activism can be for them a form of courtship and, even, of foreplay.

Most of *Te Rua*, however, focuses on the political activities of the Māori who are seeking the statues' return. Peter Huata (Peter Kaa) is one of the first to hear the cries of the ancestors. Peter is a Māori performance poet, songmaker, and storyteller, visiting Germany as part of a global tour. He is impetuous, brash, and overconfident, ready to lead others into seizing the carvings before first understanding the intricacies of museum security and international law.

Wi Kuki Kaa, who also had a promient role in Barclay's *Ngati*, here plays Rewi, a lawyer who takes the lead in the planning and negotiations with, first, the museum and, finally, the Berlin police. Rewi has lived abroad many years and achieved extraordinary worldly success. This success has cost him his wife, who has left him to return to their Wairarapa coast home. Rewi's work has also led him to become alienated from his children, who also now live back in Wairarapa. It looks for a while as if Rewi might choose to return to the village and renew relations with his relatives and children, but first his law business and then the carvings call him back to Berlin. No one in *Te Rua* is more flawed than Rewi, and no one is more essential to the political campaign to win back the carvings.

At film's end, Rewi and Peter, as well as several other Māori who have flown to Germany to help, are led off to jail. They have stolen valuable public property for purposes of extortion and they have refused to follow numerous police orders. We have reason to believe that they will be incarcerated for quite some time, but, in the logic of the film, personal flaws and problems count for little. The three carvings are being sent home. In the concluding words of the community spokesman, "The others go to prison. The main thing is, we have our granny back. You know what that means? We're all together now." *Te Rua* thus celebrates the power of community-oriented political action to achieve community goals while acknowledging the personal sacrifices that such action may require.[4]

Though he received New Zealand Film Commission money to produce both *Ngati* and *Te Rua*, Barclay has since been granted no national funds for a feature film. *Te Rua*'s endorsement of direct political confrontation likely helped dissuade mainstream funders from bankrolling Barclay's further efforts. Another Māori feature with political content, Don Selwyn's *The Māori Merchant of Venice*, was also repeatedly refused New Zealand Film Commission funds. On the other hand, the New Zealand Film Commission did help fund *Once Were Warriors* three years after *Te Rua* and has subsequently assisted with another Māori-directed feature, *Eagle vs Shark*. Neither of these later films (discussed in chapter 11) touch on any political issues. Filmmakers seeking to produce films that express political points of view will likely continue to face additional obstacles beyond the many that all filmmakers confront.

Once Were Warriors

Though not as widely viewed as *Whale Rider*, *Once Were Warriors* remains the most critically acclaimed film ever made about Indigenous Pacific Islanders. Stuart Dryburgh, the film's cinematographer, had already received an Academy Award nomination for *The Piano* (1993). After *Once Were Warriors*, Dryburgh went on to shoot, among others, *Lone Star* (1996), *The Portrait of a Lady* (1996), *Kate & Leopold* (2001), *Bridget Jones's Diary* (2001), and *The Beautiful Country* (2004). Lee Tamahori, the Māori director of *Once Were Warriors*, parlayed its success to become an A-list director in Hollywood, making such large-budget films as *Mulholland Falls* (1996), *Die Another Day* (2002), and *xXx: State of the Union* (2005). All the actors in *Once Were Warriors* were widely praised. Roger Ebert, for example, raved that Temuera Morrison (as Jake) is "as elemental, charismatic and brutal as the young Marlon Brando." He recommended both Morrison and Rena Owen (as Beth) be considered for Academy Awards. (They would not be.) Cliff Curtis, with a secondary but essential role as Bully in *Once Were Warriors*, has gone on to become probably New Zealand's best-known international actor, with prominent roles in *Crossing Over* (2007), *Live Free or Die Hard* (2007), *Sunshine* (2007), *10,000 B.C.* (2008), and, of course, *Whale Rider*.

Once Were Warriors, based on Māori Alan Duff's novel of the same name, was path-breaking in many ways. While the four preceding Indigenous films of Oceania had focused on rural lifestyles and had, more or less explicitly, encouraged a nostalgia for village life, *Once Were Warriors* acknowledged the reality that an increasing number of Pacific Islanders were growing up in cities, with little or no memory or interest in ancestral lands and traditions. *Once Were Warriors* broke startlingly new ground as well with its raw and bloody depictions of domestic violence. Tamahori used his earlier experience at making television commercials and Dryburgh's sophisticated camera movements to create sickeningly graphic scenes more painful to view that those offered in most earlier domestic dramas. Sometimes viewers have bolted from their seats to escape. "Be advised: this is not 'entertainment,'" reviewer Sarah Chauncey warned.[5] Many viewers have gone on to associate the domestic abuse shown in the film to deeper problems, especially to a supposed sense of alienation that many Indigenous people experience if their connections to traditional places are severed. Once Were Warriors' "dark themes apply to the oppressed all over the world," one reviewer proclaimed in the Washington Post.[6] Such searching for broader themes, however, probably too easily allows viewers to overlook the immediate and concrete cause of all the bad behaviors depicted in the film. Every fight, failure, misfortune, and heartbreak in Once Were Warriors results from someone's drunkenness.

Jake abandons his job, because he'd rather be at the pub with his mates. Jake and Beth neglect Nig, their eldest son, because they are too busy drinking. They allow Boogie, their second son, to be sentenced to a detention home because they've spent the night fighting and drinking. Jake loves Beth when he is sober and beats her brutally when he is drunk. Beth loves Jake when she is sober, but entices him to pummel her when she (and he) is drunk. Jake and Beth are too dominated by alcohol to notice when Jake's friend Bully rapes their thirteen-year-old-daughter in their own home. It is the aftereffects of too much drinking, also, that keep Beth from recognizing how traumatized that daughter is after the rape. Beth's daze leads to the girl's suicide. And, finally, we are shown that it is only because Beth has finally stopped drinking that she seems, in the last scenes of Once Were Warriors, to be beginning a better life for her remaining children and herself.

Understanding Once Were Warriors to be more about alcoholism than Indigenous alientation may help explain why the film was generally embraced so positively by Pacific Islanders throughout Oceania. Outsiders tended to find that the film confirmed their belief that many "oppressed" minority parents should be charged with domestic and child abuse. Pacific Islanders, however, instead often celebrated Once Were Warriors as a long overdue movie finally putting people like themselves up on the big screen. Outsiders tended to see a parade of negative representations of urban Māori adults, but many Māori felt gratitude that Māori actors and Māori stories were at last starring in a film with high production values and a (relatively) large budget. Outsiders seemed ready to conclude from Once Were Warriors that urban Māori are generally a violent and tragic "race," but Pacific Islanders more often found that the film demonstrated that some people do bad things when they drink too much. *Once Were Warriors* illustrated for them the problem of irresponsible drinking and not any broad generalizations about the social situation of contemporary Indigenous people.

Scenes emphasizing the dangers of excessive drinking had already appeared in *Tukana*. *The Land Has Eyes* and *Samoan Wedding*, considered in the next chapter, also associate some bad behaviors with alcoholism. No film in Oceania, however, and few from elsewhere, have focused on the ugliness of alcohol abuse as starkly as *Once Were Warriors*. It probed this dark topic so deeply that no successor will likely soon appear.[7]

Chapter 11

Oceania's Indigenous Films after 2000

The images are precious as the ancestors appear in those images.

Merata Mita

Once Were Warriors sparked an interest in Indigenous-made films across Oceania and far beyond. Unfortunately, however, the film did not noticeably improve Pacific Islander access to production funds, and no further Indigenous features appeared in the region for eight years. Then, with a rush, six new films appeared, led off by two films in 2002, the first entirely Māori language film, *The Māori Merchant of Venice*, and the global hit *Whale Rider*. *Whale Rider* grossed over forty million dollars worldwide and has probably been viewed by more people than have seen all other Indigenous films combined. Because its director, Niki Caro, is not Indigenous, some people exclude *Whale Rider* from the category of Indigenous film. Nonetheless, however categorized, *Whale Rider* has been very influential and deserves further examination here.

Whale Rider

Most of the pioneering, pre-2000 Indigenous films of Oceania include strong female characters. *Mauri* contrasts the flaws of Māori and Pakeha men with three generations of generally wise and healthy Māori women. Powerful women guide men in *Te Rua* as well, as Rewi's wife and, especially, Nanny Matai seem to possess knowledge that men in the film generally lack. Beth Hecke in *Once Were Warriors* also seems on the way to becoming a leader like the older women who guide the young in *Mauri* and *Te Rua*. Still, it is in *Whale Rider* where gender relations are most at the center.

Whale Rider traces the trials of a young girl, Paikea (Keisha Castle-Hughes), named Kahu in the original novel. Paikea is rejected as a candidate to become a chief by her grandfather, Koro (Rawiri Paratene), the current village chief, because tradition decrees that chiefs must be male. The plots of both the novel and the film depend on scenes where the girl's increasing knowledge clashes with Koro's unyielding commitment to patriarchal traditions. The girl is as steadfast in her pursuit of her grandfather's approval as her grandfather is in insisting she can be of no help. In the film, Paikea disobeys commands, ignores protocol, and profanes sacred spaces. Her worst outrages include secretly observing Koro teaching boys how to wield a war club, the *taiaha*. Koro catches her, as he always does, and fumes, "You have broken the tapu of this school, on this *marae*, the one place where our old ways are upheld. The knowledge that's been passed down from your ancestors from my grandfather to me, to those boys. It is broken."

In the end, in both novel and film, Koro proclaims that he has been fundamentally wrong. The young girl, Kahu/Paikea, has excelled at various chiefly tests as Koro's male students have not. Kahu/Paikea even manages miraculously to retrieve Koro's pendant (made of stone in the book and of whale's tooth in the film) deep from the ocean floor. And, in the tradition of male film heroes, Kahu/Paikea successfully ends both novel and film by riding a giant whale, climbing atop him in the shorebreak, then guiding him out to safety in the ocean deep.

11-1 Paikea dressed to dance (© www.whaleriderthemovie.com)

The giant whale is spiritually connected to Koro and his people, and so the whale's rescue seems to signal a revitalization of the entire village and, to a degree, of all of Aotearoa's Indigenous peoples. The spiritual connection of the ancient whale and the young girl anticipates a similar association between the warrior woman and young girl that Rotuman writer-director Vilsoni Hereniko exploits in *The Land Has Eyes* (discussed below). *Whale Rider* stands apart from all other Pacific Islander feature films, however, by first rehearsing its tribe's many traditional gender differences and then abruptly sweeping them away, with no rationale or explanation. The long history of male-only chiefs that Koro was himself taught and subsequently maintained is suddenly abandoned.

The film ends with Paikea sitting proudly beside Koro in the center of her father's immense, recently completed *waka* (canoe). Paikea has saved whale and people. The decay of the tribe has apparently been reversed. Audiences seem encouraged to conclude that there is nothing a woman cannot do or, at least, nothing a man can do that a woman cannot do, too. Accordingly, the Girl Scouts of America have adopted the film as an instructional tool to help empower their members.[1]

Through the character of Koro's wife, Nanny Flowers (Vicky Haughton), the film alludes to other Māori tribes with traditions of female chiefs and heroes. Still, it is difficult to see the film without suspecting its celebration of a female hero is a product of those strains of Anglo-American feminism that seek not to alter existing structures of inequality so much as to make sure that women have the right to assume powerful hierarchical roles traditionally reserved for men. The importation of this contemporary western idea to a Māori story should not be simply attributed to Caro, its western screenwriter and director. Witi Ihimaera has explained that the short novel that inspired the film grew out of his desire to counteract the many movies his then-young daughters were seeing in the 1980s.[2] As they walked out of one, a daughter asked Ihimaera, "Daddy, why are the boys always heroes while the girls yell out, 'Save me, save me, I'm so helpless.'"[3] Caro's film follows Ihimaera's short novel, then, in what he says is the "socking it to the guy thing."[4]

Ihimaera (and his daughters) may have been influenced by western feminism, but storytellers in Oceania certainly have their own, older traditions of strong women to draw upon. Oceanic films made both before and after *Whale Rider* have portrayed these women enacting influential roles such as women have often played in societies across the Pacific. These pre-cinematic traditions of commanding women will likely guide Pacific Island filmmakers for many decades to come.[5]

The Māori Merchant of Venice

Indigenous language preservation is another important theme in Oceania's Indigenous films. *Tukana's* and *The Land Has Eyes'* reliance on Tok Pisin and Rotuman, respectively, has helped to validate the continuing vigor of both these languages. Most Māori-directed features include both Māori and English to similarly encourage the continuing use of Māori in place of or, at least simultaneously with, English. *The Māori Merchant of Venice* (known in Māori as *Te Tangata Wahi Rawa o Weniti*), however, merits special attention. Veteran Māori actor and director Don Selwyn directed and co-produced this cinematic version of Pei Te Hurinui Jones's 1945 translation of Shakespeare, making this not only the first Shakespeare film to be produced in New Zealand but also the first and, so far, the only feature film to exclusively use the Māori language.

There are deep affinities between Shakespeare's poetic diction and the oracular and metaphorical formal Māori speech that translator Jones adopted for his script. (Jones also created Māori translations of *Julius Caesar* and *A Midsummer Night's Dream*.) Selwyn says that Jones's translation "captures the essence of how Māori language would have been spoken before the arrival of Europeans."[6] The classical, almost operatic Māori heard in the film resonates with how Shakespeare's poetic lines sound to modern English-speaking audiences. *The Māori Merchant of Venice* simultaneously suggests that Māori language and traditions are equal to those of both Elizabethan and present-day England. "It is important to keep the poetic side of the [Māori] language active," Selwyn explains. "We need something more than the cryptic and colloquial translations from modern-day English that are common in Māori now."[7] As Selwyn hoped, the film has been used in schools across New Zealand to teach both Shakespeare and Māori culture.

The Māori Merchant of Venice recreates the play's Venice scenes from shots of Italian-inspired buildings in Auckland and of inner-harbor waterways and wharves. When the scenes move to the imagined land of Peremona (Belmont, in Shakespeare's play), the film locates itself in New Zealand by incorporating Māori art, music, and culture in both its design and staging. So, for example, when the Prince of Morocco arrives to seek Portia's hand in marriage, he is given a ceremonial Māori welcome with conch shell and *karanga* (a female cry of welcome), counterpointed by Moroccan trumpets and song. The suitors put their case to Portia (Pohia in Māori, played by Ngarimu Daniels) accompanied by Italian-style operatic arias (performed in Māori by William Winitana and Mere Boynton) intermingled with traditional Māori wind instruments, played by Māori music expert Hirini Melbourne.

Because of its many virulently anti-Semitic scenes, after World War II *The Merchant of Venice* became one of Shakespeare's most controversial plays. *The Māori Merchant of Venice* exploits the play's racism in a startling way by calling attention to the parallels between how the Jews and the Māori have been treated by white Christians. The crucial scene where Antonio (Anatonio in Māori, played by Scott Morrison) promises Shylock (Hairoka in Māori, played by Waihoroi Shortland) a pound of his own flesh if he fails to repay a loan is set in an art gallery. Surrounding the actors are paintings by the contemporary artist Selwyn Muru depicting the destruction of the Māori Parihak community by nineteenth-century white settlers.[8] As the scene ends, audiences see Muru himself at work on a canvas where he has scrawled the word *holocaust*. The word serves as a reminder early in the film that some Māori have for over one hundred years been comparing their search to recover their homeland to the Jews' search for the promised land. Some have even referred to a Māori holocaust.[9]

Shylock's search for justice in *The Māori Merchant of Venice* is presented as a search for justice for the Māori as well as for Jews. Portia's climactic manipulation of the law to deny payment to Shylock is thus staged to recall "the court battles between Māori political activists and the New Zealand government over differing interpretations of key clauses about land ownership as expressed in the Treaty of Waitangi."[10] This minority-centric approach is unique within the 400-year history of the play's performances. Unlike in earlier stagings, *The Māori Merchant of Venice* presumes that its audience will sympathize with the Jewish rather than with the Christian characters. Laurence Olivier pioneered this transition in perspective with his famous Shylock in the British National Theatre production of 1970. Olivier submissively exited after his last speech ("I am content") and then, off-stage, roared "an anguished wail that shook the theatre."[11] *The Māori Merchant of Venice* extends this wail, metaphorically, to the language, setting, acting, and very pulse of the play.

The Land Has Eyes

While exploring the importance of politics, *Te Rua* simultaneously illustrates the influence that invisible forces often exert in the lives of Pacific

Islanders. *Tukana,* similarly, points to the importance of sorcery, while *Ngati* and *Mauri* each evokes the presence of ancestors in the everyday lives of the living. Though all these early features, as well as *Whale Rider,* integrate unseen forces into their stories, Vilsoni Hereniko's *The Land Has Eyes* (in Rotuman, *Pear ta ma''on maf*) alone uses spirits as one of its central protagonists. The origin story of the Warrior Woman, Tafate'masian (Rena Owen), fills the first eight screen minutes as a modern-day girl, Viki (Sapeta Taito), is taught by her father (Voi Fesaitu) that the Warrior Woman was the pioneer settler on her island of Rotuma. The many-centuries-old Warrior Woman then guides Viki throughout much of the rest of the film as Viki learns the truth of her father's teaching that "the land has eyes and teeth and knows the truth."

11-2 The Warrior Woman

Hereniko has said, "*The Land Has Eyes* has the potential to make people aware of our spiritual and enduring relationship with the land and to see the land as a living human being."[12] Such an ambition, of course, is unlikely to be achieved with a single film. Still, *The Land Has Eyes* is significant for the many ways it attempts to make invisibles visible, to show that the deceased, weather, sea, and land can be conscious participants in everyday Rotuman life. Versions of the proverb that gives the film its name recur throughout the film, including once when Viki's churchgoing mother, Maurea (Ritie Titofaga), complains to her father, "How can you believe in the land more than Jesus?" A mistranslation of the proverb from English to Rotuman by Noa (John Fatiaki) even sparks the film's climax, rousing the land to come alive and burst through the door of the government building to display its teeth and eagerness to reveal the truth.

The Land Has Eyes also makes the invisible visible through repeatedly showing Viki becoming a present-day manifestation of the Warrior Woman. Viki cultivates scarlet featherwork and ruby torch ginger, materials also cultivated by the Warrior Woman. Viki paints her cheeks with blood-red stripes, like the Warrior Woman. In times of crisis—upon her father's death and when being mistranslated by Poto before Clarke (James Davenport), the white colonial magistrate—shots of Viki and the Warrior Woman are intercut. The two never appear together on-screen. Instead, their images rapidly succeed each other, showing first one, then the other, in similar scarlet colors, or with the same red-striped cheeks, or holding identically decorated fans, or, most memorably, in stunningly aqua underwater shots, with first one and then the other bobbing along the sandy ocean floor.

The fusing identities of Viki and the Warrior Woman recur in the climactic scene inside the government building. Here, the land spirits, Warrior Woman, and Viki merge to create a whirlwind that brings justice to Viki's deceased father and her family. The white magistrate looks on with amazement, then asks Viki, "Could you tell me what happened then? I think the chiefs understand, but I don't." Magistrate Clarke's on-screen bewilderment anticipates that of many in continental audiences who sometimes, too, are confused by the ending. Alan Howard reports some viewers of The Land Has Eyes cannot see the invisible forces Hereniko invokes and so believe that the film argues that white colonials possess ultimate power.[13] However, for viewers who recognize the Oceanic traditions of oral storytelling within which Hereniko is working, the invocation of invisible forces in The Land Has Eyes will seem but the latest attempt to find ways to transfer to screen experiences commonplace across most Pacific Islands. For these viewers it will be clear that ancestral forces and Pacific Islanders—not white governors—are the heroes of The Land Has Eyes.[14]

Three Genre Films

Both Whale Rider and The Land Has Eyes are coming-of-age films. Still, both seem more driven to tell a story about Pacific Islanders than to meet expectations associated with cinema's coming-of-age genre. The Māori Merchant of Venice is also a genre film, one of hundreds of movies that put Shakespeare on-screen. Nonetheless, a celebration of the Māori language drives this film at least as much as, if not more than, the genre of cinematic Shakespeare. Now, however, with the release within two years of one another of the three latest Pacific Islander films, earlier celebrations of difference seem to be metamorphosing into celebrations of assimilation. *Naming Number Two, Samoan Wedding,* and *Eagle vs Shark* so completely embrace their different genres' expectations that their Pacific Islander characters appear to differ little from the non-Indigenous peoples with whom they share islands.

Naming Number Two (also known as *No. 2*) is a family drama about first-, second-, and third-generation immigrant Fijians living in Auckland. It tells a story, however, that could as easily be about Hawaiian, Mexican, Scandinavian, or many other immigrants. The film is based on first-time director Toa Fraser's own screenplay, which, in turn, grew out of his earlier award-winning play, *No. 2*. The play used but a single actor, the Irish-Fijian Madeleine Sami, who acted all the drama's multiple roles. The film, however, relies on more traditional casting and has veteran American actor Ruby Dee in its lead. Both play and film were built in part on Fraser's perspective as a child of a British mother and a Fijian father. Fraser moved from England to New Zealand in 1989 when he was fourteen, and *Naming Number Two* borrows from his Fijian family's experiences of living for the last fifty years in Mt. Roskill, a working-class suburb of Auckland. The mixing of peoples and cultures in Mt. Roskill plays a prominent role in the film.

Dee's character, Nanna Maria, is an aging immigrant Fijian matriarch who one morning suddenly decides that her grandchildren must prepare a "great feast" in the old style so that the family can gather and she can name her successor. The family, unfortunately, is in complex disarray. Different factions no longer speak to one another and Nanna's two sons, Percy (Pio Terei) and John (Nathaniel Lees), are the most bitterly divided of all. Numerous crises come and go, as well as many characters, some of whom are already in the family and some of whom, perhaps, are on the way to gaining membership. Nanna despairs at one point and retreats to her bed; a series of flashbacks reveal the pampered, aristocratic life she once led in Fiji, before her philandering husband moved her to New Zealand after World War II. Nanna's fate works out as is expected in a family drama like this, as do most of the other conflicts and tensions.

Fraser's aim to create a genre film with wide appeal and little cultural specificity is illustrated by his casting of the African American Dee as Nanna. Dee was a pioneer in Hollywood films in the 1950s. She starred opposite Sidney Poitier in *A Raisin in the Sun* (1961), perhaps the single most influential film about black Americans ever made. Dee has worked steadily since, appearing in dozens of American films as well as in stage and television shows. Along with her late husband, actor Ossie Davis, Dee was also an important civil rights activist. She brings to *Naming Number Two* the compelling performance required in a film that centers its plot and most of its scenes on a single character.

The other actors who play Fijians in the film are similarly non-Fijians. Most are Polynesian and, though audiences outside Oceania may not recognize the difference, the divergence in physical appearance, history, and cultures between Fijians and Polynesians is considerable. In many places today, of course, it has become unacceptable for outsiders to play roles that represent them as Indigenous people. Still, in genre films the off-screen ethnicity of actors matters less than their ability to carry each genre's familiar roles. This casting strategy likely decreases opportunities for many Indigenous actors who already face more than the usual obstacles in finding roles. If ethnic Fijian actors are not to be cast in large ensemble films about Fijians, for example, it is difficult to know where Fijian actors will find work.

Samoan Wedding (2006), also known as *Sione's Wedding*, is also much shaped by its genre as a buddy comedy, though it does use Samoan actors to play its many Samoan roles. The setting once more is Auckland, as in *Naming Number Two*, but now the immigrants are predominantly Samoan rather than Fijian. Chris Graham, the director, is not Indigenous, but much of the film was under the creative control of Samoan Oscar Kightley. He co-produced and co-wrote the screenplay as a vehicle for himself and some other members of the Naked Samoans, a New Zealand comedy troupe whose work includes the inspiration and voices for *bro'Town*, a popular animated television series. *Samoan Wedding* traces the misadventures of four thirtyish, second-generation Samoan men who use their long friendship as a shield against mounting community pressures demanding that they grow up. These four principals are the familiar male "slackers" that have anchored many recent comic films. The film's plot and dialogue could be transferred to many cities across the contemporary English-speaking country.

The four Samoan buddies, Michael (Robbie Magasiva), Sefa (Shimpal Lelisi), Stanley (Iaheto Ah Hi), and Albert (Kightley), adopt hip-hop styles and pursue many activities familiar to audiences from Hollywood movies that stereotype black male Americans. The four even retreat to an outdoor basketball court to shoot hoops when crises require they find a place to share some serious talk. (Their performance on the court suggests their basketball skills, too, are quite immature.) In one of the film's several running gags, the buddies repeatedly assert their right to be authentic practitioners of hip-hop against the supposed inauthenticity of a white character, Derek (David Van Horn), whose embrace of American black culture they vilify.

The friends' very different idiosyncrasies drive the film, which concludes in an elaborate wedding scene where each man gets what he wanted most all along. Spread throughout is much of the banter one would expect from a professional comedy troupe, as well as many effective sight gags. The laughs are frequent and helped *Samoan Wedding* break box office records in New Zealand, where it received a long and wide 2006 release. Much of the enthusiastic reception was led by Pacific Islanders living in New Zealand. Auckland, the setting for *Samoan Wedding*, now has a larger population of residents with origins in other Pacific Islands (about 15 percent) than it does Indigenous Māori (about 10 percent). Pacific Islanders thus are becoming one more group, like the earlier Europeans, settling in Māori lands, more or less uninvited. When one of the buddies says, "*Et tu*, Brute," another asks, "Why are you speaking Māori?" This suggests that Pacific Islander immigrants to New Zealand may have no more knowledge of their host Indigenous culture than do most white settlers.

As films offering stories of Samoans and Fijians, respectively, *Samoan Wedding* and *Naming Number Two* seem to belong to the category of Indigenous film. Yet, because they are about immigrants far from their homelands, both differ from the other films discussed in this chapter as well as from most films considered in this book. *Samoan Wedding* and *Naming Number Two* might better be labeled "diasporic Indigenous films," a category that is likely to fit an increasing number of films, as more native peoples in the Pacific and elsewhere emigrate from their ancestral lands.

Samoan Wedding and *Naming Number Two* fulfill their separate genre expectations with tight precision partly by suggesting that the Indigenous immigrant communities that each depicts are well assimilated into the dominant New Zealand society. The Samoan immigrants in *Samoan Wedding* and Fijian immigrants in *Naming Number Two* do still live mostly among other immigrants like themselves, but, the films show, they also frequently form friendships, date, and sometimes even marry people from the other ethnic groups that surround them. The offbeat romantic comedy *Eagle vs Shark* goes even farther to suggest that consequential cultural differences may soon no longer exist.

Māori director and writer Taika Waititi (aka Cohen) had previously made two widely praised short films, *Tama tu* (2005) and *Two Cars, One Night* (2003). The latter was nominated for an Academy Award for Best Short Film. These short films used Māori characters and situations, but *Eagle vs Shark* presents a society where Māori, Samoan, and white characters have become interchangeable.

Lily (Loren Horsley) is an abruptly unemployed Meaty Burger counter worker. Her desired boyfriend, Jarrod (Jemaine Clement), clerks at an electronic game store. Lily crashes Jarrod's "dress as your favorite animal" party wearing a dumpy shark costume; Jarrod awkwardly hosts in a crude eagle costume. Romantic sparks fly when Jarrod sees Lily is a great video gamer. Soon, after a comically brief sex scene, the two head off together to Jarrod's hometown, driven by Lily's geeky brother. Once there, audience sees that Jarrod has a white father (Brian Sergent), wheelchair bound, except when in a hurry. Jarrod's mixed-race sister (Rachel House), with her white husband (Joel Tobeck), peddles hideous exercise clothes and potentially carcinogenic makeup. Jarrod's mother turns out to have run off to Australia and not be dead, as Jarrod had told Lily. Lily inspects family photographs that suggest the absent mother may be Māori or, perhaps, has origins on some other Pacific Island. (The dead brother shown in these photos is writer-director Waititi himself). Race and culture, however, are irrelevant to the plot.

11-3 Jarrod and Lily in their eagle and shark costumes

Jarrod arranges a fight in his old schoolyard with the bully (David Fane) who frequently harassed Jarrod during high school. Family and friends assemble to witness the moment when Jarrod discovers the bully is now in a wheelchair. The bully apologizes for his decade-old misdeeds but, in a startlingly unexpected and hilarious moment, Jarrod nonetheless attacks. The bully tumbles from his chair and the two roll across the pavement, perhaps fighting to a draw, certainly providing Jarrod with a public humiliation once again.

Eagle vs Shark was developed partly with assistance from the Sundance Institute and, after its premier at the Sundance Film Festival in 2007, was bought by Miramax, a major global distributor that launched the film in North America with a modestly expensive publicity campaign. Reviews were generally positive, with one writer even gushing that *Eagle vs Shark* is "the best indie romantic comedy of all time."[15] It may, indeed, be the funniest film ever made by an Indigenous director. Certainly, also, *Eagle vs Shark* challenges assumptions about what constitutes an Indigenous film. Omitting it completely from the archive of Indigenous films would suggest that Indigenous films must avoid showing Indigenous people well integrated into dominant societies. Including it, however, suggests that Indigenous directors make Indigenous films even when they include no distinguishing Indigenous content. As I have said before, it seems best to let the specific Indigenous people represented in any film decide if they will embrace the film as their "own."

The Oceanic Film Tradition

Indigenous films have now been made in Oceania for twenty-five years, sufficient time for trends to appear. The theme of intergenerational conflict, so prominent in the region's first Indigenous film, *Tukana*, continues to prove fruitful, even in the three recent genre films. Similarly, an interest in children and childrearing remains as strong now as it was when *Mauri* put this issue at its core. Spirituality, prominent in Pacific Islander films since the beginning, also seems likely to play a role in Oceania's films for some time to come.

On the other hand, politics, the central theme of *Te Rua*, has not been the topic of any of the many films made since. And, while all the early films took place in rural areas, since *Once Were Warriors*, cities and suburbs have become the most common setting. Finally, and perhaps most significantly, explorations of conflicts between traditional and introduced customs, like those at the center of *Tukana, Ngati,* and *Whale Rider*, seem to be attracting diminishing interest, the recent *Naming Number Two* notwithstanding. The fading interest in differences seems

at least in part to be caused by the desire of the new generation of Indigenous filmmakers in Oceania to make films that fit within the recog-
nized genres of commercial cinema. These genres do not easily allow for
an emphasis on the ways that Indigenous—or any—people differ from
dominant western cultures.

The earliest films from Indigenous filmmakers in Oceania—the films
discussed in chapter 10—frequently celebrated the uniqueness of Pacific
peoples and traditions. They aimed to encourage pride within the communities represented, and their resulting cultural specificity helped
make these films stand apart from mainstream productions. Though cel-
ebrating traditions and increasing pride continue to be important goals,
as Sean Mallon and Pandora Fulimalo Pereira warn, any art that emphasizes how much Pacific Islanders differ from Pacific settler cultures can
also have negative consequences. These artworks, including films, can
"marginalize, create points of conflict and tension, and alienate ourselves
from others."[16] Films that emphasize older Pacific Islander traditions may
suggest to both Indigenous and non-Indigenous viewers "that Pacific
cultures lack innovation, creativity, and the ability to re-interpret."[17]
Films that emphasize differences will also generally be of limited interest
to audiences outside of the communities being represented on-screen.
Mass audiences are more likely to turn to genre films, to films like *Eagle
vs Shark*, *Samoan Wedding*, and *Whale Rider*, for people usually watch
movies to see what is already familiar to them rather than to increase their
knowledge about Pacific Islanders or any little-known peoples.

Determining when to spotlight Indigenous differences and when to
emphasize cultural commonalities will continue to present challenges for
filmmakers in Oceania. Films that affirm contemporary western values
are more likely to find funding and a wide audience than are films such
as *Tukana*, which, for example, endorses pre-contact gender roles. Indigenous films such as *Ngati, Mauri,* and *Te Rua*, which recommend
choosing community obligations over individual desires, are similarly
unlikely to become popular among audiences accustomed to individu-
alistic heroes. Pacific Islander filmmakers thus face choices like those
familiar to many artists, choices about whether to aim to make art mostly
for their own communities or for the global masses.

Chapter 12

The Indigenous Films of Australia

Film is the white man's dreamtime—and more often than not it
turns out to be the Aborigine's nightmare.

Archie Weller

The Indigenous people of Australia have made dozens of documentaries
and short fiction films but, so far, only five features: *Jindalee Lady*,
beDevil, Radiance, Beneath Clouds, and *Ten Canoes*.[1] (A sixth feature,
Yolngu Boy, has been widely embraced by the Arnhem Land Aborigine
community it represents, and so will also be discussed in this chapter.)
Many troubles surrounded the first feature by an Aboriginal director,
Brian Syron's *Jindalee Lady* (1992), and these troubles likely discouraged
some subsequent efforts. *Jindalee Lady* is now seldom listed even in many
books and on Web sites that chronicle the history of Australian films.

Tracey Moffatt's *beDevil* (1993), the second feature by an indigenous
Australian, was viewed much more widely than *Jindalee Lady* but created
its own difficulties for aspiring Aboriginal filmmakers. There was,
first, the considerable problem that in 1993 Moffatt was already well on
her way to becoming, as she now is, probably the best-known contemporary Australian visual artist in the world. Moffatt's previous and
subsequent work in photography and video installations have led many
to view *beDevil* more in the context of the global art scene than as a feature
film. And, indeed, *beDevil* does appear to be directed more at a western-
trained aesthetic elite than at ordinary film audiences. Moffatt even
worked to discourage viewers from looking at *beDevil* as the work of an
Indigenous woman. "I am Aboriginal," Moffatt has said, "but I have the
right to be avant-garde like any white artist."[2] *BeDevil*, then, provided
little guidance for filmmakers seeking to make films for and about
Australia's First Peoples.

Rachel Perkins's *Radiance* (1998), the third feature directed by an Aborigine, is much more accessible than either of its predecessors, but it, too, may have discouraged some successors. *Radiance* is based on a play and screenplay by a white man, Louis Nowra, and the presence of his perspective throughout *Radiance* (as discussed below) may have compromised the film's usefulness as a model for Aboriginal filmmakers wishing to make feature films.

Of course, the main obstacles that Aboriginal and Torres Strait Islander filmmakers face can hardly be blamed on *Jindalee Lady, beDevil,* or *Radiance*. The first white colonizers treated Australia's First Peoples as occupiers of the lowest possible rank of human development. Subsequently, in what Michael Leigh estimates have been more than 6,000 films of various lengths and intents, white-made films have commonly represented Aborigines and Torres Strait Islanders as vestiges of a dying race, or, less often, as faithful companions to whites, as victims, or as criminals.[3]

Australia's First Peoples were not even granted status as legal citizens of Australia until 1967. Only since then has it become common for outsiders to focus less on the supposed poverty of Australia's Indigenous cultures and more on the unusually rich repertoire of arts, languages, and other symbolic practices that Aborigines and Torres Strait Islanders possess. The continent's first inhabitants may have had comparatively little interest in the material culture of everyday life, Marcia Langton concludes, but it is clear that they simultaneously excelled in elaborating "[m]ultilingualism, linguistic devices and codes, dance and musical traditions, and the visual arts."[4] What Langton calls "the Aboriginal worldview or cosmology" is thus available to provide contemporary Aboriginal filmmakers with a rich foundation upon which to build a distinctive and diverse cinema.[5] And Aborigines and Torres Strait Islanders can in addition, of course, simultaneously draw upon their varied experiences of settler and immigrant cultures.

Adapting technologies to express an Aboriginal perspective can help relieve the pressure many Aboriginal people feel to become more assimilated into the settler culture surrounding them. The films by the pioneers discussed in this chapter demonstrate Langton's contention that it is not filmmaking itself but filmmaking by outsiders that abets the many threats to Aborigine survival and diversity.

Jindalee Lady

As mentioned, *Jindalee Lady*, the first feature made by an Indigenous Australian, disappeared from view amid multiple controversies. The Australian Film Commission (AFC) refused funding to help with post-production, and Brian Syron, its Aboriginal director and co-writer, filed a complaint with the Human Rights and Equal Opporunity Commission that argued, in part, that the AFC "doesn't have the right to deny people who have had the experience the chance to reproduce it and communicate with their own people. I don't think that any white person in this country has the right to do that."[6] The Commission eventually yielded and set up its own "Indigenous Branch" in 1993 to try to avoid further disputes.

Controversy continued, however, when the same AFC published a high-profile short book by Aborigine critic Marcia Langton that included substantial criticism.[7] *Jindalee Lady*'s producers filed a complaint in Australian Federal Court alleging that Langton's evaluation had helped prevent the film's sale and distribution. The AFC fought the charge and, in 1997, before the scheduled court hearing, *Jindalee Lady*'s producers withdrew their claim and agreed to pay the AFC for its pre-trial costs.

Syron had established himself as a successful director, actor, and acting teacher, both in the United States and in Australia, before undertaking to make *Jindalee Lady*.[8] He died of leukemia in 1993 before his film's inability to find an audience had become evident. Syron wanted *Jindalee Lady* to advance "the cause of Aboriginal people" since, he believed, films by white directors had mostly "reinforced what white Australians think about us. Low life. It's negative images, reinforcing negative images all the time in the minds of the children about what Aboriginal people are."[9]

Jindalee Lady worked aggressively against these negative stereotypes by focusing on young Lauren (Lydia Miller), who, over the course of the film, becomes an increasingly successful fashion designer. She is intended to be, like Syron described himself, "very middle-class, . . . a bourgeois black, or an uptown nigger."[10] Lauren is married to David (Patrick Ward), a white music executive, but falls in love with Greg (Michael Leslie), an Aboriginal man, himself a successful photographer. Lauren learns she is pregnant with her husband's child but still leaves him for Greg, who is encouraging her to better integrate her Indigenous heritage into her personal and business life.

Langton's influential book criticized *Jindalee Lady* for being "caught in the grip of a paternalistic impulse."[11] Langton also argues that the film's small budget constitutes no excuse for its avoidance of the broader economic and political issues facing Australia's First Peoples. Langton complains that the film focuses too much on what she calls "Aboriginal Australian yuppies," and she interprets the cinematic death of Lauren's baby by sudden infant death syndrome (SIDS) as a sign that the film intends to blame a black "successful careerist mother" for maternal negligence. Langton also attacks a remark by a white woman and friend of Lauren's in the film who says, "You, Lauren, have made it." Langton asks, "Is this what every striving Aboriginal person is supposed to want to hear: approval and blessing from the white capitalist world?"[12]

The controversies as well as distribution problems associated with *Jindalee Lady* provided a doleful beginning for First Peoples' filmmaking in Australia. The example of *Jindalee Lady* suggested that Indigenous films that did not focus on social problems might be attacked, as Langton had attacked *Jindalee Lady*. On the other hand, films that did focus on Aboriginal problems seemed equally likely to be criticized for perpetuating the very negative stereotypes that Syron wished *Jindalee Lady* to avoid.[13]

The Indigenous Australian features that followed Syron's pioneering film have struggled to devise strategies to negotiate ways through this dilemma.

Tracey Moffatt

Tracey Moffatt is now one of the best-known and highest-earning artists based in Australia.[14] Moffatt was, however, just beginning to accumulate renown when she wrote and directed *beDevil*, released in 1993, just a year after *Jindalee Lady*'s brief appearance. Moffatt's previous work had included photographic tableaux and two short films, *Nice Coloured Girls* (1987) and *Night Cries: A Rural Tragedy* (1989). The latter attracted much critical interest for its reworking of representations of the relations between an adoptive white mother and her Aboriginal daughter, themes famously explored in *Jedda* (1955), a classic Australian film directed by the non-Indigenous Charles Chauvel. Released four years after *Night Cries*, *beDevil* enhanced Moffatt's reputation among art critics. However, while Moffatt has since produced several more short films and video installations (including *Heaven* [1997], *Lip* [1999], *Artist* [2000], and

Love [2003]) as well as mounted photographic exhibits at some of the most prestigious galleries in the world, she has not made any more feature films.[15]

Moffatt's *beDevil* attracted attention not only because Moffatt was already an emerging artist but also because the film was widely labeled as the first feature film by an Aboriginal woman. In fact, it may have been only the second feature ever made by any Indigenous woman anywhere, probably preceded solely by Māori Merata Mita's *Mauri* (see chapter 10).

BeDevil's multiple innovations included a prominent interweaving of documentary film techniques, where characters, for example, reach out and rub the camera lens or speak directly to other characters inviting them to "come and meet the camera people." Sometimes, too, this documentary look is emphasized by having key actions that are seen by characters nonetheless "missed" by the camera, which seems unable to turn, seek out, or film crucial narrative events. *BeDevil*'s acting, as well, sometimes seems to suggest real people are behaving awkwardly not because they are amateur actors but because they feel uncomfortable in front of an intrusive camera.

BeDevil further upsets fiction film conventions by mixing naturalistic settings with "unnatural," aggressively stylized interiors and exteriors. These stylized scenes refine techniques that guide Moffatt's earlier short, *Night Cries: A Rural Tragedy*. Both *beDevil* and *Night Cries* seem more to show "moving paintings" than the expected moving action of ordinary feature films. *BeDevil*, especially, anticipates some of the same startling hyperimaginary, antinaturalistic characteristics that have since made Moffatt's photographs so well known in the commercial art world.

Still, probably the most bedeviling aspect of *beDevil* is its refusal to provide a coherent narrative. This faux-documentary sometimes seems to be perversely assembled to actively thwart rather than encourage the audience's understanding. As one reviewer complained, "The film is very much the author's space: one wonders what the film tells us about anybody but Tracey Moffatt."[16]

BeDevil offers three distinct episodes, separately labeled "Mr. Chuck," "Choo Choo Choo Choo," and "Lovin' the Spin I'm In," but no characters appear across episodes. The actors are of various ethnicities and mixed ethnicities, sometimes clearly and, as often, confusingly presented. (So, for instance, the little blond girl in "Choo Choo Choo Choo" is played by blond Aboriginal actor Karen Saunders.) *BeDevil* pictures an Australia where ethnic histories and presents overlap. "For me," Moffatt explains, "Australian society is now a very mixed society, very multicultural—a hybrid society."[17] There are Chinese Australians, Anglo-Australians, Torres Straits Islanders, and Aborigines, but as Catherine Summerhayes points out, few characters are what they first seem. They are "slightly mysterious people who are in the middle of a larger story (which is in fact the story of their lives)."[18] That "larger story," however, is not made available to viewers.

12-1 Tracy Moffatt as Ruby in *beDevil*

Audiences are left bewildered not only by the lack of narrative progression within the three episodes but also by a lack of connections across the three. Just such bewilderment, however, seems to have been part of Moffatt's purpose. "*Bedevil* is a very playful, old-fashioned word that no one really uses anymore," she has explained. "It means 'to haunt and taunt.' The style of the film is teasing." As Moffatt further spells out, "You're following characters who are haunted by something, and I suggest perhaps we're all a little haunted in a way, and we probably don't ever come to terms with it."[19] By refusing to "come to terms" with the issues it raises, *beDevil* exposes feelings and issues more than it comments on or resolves them.

Early in her career, even before making *beDevil*, Moffatt discovered her work was of interest mostly to sociologists and anthropologists. "It was never looked at as art," she has lamented. "I was written about as a social commentator."[20] Moffatt subsequently made artistic choices about subjects, presentations, and commercial galleries in order to escape being categorized as an Aboriginal artist. If Moffatt had continued to be associated with Australia's First Peoples, she may not have become, as she has, one of the highest-paid visual artists in the world.

On the other hand, Moffatt's success at discouraging viewers from seeing her work as Aboriginal simultaneously tends to set both *beDevil* and Moffatt's other short films apart from the emerging tradition of First Peoples' filmmaking. Moffatt's view that Australia's indigenous peoples are best understood as but one of many components in a multicultural society seems to position her in opposition to those who seek to emphasize the rights of primacy and autonomy for the continent's First Peoples.

Two Films by Rachel Perkins

The precipitous disappearance of *Jindalee Lady* and the narrow art-house ambitions of *beDevil* served as cautions for Rachel Perkins when she accepted Louis Nowra's invitation to adapt his play, *Radiance,* for the screen. The then twenty-six-year-old Perkins determined to make a film that would escape the fates that had overtaken the only two previous features made by Aboriginal directors. Perkins, with Nowra, aimed *Radiance* at a broad audience, which, in Australia, necessarily meant an audience composed principally of white people. As Perkins explains, "For me a lot of Indigenous films with Indigenous content have been portraying the characters as social problems, not as individuals, and that for me is what *Radiance* didn't [aim to] do. The Aboriginality of the women informed the characters, but it was about them as women and as sisters."[21]

Radiance develops themes pursued but three years before in two critically praised non-Indigenous Australian films, *Vacant Possession* and *Hotel Sorrento* (both 1995). Both of these, like *Radiance,* focus on daughters returning to their family homes to attempt reconciliations around the death of a parent. In another attempt to attract an audience, Perkins altered the indeterminate ending in Nowra's original play (which had a bewildered Nona leaving her two older sisters behind) to create instead a happy ending. So, in *Radiance,* after a cleansing house fire, the three sisters unite as a family and sit together in a car, adorned similarly in sunglasses and wigs, joking, preparing to drive off to share a common life.

This feel-good conclusion fits with *Radiance*'s development of all three sisters as good and likable people. Each is complex and interesting in different ways, as Perkins says, "informed by" but not defined by being an Aborigine. Mae (Trisha Morton-Thomas) has sacrificed her professional and personal life to move back home and care for an ungrateful, declining mother. Cressy (Rachel Maza) has worked desperately to overcome her childhood abandonment and achieve success as an opera singer. Nona (Deborah Mailman), the youngest, is as yet an irresponsible party girl struggling to find her place in the world. Still, Nona's infectious enthusiasm and bubbly personality eventually charm her sisters, as she charms audiences as well. (Deborah Mailman won the 1998 award for Best Actress from the Australian Film Institute.)

There had never before been a film with strong parts for so many Aboriginal women. And, by emphasizing a story about sisters rather than a story about Aborigines, *Radiance* avoided historical and political issues that could have made white audiences uncomfortable. The plot does rely on incidents of child removal, rape, and physical dispossession, problems that many associate with settler dominance of Australia's First Peoples. But, as Ceridwen Spark points out, *Radiance* disconnects these social problems from the country's history of white colonization and settlement.[22] The child removal in *Radiance* is presented as having been deserved or, at least, to have been passively encouraged by the recently deceased mother. The stereotype of the uncaring and irresponsible Aboriginal mother willing to give away her children is then in *Radiance*, if not validated, to some extent repeated once again. (A memorable, heartbreaking scene of forced child removal would appear four years later in white director Phillip Noyce's *Rabbit-Proof Fence*; see chapter 1.)

The rape that provides the central plot twist in *Radiance* is associated with a black, not a white, man. Indeed, Nona's new knowledge about this rape signals the end of her dream of finding an Aboriginal man, a "black prince," to make her life better. And, finally, though the impending dispossession (loss of the family house) that precipitates Mae and Cressy's triumphant arson is caused by a white man, in *Radiance* it is not his race but his maleness that is associated with this and many other evils. In general, then, *Radiance* suggests the sisters' various difficulties are universal family problems or, maybe, universal female problems. If there are systemic troubles for these Aboriginal women in *Radiance*, it seems they are troubles shared with all women, and their cause is men.

Perkins's other films make it clear, however, that *Radiance* does not summarize her view of the condition of Australia's First Peoples. She had earlier produced *Blood Brothers* (1992), four one-hour television documentaries focused on the lives of four prominent, exemplary Aboriginal men. The first hour, called *Freedom Ride* and directed by Perkins, examines the life of Perkins's father, Charles Perkins, who, among other accomplishments, in 1965 helped organize mobile demonstrations to draw attention to the segregated customs then current in much of rural Australia.

A few years after *Radiance,* Perkins co-wrote and directed *One Night the Moon* (2001), at fifty-seven minutes neither quite as long as most features nor as short as most short films. *One Night the Moon* further demonstrates that the apolitical stance of *Radiance* was a reflection of that film and not a perspective Perkins herself endorses. At the end of *One Night the Moon,* before the credits, Perkins includes a long written quote attributed to her father, described on-screen as, "Charles Perkins (First Indigenous Australian to graduate from university)." The quote's final sentences are:

> Our land, our pride and our future has been taken away from us and our people buried in unmarked graves. We wander through Australian society as beggars. We live off the crumbs that fall off the White Australian tables and are told to be grateful. This is what Australia Day means to Aboriginal Australians. We celebrate with you, but there is much sadness in our joy. It is like dancing on our mother's grave. We know we cannot live in the past but the past lives in us.

One Night the Moon is based on a true story of events in the Australian interior in 1932. (An earlier documentary version, *Black Tracker* [1997], was produced and directed by Michael Riley, grandson to Alexander Riley, the black tracker the two films describe.) In Perkins's film, a young girl (Memphis Kelly) goes missing and, when the police suggest they use Albert (Kelton Pell), an Aboriginal tracker, the white father (Paul Kelly) refuses. He insists, "I'm not having some blackfella leading the search party." The police defer to the father, but the subsequent weeks of searching go for naught. Finally, the mother (Kaarin Fairfax) asks the tracker to use his skills to find and return the girl's body. The tracker complies, because he has been agonizing all along about not being allowed to save the girl's life.

One Night the Moon continues a preoccupation with stories about lost children that has been prominent among settler Australians since the nineteenth century. Four widely viewed earlier Australian films, John Heyer's documentary *The Back of Beyond* (1954), *Walkabout* (discussed in chapter 3), *Picnic at Hanging Rock* (1975), and *Evil Angels*

(1988, starring Meryl Streep), explore this theme, too. *One Night the Moon* is, however, the first to associate a fear of the outback with settler attempts to assert mastery over it. The father sings, "This land is mine," and continues by associating his ownership with deeds, banks, and "working hard just to make it pay." The tracker sings a reply, "This land is me. . . . This land owns me," and, in closing his solo, declares, "You only fear what you don't understand." The father's lack of understanding of the nature of "his" land and his simultaneous unwillingness to acknowledge the tracker's deeper understanding leads to the death of his child.

Perkins has directed no further features since *One Night the Moon* but has become a central figure in the push to increase government support for more Indigenous films. She is working as well with Australia's Indigenous Television Working Group, which aims to create a national indigenous TV service to help revitalize diverse Aboriginal languages and cultural practices across the continent.

Yolngu Boy

Yolngu Boy, shot in 1999 but not released until 2001, has been widely and correctly praised for its many differences from earlier films that represented Aborigines. Among other innovations, *Yolngu Boy* focuses on Aborigine youth, on three fifteen-year-old boys trying in different ways to integrate older traditions with the modern settler culture that is increasingly penetrating their Northern Territory ancestral lands. Several First Peoples' films have had prominent child characters (e.g., *Mauri, Ngati, Whale Rider*), and others have offered stories of young adults (e.g., *5th World, Smoke Signals*); however, *Yolngu Boy* and, later, *Beneath Clouds* were the first to tell stories about teenagers, the people who most often buy movie tickets and at whom, as a result, the majority of commercial films are aimed.[23] Teens, too, in Australia, as in much of the world, are probably more influenced by what they see on-screen than are adults. It may be doubly important, then, that Indigenous filmmakers make films that target this age group.

Yolngu Boy is an adventure-quest film aimed at youth through its plot and editing as well as through its choice of main characters. The boy protagonists were childhood friends who have now reached turning points in their lives. Lorrpu (John Sebastian Pilakui, a Tiwi Islander) is preparing to follow the dream that all three once had to become knowledgeable in the traditional customs of their people. Milika (Nathan Daniels, also a Tiwi Islander) has not yet rejected that dream but is more passionate about rugby than about practices more associated with the Yolngu past. Botj (Sean Mununggurr, a Yolngu), the third friend, has fallen farthest from the once-shared dream. He returns home at the film's start after three months in youth detention and soon is in trouble again. Lorrpu hatches a plan for the three friends to "go bush" and travel to Darwin, 300 miles away, to seek the guidance and protection of the Aboriginal elder Dawu (Nungki Yunupingu).

Much of the film follows the boys' progress through the northern Australian outback, from Yirrkala through Kakadu National Park, as they struggle with their lack of preparation for such a journey and with their estrangements from one another. Relying on both old and new methods, the boys gradually become more comfortable and more skilled. Their journey culminates in an extraordinary descent down spectacularly steep cliffs; they cling to one another and to the traditional three-strand banyan tree rope they have together fashioned. On level ground at last, the boys celebrate by removing their clothes and jumping into a large waterhole. The three laugh and play in the water in a scene that recalls an earlier nude swimming scene with David Gulpilil and Jenny Agutter in *Walkabout*. Both scenes present iconic depictions of innocent joy, though *Walkabout* emphasizes eroticism while *Yolngu Boy* celebrates friendship. The boys' idyll is interrupted by a flock of tourists, who float toward them on tacky pink intertubes. Their journey of renewal, friendship, and discovery across Australia's northeastern wilderness has abruptly ended; a cut-rate tourist bus transports them the rest of the way.

The streets and stores of Darwin clash sharply with the harmonious world the boys have just traversed. They quickly discover that the skills and friendship that sustained them in the bush provide little protection in the city. Though *Yolngu Boy* offers audiences scenes of wonderful wisdom-granting adventures, it does not conclude by pretending that a few weeks living on their own can solve any of the boys' more systemic problems.

Yolngu Boy's visual style is as much crafted for a youthful audience as are its protagonists and story. First-time director Stephen Johnson's best-known previous work was in making music videos for Yothu Yindi, a groundbreaking, mostly Aboriginal band that combines traditional music with modern western instrumentation.[24] Yothu Yindi provided several songs for *Yolngu Boy*'s sound track, and Johnson included music video techniques such as rapid cutting, meaning-making montages, and accelerated helicopter shots to accompany this and other youth-oriented contemporary music. Importantly, as well, Johnson intercut shots of Yolngu symbols and ceremonies, as he does also in his Yothu Yindi videos, to illustrate how thoroughly the traditional and the modern coexist in contemporary Aboriginal lives.

Images of Baru, the Gumatj tribe's revered crocodile spirit, recur throughout *Yolngu Boy*, interspersed among scenes from circumcision and manhood initiation ceremonies, Yolngu practices not usually open to outsiders. Neither director (Johnson) nor scriptwriter (Chris Anastassiades) are Indigenous, but the film was produced in part by Galarrwuy Yunupingu, chair of the Northern Land Council, and by his brother Mandawuy Yunupingu, the lead singer of Yothu Yindi. The Yothu Yindi Foundation, established to support the development and teaching of Yolngu culture, even partially funded the film. The Yunupingu brothers brought the filmmakers together with the Arnhem Land Indigenous communities that the film depicts, and many community members were involved in both the development of the script and in monitoring the daily shooting production. Johnson's own origins in Australia's Northern Territory and his earlier work with Yothu Yindi added to his credibility.[25]

Though not Indigenous by the strictest of definitions, then, *Yolngu Boy* belongs far toward the Indigenous end of the Indigenous to non-Indigenous continuum of films. It tells a story of Aborigines with barely a mention of white people, and does so with careful attention to cultural protocols and to community concerns. *Yolngu Boy* suggests it is sometimes necessary to know more than the tribal status of the director to determine if a film presents an Indigenous point of view.

Beneath Clouds

Released just two years after *Yolngu Boy*, Ivan Sen's *Beneath Clouds* also focuses on contemporary Indigenous teens. Like the three boys at the center of *Yolngu Boy*, the two teen stars of *Beneath Clouds* had had no previous acting experience. Both were chosen, in part, because they came from circumstances like those of the characters they would play, a strategy also used in casting *Yolngu Boy*. Dannielle Hall is Lena in *Beneath Clouds*, a light-skinned, blue-eyed teen with a drunken Aboriginal mother and a recently arrested younger brother. She runs away from her small town in search of her long-absent, Irish-Australian father. Lena believes, probably mistakenly, that he lives in Sydney and will welcome her arrival. Damian Pitt plays Vaughn, an escapee from a youth detention facility. He is trying to make it to a town near Sydney to have a last visit with his dying mother, who had abandoned him years before. The two fugitives are thrown together as they hitchhike hundreds of miles southward across the Australian countryside.

Vaughn mistakes Lena for white and treats her alternately with distrust, disdain, and curiosity. "I never knew any whitefella before," he tells her. "Not like you anyway." Lena, on the other hand, believes she already knows Vaughn far too well. "I've seen plenty of boys like you before," she tells him. He seems to her the stereotypical Aboriginal male she hopes to escape through running away from her mother, brother, and small town.

Cinematic male-female relationships that begin like this, in antipathy and misunderstanding, typically end in romance. *Beneath Clouds*, however, aggressively rejects this cliché. Vaughn and Lena come to understand each other a little, but their journey does not lead to love or, even, to the promise of a friendship that might outlast the film. *Beneath Clouds* not only eschews a sentimental end, it also refuses to provide both Lena and Vaughn with typical character arcs. Each begins angry and wary and so, mostly, do they remain. At film's end the two are quietly opening a little to the possibility of emotions beyond anger and wariness. But, while their circumstances have changed, perhaps for the worse, Lena and Vaughn remain much the same scarred, defensive, solitary people they were at the film's beginning.

Sen, with Alister Spence, composed and performed original music for *Beneath Clouds*, and, Sen says, he had selected much of the music even before casting the actors. "I always had intentions of exploring the Irish pipes to represent Lena's romanticized feelings about Ireland and her father. Distorted electric guitar was a main factor when representing Vaughn's aggressive state of mind."[26] Both diegetic and non-diegetic sounds carry much meaning for Sen, and he often allows the soundscape to "speak" at moments when most directors rely on dialogue. Sen generally encourages his teen actors to emote more often with their actions and body language than with words. He therefore uses few two shots, preferring instead alternating close-ups not as his actors speak but as they look or listen.

Sen's emphasis on faces fits with his similar inclusion of extended shots that dwell on the vast, unmoving landscape through which Lena and Vaughn pass. The two begin their separate escapes in areas of flat, rural isolation and then, after many miles, gradually enter more hilly and populated lands. Finally, they encounter disaster near Sydney in the film's final scenes, set amid high-power transmission lines, a nuclear power plant, and suburban sprawl.

Beneath Clouds culminates in a pivotal scene where white highway patrol officers confront Lena and Vaughn at the bottom of the same cliff where Vaughn has told Lena white "farmers chased all the blackfellas up there a long time ago. They just shot them and pushed them off. Now, no one gives a shit. I suppose they've got their own shit to worry about." The violence that erupts in this place, first from the police, then from Vaughn, and finally, unexpectedly, nearly from Lena herself, continues this history, connecting the teens with their ancestors in ways they can feel but not understand.

Sen had earlier won acclaim for several short films, including the thirty-five-minute *Wind* (1999), depicting mid-nineteenth-century rural Australia. *Beneath Clouds* further enhanced Sen's reputation, winning both critical praise and dual awards at the 2002 Berlin International Film Festival and at the 2002 Australian Film Institute Awards. These successes thrust Sen into a situation something like that which Tracey Moffatt faced earlier. Many wanted to treat *Beneath Clouds* as a film about social problems, as a general statement about the perilous situation of Aboriginal teens in contemporary Australia. Sen resisted, telling one interviewer, "I just wanted to write a story about a couple of kids who I kind of knew and one of them was me."[27] And, he informed another interviewer, "I'm really keen for a wider cross-section of Australians to see it and accept these kids as kids who happen to be indigenous."[28] Sen said that he, too, wanted to be seen not as an Indigenous director but as a director who happened to be Indigenous. "I'm not interested in using cinema to talk about social issues," he declared and, as if to prove it, announced plans in 2002 to set his next film in New Mexico, USA, in part to make sure that he did not become pigeonholed as a maker of films about Aborigines.[29]

Circumstances changed, however, and Sen remained in Australia after *Beneath Clouds* to direct two documentaries. The first, *Yellow Fella* (2005), reprises Sen's interest in the theme of mixed parentage. It examines the life of Aboriginal actor Tom E. Lewis, who gained fame for his starring role in *The Chant of Jimmie Blacksmith* (1978). Sen's next documentary, *Shifting Shelter 3* (2006), returns to the lives of four young

Aborigines he had interviewed for two earlier documentaries, *Shifting Shelter* (1995) and *Shifting Shelter 2* (2001). *Shifting Shelter 3* juxtaposes some of these earlier interviews with how the four understand their lives now that most are about twenty-five years old. A later documentary, *Broken Borders* (2006), shifts Sen's focus from rural to urban Aborigines as he mixes archival footage, shot in the 1960s and 1970s of people moving off traditional lands into towns and cities, with interviews of Aborigines who live in Sydney today.

Sen's post–*Beneath Clouds* documentaries have been widely viewed in Australia and demonstrate how often the desire to make feature films can be thwarted by the realities of the marketplace. Sen says he has discovered that "feature filmmaking, especially in this country, is a part-time job. So you have to do your number one job and do features on the side." Sen maintains he still hopes to make films that go beyond "stories about my family and Indigenous experience" to "inspire the imagination on a universal level."[30] For now, however, with *Beneath Clouds* and his succeeding documentaries, Sen has used his skills to help fill the need for more films by Aboriginal directors that tell mostly Aboriginal, not "universal," stories.

Community Filmmaking in *Ten Canoes*

Most Aboriginal films reflect the experiences of Australia's First Peoples who reside in what Marcia Langton describes as "settled Australia," an immense region that stretches in a broad arc across the continent from Cairns to Perth. Many small Aboriginal communities flourish in this region, more and less well integrated into the more populous settler cities and towns that surround them. There is, as well, says Langton, an immense second region, "'remote' Australia where most of the tradition-oriented Aboriginal cultures are located."[31] First Peoples in remote Australia tend to occupy traditional homelands where, to varying degrees, they continue the peripatetic and communal lifestyles of their ancestors. *Yolngu Boy* depicts teens torn in their choices between settled and remote Australia. *Ten Canoes*, however, was made entirely for, about, and mostly by these remote Aboriginal people.

As described in chapter 3, *Ten Canoes* begins with the voice of an unseen English-language narrator, David Gulpilil, who establishes a playful tone before interrupting himself with laughter. Gulpilil then begins again, telling about his ancestors from very long ago and the story of a goose-hunting expedition where, the audience discovers, the principal event is the meandering telling of yet another story, this one set at the very beginning of time. Though complicated in structure, these three levels—the voice-over narration, the goose-hunt frame tale, and the very ancient events—are clearly differentiated on-screen, enabling viewers to relish the intertwining of Gulpilil's modern-day mock commentary with tales from long and from very long ago.

The frame tale is shot in black and white and follows ten men as they hike deep into the Arufura wetlands. The men are seeking trees for constructing the unique bark boats their people have used for centuries in their hunts for magpie geese and their eggs. The leader, Minygululu (Peter Minygululu), discovers that young Dayindi (Jamie Gulpilil, the son of David Gulpilil), on his first goose-egg-hunting expedition, is interested in Minygululu's third and youngest wife. Minygululu begins to tell Dayindi a long story about their ancient ancestors. This story stretches on for days, as the ten men carefully build and launch their canoes, then pursue the many demanding activities required for a successful goose-egg hunt.

The tale that Minygululu narrates about the ancestors at the beginning of time is shown in color, so the jumps back and forth from these scenes to the black-and-white frame tale are easily distinguished. This ancient tale includes an older man with three wives as well as a younger man, Yeeralparil (also played by Jamie Gulpilil), who like Dayindi is also interested in the older man's youngest wife. Dayindi grows progressively eager to find out how his counterpart, Yeeralparil, in the ancient story will fare in his parallel search for love.

Neither young protagonist in either story gets quite what he or, probably, what audiences expect. Still, as David Gulpilil concludes once the hunters have returned with their bounty, "Now you've seen my story. It's a good story. Not like your story, but a good story all the same." Gulpilil's mocking voice throughout the film seems aimed at reflecting some of the oral storytelling traditions that *Ten Canoes* translates to the screen. Indeed, *Ten Canoes* evokes oral traditions far more directly than do most Indigenous films, creating a cinema experience that is almost as aural as it is visual. Luke Buckmaster compares Gulpilil's narrator to a "restless Dreamtime god giggling all-knowingly while sipping booze and brewing mischief from that great boomerang in the sky."[32] Beyond such hyperbole it is clear that Gulpilil, the storyteller, is controlling the pace and tone throughout.

12-2 Living in creation time in *Ten Canoes*

Ten Canoes' departures from expectations extend beyond its prominent use of a narrator and parallel narratives. Even the way the film was
conceived and produced differed significantly from most feature films,
including those produced by the four Aboriginal directors already discussed in this chapter. Though a non-Indigenous man, Rolf de Heer, is
listed as producer, co-director, and writer for *Ten Canoes*, most key
decisions about the film were made by members of the Yolngu community in northeast Arnhem Land.

The impetus to make an Aboriginal-centered film in Arnhem Land
came first from Gulpilil, while he was working with de Heer on *The
Tracker* (see chapter 3). The two resolved to make a film together,
with Gulpilil as co-director. They visited Gulpilil's home village of
Ramingining and, after consultation with Richard Birrinbirrin and
Bobby Bunungurr, among others, decided the film should take place before Europeans had entered the area. Gulpilil next determined that the
film must be built from a photograph of ten men in ten canoes taken by
white anthropologist Donald Thomson in the mid-1930s. This photograph is one of 4,000 ethnographic plates that have become priceless parts
of several Australian museum collections. Prints of a few of these plates
have also found their way back to the Yolngu at Ramingining and been
reappropriated as important cultural artifacts, as a legacy from the ancestors who lived in what some now call "Thomson Time." Gulpilil hoped
the proposed film would transform these precious Thomson Time images
from still into moving pictures.

Gulpilil pulled out of the project shortly after his vision was accepted.
The outsider de Heer was thus left to develop the screenplay during
periodic visits with the Yolngu community that had little experience of

filmmaking. The resulting script with parallel stories respected the community's determination to center the film on the activities associated with the goose-egg hunting that is evoked by the ten canoes picture. Because this hunting had been discontinued years before, many in Ramingining hoped the film would at least help revive the craft of bark-canoe building if not the hunting of geese and eggs themselves.

Thomson Time unfolded in black and white, so the film's scenes depicting that time would also have to be in black and white. Unfortunately, de Heer had already received funding to produce a color film, so he proposed that *Ten Canoes* include a second story, placed in the mythical age before Thomson Time. This ancient time could be shot in color, as in mythical time anything is possible. Including a second, parallel story also solved a second problem. The Ramingining Yolngu had identified most of the people in the Thomson photographs as their grandparents and ancestors. They did not want to make a movie that either denigrated any of their ancestors' memories or that suggested that the revered Thomson Time was a period of conflict. A film without conflict would, however, displease non-Indigenous funding agencies, so the creation of a second story set in mythical time provided a way to introduce elements of drama into the film.

The Yolngu at Ramingining cast roles for the film based on who was most closely related to each person pictured in the ten canoes photograph. This usually worked but sometimes had to be further adjusted since the relationships acted in the film also had to conform to prescriptions about present-day kinship relations. Brothers could not be married to sisters in the film if this was not acceptable in their off-screen lives. When someone who met the culturally appropriate rules was found, he or she got the part. The resulting performances were surprisingly convincing, as de Heer speculates, since the actors "were not playing their ancestors, they *were* their ancestors." Because in assuming their roles each day they were "*being* their ancestors, they could do it with relative ease and continuity."[33]

Props and costumes, too, were chosen and made by the cast and their families who, of course, accompanied the crew from place to place throughout the shoot. Work was divided by gender, as was customary, with men making the spears, axes, and canoes, and women making the huts, dilly bags (traditional woven bags), and body decorations. Many were making these tools for the first time. Work sometimes went slowly but created an increasing sense of community pride.

Constructing the bark canoes posed especially difficult problems. No examples survived to serve as models, and only a few of the older men had ever built one. Still, the right kind of tree was eventually found. The long bark was pried loose, soaked overnight, stretched and softened over a fire, stitched with the correct fibrous plant string, then reinforced with sticks from yet another plant bent into just the right shape. The Thomson photograph had to be consulted at the end of the process, to determine how to sew the prow. When the first bark canoe was finally completed, the Yolngu men kept walking around it, admiring their work. De Heer writes, "This one canoe was a small miracle, even for the Yolngu. . . . [F]orgotten aspects of their culture were being brought back from the brink of extinction, and they knew it."[34]

12-3 Planning strategy in *Ten Canoes*

All dialogue in *Ten Canoes* is spoken in one of the several Indigenous languages of the region, most frequently Ganalbingu and Mandalpingu. It is the first feature film to be made entirely in the languages of Australia's First Peoples. Some prints of the film provide subtitled translations of these languages, but prints for the Yolngu themselves do not. There is one version with Gulpilil's voice-over narration in Mandalpingu as well as one in English for international audiences. Making Aboriginal films in Indigenous languages is, of course, important to demonstrate their continuing value, especially to younger Aboriginals who, even in remote Australia, are increasingly exposed to media in English.

Frances Djulibing said of her role as Nowalingu in *Ten Canoes*, "It is my destiny to do this, so all over the world they can see how my ancient ancestors had been like this before." Even more important, she believes, *Ten Canoes* "is for the kids' future, so when they grow up they're gonna see, because not enough of the older people is trying to teach the younger kids."[35] The film has proven to be a vehicle for teaching the Yolngu at Ramingining new technologies, as well as more about Thomson Time and the ways of their ancestors. Several production spin-offs have been labeled Many Canoes and include, among others, projects (1) to teach the young people of Ramingining how to make their own documentaries, (2) to build a Web site that provides information about the region's environment, cultures, and people, (3) to design a book featuring a sample of the Thomson photographs with accompanying stills from the film that are based on Thomson's images, (4) to restore a moribund community closed-circuit television studio, and (5) to help produce a television documentary, *The Balanda and the Bark Canoes*, first broadcast in Australia in July 2006.

As these Many Canoes projects make clear, both the Indigenous and non-Indigenous co-creators of *Ten Canoes* wanted the film to work as an enhancement to Yolngu community traditions rather than as one more imposition of foreign ideas and technologies. For now, at least, this goal seems to have been met. *Ten Canoes*, the newly made bark canoes, and much else are now being assimilated into the oral traditions of the First Peoples of Ramingining much as the Thomson photographs once were. The old persists in new forms. "That story is never finished," Gulpilil reminds us. "That *Ten Canoes* story, it goes on forever because it is a true story of our people, it is the heart of the land and people and nature."[36]

Future Aboriginal Films

Whether made in settled or remote Australia, all Indigenous films participate in what Aboriginal playwright John Harding calls a "politics of survival." A "real black film," he asserts, proclaims to whites and Aboriginals alike that "we are still here, reclaiming the images of our identity, and still at war for land rights and compensation."[37] All films that make these claims remind audiences that the fashion designer and photographer in *Jindalee Lady* and the internationally successful opera singer in *Radiance* are no more (or less) Indigenous than are the remote-living Yolngu and Tiwi Islanders acting in *Yolngu Boy* and *Ten Canoes*.

Films by Aborigines present this range of lifestyles, along with much else. The complexity and variety of cultures that existed across Australia when white settlers arrived dwarfed the comparatively narrow range that existed within the cultures of Europe that the settlers left behind. In 1770, for example, Aboriginal and Torres Strait Islander peoples spoke an estimated two to three hundred mutually unintelligible languages. About fifty of these languages survive across contemporary Australia, as do many other manifestations of the varied pre-contact cultures that created them. Consequently, though Torres Strait Islanders and Aborigines altogether today comprise only about 2 percent (500,000) of Australia's total population, their collective visual and oral traditions equal, and likely even surpass, the degree of complexity found among the entire rest of the settler population. Aboriginal filmmakers can thus develop their films from both their own traditional diversity as well as from the new things that settler cultures provide.

Chapter 13

Future Indigenous Films

We need to connect with other people and share, because even though we may not be a majority of the world population, we are superior in diversity and in richness, and if we are able to bring together all of our knowledge, we will be able to develop and create a better world that we all can survive in and improve our life.

Marcelina Cárdenas

This book has focused on Indigenous films from regions where English is either the dominant language, as in Australia and North America, or a language in frequent use, as in the Arctic and Oceania. The neglect of other regions does not mean that Indigenous features are not also appearing in Africa, Asia, and Latin America. Several of the thousands of distinct Indigenous people living in these non-anglophone regions are also now producing their own fiction films. However, so far few of these have been shown or are available in North America.

Africa, of course, has a relatively long history of film production and is even home to a video-making explosion in Nigeria that some say makes that country now the largest producer of fiction features in the world. Most of these hundreds of Nigerian-made movies in what is often called "Nollywood" are being made by tribal peoples, as Indigenous peoples are commonly labeled in Africa. When a particular tribal people dominates the government of a country, however, the films they make do not fit easily within the ordinary understanding of Indigenous film. Films made by minority tribes within African countries do fit the category, but designating some African films as Indigenous while excluding others can be confusing. So, for example, since the Zulu currently dominate South African politics, a film such as *Yesterday* (2004) that uses the Zulu language might not be labeled Indigenous while films foregrounding minority South African tribes (e.g., the Xhosa-langauge *U-Carmen e-Khayelitsha* [*Carmen in Khayelitsha*], 2005) likely would be.

Issues of definition are equally complicated when one looks north to North Africa and the Middle East. Though peoples across this region are often identified by tribal affiliation, they are as often defined by their relationship, or lack of relationship, to Islam. The Kurds, for example, live across a homeland that includes four countries. Most Kurds are nominally Muslim and yet most, too, retain a culture and identity quite separate from the Muslim peoples that surround them. Though the Kurds fit all four characteristics of an Indigenous people described in chapter 5, they are omitted from many lists of First Peoples. Meanwhile, Kurdish filmmakers are creating an impressive archive of feature films. The best-known Kurdish filmmaker, Bahman Ghobadi, won the Cannes Caméra d'Or award for his *A Time for Drunken Horses* (*Zamani barayé masti asbha,* 2000), and subsequently made the well-received *Niwemang* (2006) and *Turtles Can Fly* (*Lakposhtha hâm parvaz mikonand,* 2004). Ghobadi, however, is not commonly grouped together with other Indigenous filmmakers.[1]

Complexities surrounding, as well as opportunities for producing, Indigenous films abound across Asia as well. The Tibetans, for example, are now commonly labeled as "Indigenous" though they were not so labeled before the Chinese intensified their efforts to erase Tibet's status as a separate country. Similar government-sponsored repressive practices against native peoples are common within China's traditional borders as well as within many other countries across Asia. It is thus often very difficult, not to say dangerous, for Indigenous peoples in Asia to produce identity-affirming films.

India contains the most numerous Indigenous populations of any single country in the world. The people there officially identified as Adivasis make up about 8 percent of the country's total one billion people. The potential for feature filmmaking among these approximately 800,000 Indigenous people is thus immense. K. J. Baby's *The Cage* (*Guda,* 2003), made in the tribal language of the Kattunaikkars in India's northern Kerala region, is a harbinger of the eventual torrent of Adivasis films that are likely one day to appear. So, too, is Ahsan Muzid's more recent *The Fortunate One* (*Sonam,* 2006), which tells a story in the Monpa dialect of the Brokpas, yak shepherds, who live in the Himalayas of India's easternmost state, Arunachal Pradesh.

The diversity of Asia-based Indigenous films will be further increased by filmmakers on the continent's island outskirts, from films made one day, for example, by some of the 150,000 Ainu in Japan and by some of the almost 500,000 First Peoples currently living on Taiwan and speaking fourteen different languages. The Philippines, farther out in the Pacific, is also home to several dozen Indigenous peoples, most with a distinctive language of their own. Three films by Kanakan Balintagos, a member of the Palaw'an tribe who also goes by the name Auraeus Solito, hint at the future richness that may be found in Indigenous Filipino filmmaking.[2] Balintagos's debut feature, The Blossoming of Maximo Oliveros (Ang Pagdadalaga ni Maximo Oliveros in Tagalog [2005]), chronicles the coming of age of a gay twelve-year-old, Maxi (Nathan Lopez), living in Manila with his family of petty thieves. Tuli (2006) moves to a rural setting and to a female protagonist, Daisy (Desiree Del Valle), whose abusive, alcoholic father wants her to follow in his tracks as the town circumciser. In Philippine Science (Pisay in Tagalog [2007]), Balintagos explores the competitive life of teens in an elite, residential high school much like one that he once attended.

Though not as varied as the media emerging across Asia, the Indigenous cinema of Central and South America is also abundantly diverse. Two regions, one in southern Mexico and the other in Bolivia, have already become prolific centers for the production of Indigenous documentaries and short fiction films.[3] So far, however, though dozens of fiction films under sixty minutes have been made in both these regions and elsewhere across Indigenous Latin America, there has been scant interest in making longer fiction films.[4] Two remarkable early efforts by non-Indigenous filmmakers who collaborated with Indigenous communities have yet to spawn successors. In Mexico in 1974, Rolando Klein wrote and directed a Tzeltal-language feature, Chac.[5] Independently, writer-director Jorge Sanjinés and his associated Ukamau group were attempting with Blood of the Condor (Yawar mallku, 1969) and in several subsequent films to invent a new form of cinema that represented a Bolivian Indigenous perspective.[6]

Considering Indigenous films from Africa, Asia, and Central and South America amplifies claims about the breadth of differences among First Peoples that were advanced in earlier chapters. Future films from the Adivasis in India and the Palaw'an in the Philippines are, after all, likely to be as different from each other as they are from the Inuit's Atanarjuat: The Fast Runner and the Aboriginal Beneath Clouds. Like

Indigenous peoples themselves, Indigenous films seem likely one day to display as much diversity as do all the rest of the world's non-Indigenous films combined.

Because they are so often currently struggling to maintain their differences, many Indigenous filmmakers in all regions will continue to make films primarily for the peoples they are representing. Still, a film's impact can be multiplied exponentially if it is widely seen by non-Indigenous audiences. Mechanisms of distribution are necessary to enable this impact, as distribution determines whether global audiences even have the chance to say no to an opportunity to watch an Indigenous film.

The supreme distribution prize remains a theatrical release, but such a release can come in many forms. There is, at one end of the continuum, the sort of massive global theatrical release (3,000+ screens) that no Indigenous film has ever received. Next comes distribution through a more limited appearance on hundreds of screens, the sort of release earned by *Rabbit-Proof Fence*, *Smoke Signals*, and *Whale Rider*, discussed in chapter 1. Indigenous films, like others, can also be given even smaller releases, ranging from showings on a few dozen to only one or two screens.

Success as a theatrical release on screens outside the United States does not necessarily translate into a North American release. So, for instance, though *Samoan Wedding* (as *Sione's Wedding*) and *Eagle vs Shark* both did well in wide-release runs in New Zealand, neither won even a limited theatrical release in the United States. Generally, then, it is safe to say that Indigenous films will not often find their way into most cineplexes where first-world film audiences initially see Hollywood releases.

A theatrical release, however, is not the only way to get a film widely seen. A growing number of film festivals actively promote Indigenous films. Some well-established festivals, like Sundance, have even created special programs to ensure that each year's selection includes Indigenous films. Additionally, an increasing number of festivals focus exclusively on work by Indigenous producers. The All Roads Film Project, Dreamspeakers, the Native Cinema Showcase, and imagineNATIVE are among the most prestigious such festivals, but many other both small and large festivals spread across the world are each year screening ever more Indigenous films.[7] About half of the films described in earlier chapters reached audiences mainly through their screenings at multiple festivals. Only a handful received even a small theatrical release.

13-1 2006 imagineNATIVE Film and Media Arts Festival poster

In addition to theatrical releases and film festivals, Indigenous film-makers can reach viewers through both broadcast and cable television. Already a great success through its theatrical release, *Whale Rider* later reached additional large audiences through several broadcast television showings. Three of Chris Eyre's films, discussed in chapter 2, were financed by television networks that also sponsored their premieres. *Johnny Tootall* was financed by and shown on Canadian television. Television opportunities are expanding, too, as more channels are added to home television cable "bundles." Premium channels such as the Sundance Channel and the Independent Film Channel actively promote smaller-budget films that have not been shown in theaters. As the number of specialized channels continues to increase, one day there may even be room for a subscriber-financed Indigenous Media Channel.[8]

Virtually all films that receive theatrical releases are also sooner or later marketed for sale as DVDs. Even films that premier at film festivals or on television are usually later offered as DVDs. Sales, however, are frequently meager for DVDs that have not received publicity through an earlier theatrical release. Large retail stores and mail-order DVD rental companies such as Netflix and Blockbuster will not even stock a DVD title unless it is offered to them by a distributor and, generally, distributors will not represent titles that have not had at least a limited theatrical release. Many Indigenous filmmakers are thus left trying to sell their DVDs outside of the usual retail markets. The DVD for *Mile Post 398*, for example, is sold at trading posts and stores across the Navajo reservation where it was produced. In Bolivia, Indigenous-made videocassettes are often traded in open markets, beside other, more traditional market fare. Many Indigenous filmmakers create film-specific Web sites and seek ways to publicize their films and sites to create traffic and sales. (A list of such film-specific sites is included in the Selected Filmography.) *Mile Post 398* has such a site, as does Rodrick Pocowatchit, who promotes both his films and his Web site through his blog, disarmingly subtitled, "The Useless Ramblings of a Clueless Filmmaker."

Though theaters, festivals, television, and DVDs provide multiple opportunities for Indigenous filmmakers to find audiences for their work, the popularity of at least some of these distribution channels is likely to be superseded in the next decade or so by video on demand (VOD). VOD is an emerging technique of movie distribution where consumers either stream or download the movie of their choice directly to their home imaging systems. While current mail-order DVD rental companies already carry approximately 100,000 movie titles, a mature VOD system will likely include a half million or more. Every film uploaded to the VOD system will potentially be available for viewing throughout the world, twenty-four hours a day, to anyone with an Internet connection. The quality of the viewing experience will depend on the quality of the end-user's imaging system.

Finding titles of interest in VOD will continue to be a problem, as it is now for searches across the thousands of films that make up the existing DVD archive. Still, with mature VOD cataloging systems, interested spectators should be able to find links to all Indigenous films that have been uploaded, listed by tribe, for instance, or by region, date of production, genre, language, director, et cetera. In a mature VOD system, most films mentioned in this book may one day be available for viewing with just a few clicks and, probably, a payment of a relatively modest fee. In this future distribution environment the surprises found in Indigenous feature films will likely become increasingly valued.

Increasingly valued, too, I hope, will become the diverse Indigenous peoples who make them.

Notes

Introduction

Epigraph. Kevin Gilbert, "The Flowering," in *Indigenous Australian Voices: A Reader*, ed. Jennifer Sabbioni, Kay Schaffer, and Sidonie Smith (New Brunswick, NJ: Rutgers University Press, 1998), 22–23.

1. The understanding of *Indigenous* as a label for the shared relationship of native peoples to dominant societies was developed by the Working Group on Indigenous Populations (WGIP) and other organizations affiliated with the United Nations (see, e.g., "Indigenous People" at http://www.unhchr.ch/Indigenous/main.html). The concept of Indigenous film is examined in more detail in chapter 5 below.

Chapter 1

Epigraph. John Trudell, as narrator of *A Thousand Roads*, directed by Chris Eyre (Washington, D.C.: Smithsonian's National Museum of the American Indian, 2005).

1. Doris Pilkington (aka Nugi Garimara), *Follow the Rabbit-proof Fence* (1996; repr. New York: Miramax Books, 2002).
2. Human Rights and Equal Opportunity Commission, *Bringing Them Home: Report on the National Inquiry into the Separation of Aboriginal and Torres Strait Islander Children from Their Families* (Canberra: Australian Parliamentary Paper, 1997).
3. Susan Masuhart describes the conditions at Moore River in *Sort of a Place Like Home: Remembering the Moore River Native Settlement* (Fremantle, Australia: Fremantle Arts Centre Press, 1993).
4. David Gulpilil is probably the world's best-known Indigenous actor. See chapter 3 for an examination of his films and career.
5. For histories of the fence, see http://amol.org.au/runrabbitrun/timeline.asp and http://www.thingsmagazine.net/text/t14/rabbits.htm.
6. Quoted in *Following the Rabbit-Proof Fence*, DVD, directed by Darlene Johnson (Los Angeles: Buena Vista Home Entertainment,

2002). This making-of documentary is included with the DVD for *Rabbit-Proof Fence*.

7. Gracie was later sent out from Moore River as domestic help. She married and had six children and never returned to Jigalong again. She died in 1993.

8. Quoted in A. B. Sparks, "Molly and the stolen generations: The making of rabbit-proof fence," *Angle, A Journal of Arts + Culture*, http://www.anglemagazine.org/articles/Molly_and_the_Stolen_Generatio_2044.asp.

9. Quoted in Jane Mills, "Truth and the rabbit-proof fence," *Real Time* 48 (April–May 2002): 15, http://www.realtimearts.net/archive.

10. Witi Ihimaera, *The Whale Rider* (1987; repr. New York: Harcourt, 2003).

11. For example, Barry Barclay, "An Open Letter to John Barnett, *Onfilm Magazine*, February 2003, http://www.archivesearch.co.nz/ViewEditorial.asp?EditorialID=9301&pubcode=ONF.

12. Margaret Meklin and Andrew Meklin, "The Magnificent Accident: An Interview with Witi Ihimaera," *Contemporary Pacific* 16.2 (Fall 2004): 358–66.

13. See, for example, "Our story, told to the world,"*New Zealand Herald*, January 25, 2003, www.nzherald.co.nz/index.cfm?objectid=3097871, and Rebecca Walsh, "Film puts reluctant Whangara on the map," *New Zealand Herald*. January 25, 2003, www.nzherald.co.nz/index.cfm?objectid=3097870.

14. Quoted in Bridget Carter, "Movie boasts waka plan," *New Zealand Herald*, March 14, 2003, http://www.nzherald.co.nz.

15. Quoted in *Behind the scenes of* Whale Rider, DVD (New Zealand: South Pacific Pictures, 2002). This making-of documentary is included with the DVD for *Whale Rider*.

16. See, e.g., Louisa Cleave, "Rider fans overwhelm Whangara," *New Zealand Herald*, August 8, 2003, http://www.nzherald.co.nz.

17. Alexie integrates elements from *The Lone Ranger and Tonto Fist-fight in Heaven* (New York: HarperPerennial, 1993) and also *Reservation Blues* (1995; repr. New York: Grove Press, 2005).

18. Dennis West and Joan M. West. "Sending cinematic smoke signals: An interview with Sherman Alexie," *Cineaste* 23.4 (1998): 28–33.

19. "Forgiving Our Fathers" comes from the book *Ghost Radio* by Dick Lourie (New York: Hanging Loose Press, 1998). Lourie was Alexie's editor at Hanging Loose Press.

20. Sherman Alexie, *Smoke Signals: A Screenplay* (New York: Miramax Books, 1998), 168.

21. Alexie, *The Lone Ranger*, 1993.

22. Alexie, *Reservation Blues*, 1995.

23. West and West, "Sending,"1998.

24. Alexie, *Smoke Signals*, 1998, 151–68.

25. Further aspects of *Smoke Signals* are discussed in chapter 7.

26. David Edelstein, "Four Days of the Cipher," *Slate*, June 14, 2002, http://www.slate.com/id/2066963.
27. J. Hoberman, "Let there be Light," *Village Voice*, June 5–11, 2002, http://www.villagevoice.com/film/0223,hoberman,35351,20.html.
28. Roger Ebert, review of *Atanarjuat: The Fast Runner*, robertebert.com, June 22, 2002, http://rogerebert.suntimes.com/apps/pbcs.dll/article?AID=/20020628/REVIEWS/206280303/1023.
29. Zacharias Kunuk, "The public art of Inuit storytelling," *2002 Spry Memorial Lecture* (November 25, 2002), http://www.com.umontreal.ca/spry/spry-kz-lec.html.
30. Ibid.
31. Kunuk quoted in Faye Ginsburg, "*Atanarjuat* Off-Screen: From 'Media Reservations' to the World Stage," *American Anthropologist* 105.4 (2003): 827.

Chapter 2

Epigraph. Chris Eyre, quoted in Micol Marotti, "Chris Eyre, Interview," *National Museum of the American Indian* (Summer 2005): 40.

1. Ibid.
2. Quoted in Walter Chaw, "Skins Game, An Interview with Chris Eyre," *Film Freak Central*, n.d., http://filmfreakcentral.net/notes/ceyreinterview.htm.
3. Quoted in Marotti, 2005, 40.
4. Quoted in David Melmer, "Eyre Shines at Sundance," *Indian Country Today*, February 6, 2004, http://www.indiancountry.com/content.cfm?id=1076078547.
5. Quoted in Chaw.
6. Quoted in Marotti, 40.
7. Dee Brown, *Bury My Heart at Wounded Knee: An Indian History of the American West* (New York: Holt, Rinehart & Winston, 1970).
8. Quoted in Chaw.
9. See, for example, Walter Chaw, "Review of *Skins*," *Film Freak Central*, n.d., http://www.filmfreakcentral.net/screenreviews/skins.htm.
10. Quoted in Tania Casselle, "Eyre Exposes the Heart and Muscle Beneath '*Skins*,'" *Indian Country Today*, September 10, 2002, http://www.indiancountry.com/content.cfm?id=1031666942.
11. Scott Foundas, review of *Edge of America, Variety*, January 21, 2004, http://www.variety.com/review/VE1117922887.html?categoryid=31&cs=1&p=0.
12. Quoted in "PBS: A *Thief of Time* American Mystery! Special," *Washington Post*, July 12, 2004, http://www.washingtonpost.com/wp-dyn/articles/A33769-2004Jul7.html.
13. "Rolling Rez," DVD. This documentary is included with the DVD for *Skins*.
14. Quoted in Donald Carr, "Chris Eyre Interview," *Dakota Blues Podcast, 2nd edition*, Fall 2005, http://chriseyre.org/ce_sdblues_podcast.wma.

15. James May, "Noted Filmmakers Join to Form Production Company," *Indian Country Today*, June 28, 2005, http://www.indiancountry.com/content.cfm?id=1096411143.
16. Eyre describes his emerging interest in directing a wide-release commercial film in Carr.

Chapter 3

Epigraph. David Gulpilil, quoted in *Gulpilil: One Red Blood*, DVD, directed by Darlene Johnson (Canberra, Australia: Ronin Films, 2002).

1. Gulpilil was credited as "David Gumpilil" in this film.
2. Jo Litson, "The Natural: David Gulpilil, Between Two Worlds," *Weekend Australian*, November 10, 2001.
3. David Gulpilil quoted in ibid.
4. Ibid.
5. Rolf de Heer, quoted in ibid.
6. Airlie Thomas, quoted in ibid.
7. Louis Nowra, *Walkabout* (Strawberry Hills NSW, Australia: Currency Press, 2003), 76.
8. Peter Krausz estimates that only about 50 out of 1,000 Australian-based productions have represented Aborigines in any way at all. See Krausz, "Screening Indigenous Australia: An Overview of Aboriginal Representation on Film," *Australian Screen Education* 32 (n.d.): 90.
9. Nowra, 59.
10. Marcia Langton, quoted in *Gulpilil: One Red Blood*.
11. Ibid.
12. Ibid.
13. Rhoda Roberts, "In Conversation with David Gulpilil," *Awaye Radio, Australian Broadcasting Company (ABC)*, May 24 2002, available at http://www.abc.net.au/message/radio/awaye/aw_davidgulpilil.ram.
14. David Gulpilil, quoted in *Gulpilil: One Red Blood*.
15. Ibid.
16. Walter Addiego, review of *The Tracker, San Francisco Chronicle*, March 19, 2004, http://www.sfgate.com/cgi-bin/article.cgi?f=/c/a/2004/03/19/DDG3F5MSAE1.DTL.
17. See chapter 12 for further discussion of the Thomson photographs and *Ten Canoes*.
18. Frances Djulibing, quoted in *Ten Canoes* Press Kit, 24, http://www.tencanoes.com.au/tencanoes/pdf/Background.pdf.
19. Michael Dawu, quoted in *Ten Canoes* Press Kit, 23, http://www.tencanoes.com.au/tencanoes/pdf/Background.pdf.
20. Rolf de Heer, quoted in Michael Fitzgerald, "Keeping Time with Rolf," *Time South Pacific*, May 13, 2006.
21. Michael Guillen, "2006 TIFF—Hana yori no naho & Ten Canoes," The Evening Class, Septermber 9, 2006, http://

theeveningclass.blogspot.com/2006/09/2006-tiff-hana-yori-no-naho-ten-canoes.html.

22. Descriptions of the Many Canoes projects can be found at http://www.vertigoproductions.com.au/information.php?film_id=11&display=extras.

23. *Gulpilil: One Red Blood*. See chapter 12 for further discussion of current trends in Australian films.

Chapter 4

Epigraph. Marcia Langton, "Introduction: culture wars," in *Blacklines: Contemporary Critical Writing by Indigenous Australians*, ed. Michele Grossman (Melbourne: Melbourne University Press, 2003), 83.

1. Duane Byrge, "The Land Has Eyes," *The Hollywood Reporter.com*, January 22, 2004, http://www.hollywoodreporter.com/thr/reviews/review_display.jsp?vnu_content_id=207 3833.

2. The description in the following paragraphs is taken from Alan Howard, "Presenting Rotuma to the World, The Making of the Film *The Land Has Eyes*," *Visual Anthropology Review* 22, no. 1 (2006): 74–96.

3. Ibid., 86.

4. Zacharias Kunuk, "The public art of Inuit storytelling," *2002 Spry Memorial Lecture*, November 25, 2002, http://www.com.umontreal.ca/spry/spry-kz-lec.html.

5. Freya Shiwy, "Decolonizing the Frame: Indigenous Video in the Andes," *Framework* 44, no. 1 (2003): 116–32.

6. keenynicely, "Over-rated," *Internet Movie Data Base: Pear ta ma 'on maf*, July 13, 2004, http://www.imdb.com/title/tt0390179/usercomments.

7. Sherman Alexie quoted in William H. Phillips, *Film: An Introduction* (Boston: Bedford/St. Martins, 2002), 403.

8. Chapter 7 examines several Indian films made before *Smoke Signals*.

9. Sherman Alexie, *Smoke Signals: A Screenplay* (New York: Miramax Books, 1998), 61.

10. Edmund Carpenter, *Oh, What a Blow That Phantom Gave Me!* (New York: Bantam Books, 1974), 97.

11. See chapter 5 for a broader discussion of this objection to Indigenous feature films.

Chapter 5

Epigraph. Lofty Bardayal Nadjamerrek, quoted in Nicholas Rothwell, "The New Wave," *Weekend Australian*, May 27, 2006.

1. Quoted in Alan Howard, "Presenting Rotuma to the World, The Making of the Film *The Land Has Eyes*," *Visual Anthropology Review* 22, no. 1 (2006): 57.

2. Ward Churchill, *Fantasies of the Master Race: Literature, Cinema and the Colonization of American Indians* (San Francisco: City Lights Books, 1998).

3. Vilsoni Hereniko, "Representations of Pacific Islanders in Film and Video," n.d., http://www.yidff.jp/docbox/14/box14-3-e.html.

4. Gross, quoted in Steven Leuthold, *Indigenous Aesthetics: Native Art, Media and Identity* (Austin: University of Texas Press, 1998), 22.

5. Chaat Smith, "Land of a Thousand Dances," n.d., http://redplanet.home.mindspring.com/exile/land1.htm.

6. Paula Gunn Allen, *The Sacred Hoop: Recovering the Feminine in American Indian Traditions* (Boston: Beacon Press, 1992), 224.

7. Beverly R. Singer, *Wiping the War Paint off the Lens: Native American Film and Video* (Minneapolis: University of Minnesota Press, 2001), 4.

8. Quoted in Kristen Dowell, "Indigenous Media Gone Global: Strengthening Indigenous Identity On- and Offscreen at the First Nations/First Features Film Showcase," *American Anthropologist* 108.2 (June 2006): 380.

9. Zacharias Kunuk, "The public art of Inuit storytelling," *2002 Spry Memorial Lecture*, November 25, 2002, http://www.com.umontreal.ca/spry/spry-kz-lec.html.

10. Quoted in Jerry White, "Frozen But Always in Motion: Arctic Film, Video, and Broadcast," *Velvet Light Trap* 55 (Spring 2005): 58.

11. Norman Cohn, "The Art of Community-Based Filmmaking," in *Atanarjuat/The Fast Runner*, ed. Gillian Robinson (Toronto: Coach House Books, 2002), 27.

12. "*Atanarjuat: The Fast Runner* Press Kit," http://www.isuma.ca/catalogue/other_preview/Atan_presskit.doc.

13. Kunuk, 2002.

14. See "Nunavut Series" at http://www.isuma.ca/nunavut.

15. Zacharias Kunuk, interview by Michelle Svenson, "Zacharias Kunuk Interview," *Native Networks*, April 2002, http://www.nativenetworks.si.edu/eng/rose/kunuk_z_interview.htm.

16. See Kathleen Fleming, "Igloolik Video: An Organic Response from a Culturally Sound Community," *Inuit Art Quarterly* 11.1 (1996): 26–34. See also White, 2005.

17. Geary Hobson, "The Rise of White Shaman as a New Version of Cultural Imperialism," in *The Remembered Earth* (Albuquerque: Red Earth Press, 1978), 100–108, and "The Rise of the White Shaman: Twenty-Five Years Late." *SAIL Studies in American Indian Literatures* 14 (Summer/Fall 2002): 1–11, http://oncampus.richmond.edu/faculty/ASAIL/SAIL2/142.html. Wendy

Rose, "The Great Pretenders: Further Reflections on White-shamanism," in *The State of Native America: Genocide, Colonization, and Resistance*, ed. Annette Jaimes (Boston: South End Press, 1992), 403–21.

18. Margo Thunderbird, quoted in Rose, 403.
19. Hobson, 2002, 4.
20. See Houston Wood, *Displacing Natives: The Rhetorical Production of Hawai'i* (Lanham, MD: Rowman and Littlefield, 1999).
21. Edmund Carpenter, *Oh, What a Blow That Phantom Gave Me!* (New York: Holt, Rinehart and Winston, 1972), 182.
22. Marshall McLuhan, *The Gutenberg Galaxy: The Making of Typographic Man* (Toronto: University of Toronto Press, 1962), 41.
23. Zacharias Kunuk, quoted in Faye Ginsburg, "*Atanarjuat* Off-Screen: From 'Media Reservations' to the World Stage," *American Anthropologist* 105.4 (2003): 827.
24. Patricia Grace, *Cousins* (Honolulu: University of Hawai'i Press, 1998), 235.
25. Erica Irene Daes, "Note by the Chairperson-Rapporteur of the Working Group on Indigenous populations," *UN Commission on Human Rights* (June 21, 1995), http://www.cwis.org/fwdp/International/indigdef.txt.

Chapter 6

Epigraph. Amazon video maker Mokuka, quoted in Faye Ginsburg, "Culture/Media: A (Mild) Polemic," *Anthropology Today* 10, no. 2 (1994), 9.

1. These and other projects are described on the official *Ten Canoes* Web site, at http://www.vertigoproductions.com.au/10canoes.htm.
2. Hereniko, quoted in Alan Howard,"Presenting Rotuma to the World, The Making of the Film *The Land Has Eyes*," *Visual Anthropology Review* 22 no.1 (2006): 76.
3. http://www.atanarjuat.com/production_diary/index.html.
4. Voi Fesaitu, quoted in Howard, 79.
5. Howard, 82.
6. Kunuk, interview by Michelle Svenson, *Native Networks*, April 1, 2002, http://www.nativenetworks.si.edu/eng/rose/kunuk_z_interview.htm#open.
7. Descriptions in the following paragraphs are drawn from Freya Schiwy, "Selling Out? Indigenous Media, Ayni, and the Global Market" (paper presented at the annual meeting of the *Society for Cinema and Media Studies*, Chicago, IL, March 8, 2007); see also, Schiwy, "Decolonizing the Frame: Indigenous Video in the Andes," *Framework* 44, no. 1 (2003): 116–32.
8. "Rolling Rez," DVD. This documentary is included with the DVD for *Skins*.

9. Quoted in Faye Ginsburg, "Screen Memories: Resignifying the Traditional in Indigenous Media," in *Media Worlds: Anthropology on a New Terrain*, ed. Faye Ginsburg, Lila Abu-Lughod, and Brain Larkin (Berkeley: University of California Press, 2002), http://www.ucpress.edu/books/pages/9048/9048.ch01.html.

10. Don Selwyn, quoted in Michele Hewitson, "The Man Who Colonised Shakespeare," *New Zealand Herald*, November 19, 2005, http://www.nzherald.co.nz/section/1/story.cfm?c_id=1&objectid= 10355929.

11. Eric D. Snider, review of *5th World*, directed by Blackhorse Lowe, *eFilm Critic.com*, January 24, 2005, http://efilmcritic.com/review. php?movie=11274.

12. Epeli Hau'ofa, "Epilogue: Pasts to Remember," *Remembrance of Pacific Pasts: An Invitation to Remake History*, ed. Rob Borofsky (Honolulu: University of Hawaii Press, 2000), 460.

13. Mita, interview by Karin Williams, *Merata Mita*, VHS, directed by Jeff De Ponte (Honolulu: Pacific Islanders in Communications, 1997).

14. Schiwy, 2003.

15. Sean Mallon and Pandora Fulimalo Pereira, "Pacific Art Niu Sila: Introduction," in *Pacific Art Niu Sila: The Pacific Dimension of Contemporary New Zealand Arts* (Wellington, New Zealand: Te Papa Press, 2002), 7–20.

16. Kunuk, quoted in Doug Alexander, "Zacharias Kunuk Q&A," *Geographical* 74, no. 4 (April 2002): 106.

17. Quoted in Cristina Veran, "Art & Unrest in the Andes," *Colorlines* (Summer 2004), http://www.colorlines.com/article.php?ID=53.

18. Fredric Jameson, "Third-World Literature in the Era of Multinational Capitalism," *Social Text* 15 (1986): 65–88.

19. Darrell Varga, "*Atanarjuat: The Fast Runner*," *The Cinema of Canada*, ed. Jerry White (New York: Columbian University Press, 2006), 225–33.

20. Catherine Gallagher, "Undoing," *Time and the Literary*, ed. Karen Newman, Jay Clayton, and Marianne Hirsch (New York: Routledge, 2002): 11–30.

21. Lilikalā Kame'elehiwa, *Native Land and Foreign Desires* (Honolulu: Bishop Museum Press, 1992), 22.

22. John Mowitt, *Re-Takes: Postcolonialaity and Foreign Film Languages* (Minneapolis: University of Minnesota Press, 2005).

23. Schiwy, e-mail message to author, July 29, 2007.

24. David MacDougall, *Transcultural Cinema* (Princeton, NJ: Princeton University Press, 1998), 205.

25. Schiwy, 2003, 124. See, for example, *Jorge Sanjinés y grupo Ukama, Teoría y práctica de un cine junto al pueblo* (Mexico City: Siglo XXI Editores, 1979).

26. Masayesva Jr., quoted in Steven Leuthold, *Indigenous Aesthetics: Native Art, Media and Identity* (Austin: University of Texas Press, 1998), 194.
27. Schiwy, 2007.
28. Wendy Rose, "The Great Pretenders: Further Reflections on Whiteshamanism," in *The State of Native America: Genocide, Colonization, and Resistance*, ed. Annette Jaimes (Boston: South End Press, 1992), 406.

Chapter 7

1. Sherman Alexie, "Making Smoke," *Whole Earth*, Fall 1998, http://web.ebscohost.com.
2. Richardson Morse, interview by Joanna Hearne, *Native Networks*, January 28, 2004, http://www.nativenetworks.si.edu/eng/rose/morse_r_interview.htm.
3. See *Native Networks* at http://www.nativenetworks.si.edu/eng/rose/hmod.htm.
4. Leslie Marmon Silko, "Videomakers and Basketmakers," *Aperture* 119 (Summer 1990): 73.
5. Greg Sarris, *Grand Avenue: A Novel in Stories* (New York: Hyperion, 1994).
6. Biographical details were provided by Skorodin, e-mail message to author, August 10, 2007.
7. *Trudell* (2005), written by Russell Friedenberg and directed by Heather Rae, examines Trudell's life.
8. Details on this feature can be found at http://www.crazyindn.com.
9. Sherman Alexie, *Smoke Signals: A Screenplay* (New York: Miramax Books, 1998), 7.

Chapter 8

Epigraph. Randy Redroad, quoted in Jackie Bissley, "Randy Redroad takes Indie route to success with 'The Doe Boy,'" *Indian Country Today*, February 7, 2002, http://www.indiancountry.com/content.cfm?id=1013095548.

1. Sherman Alexie, quoted in *The Business of Fancydancing* Press Kit, http://www.fallsapart.com/fancydancing/fancydancing.pdf.
2. Sherman Alexie, *The Business of Fancydancing: Stories and Poems* (Brooklyn, NY: Hanging Loose Press, 1992).
3. Sherman Alexie, *The Business of Fancydancing* DVD audio commentary.
4. Randy Redroad, quoted in Michell Svenson, "Randy Redroad Interview," *Native Networks*, April 2001, http://www.nativenetworks.si.edu/eng/rose/redroad_r_interview.htm#open.

5. Randy Redroad-Sapp, "Thru a Mythic Lens," in *Screenwriting for a Global Market: Selling Your Scripts from Hollywood to Hong Kong*, 113–18, ed. Andre Horton (University of California Press, 2004), 117.

6. Adriel Heisey and Kenji Kawano, *Fifth World: Portrait of the Navajo Nation* (Tucson, AZ: Rio Nuevo Publishers, 2001).

7. Shonie Da La Rosa, quoted in Natasha Kaye Johnson, "Diné filmmakers prepare for production," *Gallup Independent*, May 4, 2006.

8. Carole Quattro Levine, "Real versus Reel Life on the Rez," *Scene4Magazine*, May 2007, http://www.scene4.com/archivesqv6/may-2007/html/carolelevine0507.html.

9. Rodrick Pocowatchit, quoted in "About the Movie," *Dancing on the Moon*, DVD Special Feature.

10. See http://www.harmyfilms.com/harmyhome.html. The Web site explains, "Harmy was Rod's childhood teddy bear. One day, Harmy disappeared and is still at large. Hence the logo for Harmy Films, a one-eyed tattered teddy bear. Doesn't that just scream 'Important filmmaker?'"

11. From December 31, 2006. The blog is available at http://www.harmyfilms.blogspot.com.

12. Pocowatchit, quoted in "About the Movie."

13. *Imprint* (2007), *Older Than America* (2008) and *Tkaronto* (2007) were released too late to be included in this chapter.

14. Sherman Alexie, quoted in Matthew Fleischer, "Gone With the Wind," *LA Weekly*, April 11, 2007, http://www.laweekly.com/film+tv/film/gone-with-the-wind/16116.

15. Randy Redroad, quoted in Jackie Bissley, "Randy Redroad takes Indie route to success with 'The Doe Boy,'" *Indian Country Today*, February 7, 2002.

16. Phil Hall, "The Doe Boy," *IMDB Reviews*, http://www.imdb.com/Reviews/329/32929.

17. Jonathan Saturen, quoted on *The Business of Fancydancing*, DVD audio commentary.

Chapter 9

Epigraph. Anastasia Lapsui, "Cultural Creativity on Screen" (symposium, National Museum of the American Indian Symposium, New York, NY, May 12, 2005).

1. Sámi, also spelled Saami and Sami, is the preferred term for the people Europeans previous named "Lapps" and "Laplanders." Nenets is sometimes spelled "Nenet," probably because of the erroneous assumption that the terminal "s" is for the plural number. Inuit is the preferred term for peoples sometimes known as "Eskimos."

2. Willow G. Mullins and Holly Hobbes, "Finding the Path: The Politics of Passionate Research in *Ofelas* and *Our Nationhood*" (paper, presented at the annual meeting of the Society for Cinema and Media Studies Conference, Chicago, March 11 2007).

3. Stanley Kauffmann, review of *Pathfinder, New Republic,* July 2, 1990, 26.

4. Simma, quoted in Liza Bear, "Lap Give and Take," *Film Scouts Diary,* June 11, 1997, http://www.filmscouts.com/SCRIPTs/diary.cfm?Festival=mid-su97&File=midni974.

5. Biographical details are taken from the official *A Bride of the Seventh Heaven* Web site, at http://www.millenniumfilm.fi/2003_bride.html.

6. Jerry White, "Frozen But Always in Motion: Arctic Film, Video, and Broadcast," *Velvet Light Trap* 55 (Spring 2005): 52–64.

7. Kunuk, quoted in Michelle Svenson, "Zacharias Kunuk Interview," *Native Networks,* April 2002, http://www.nativenetworks.si.edu/eng/rose/kunuk_z_interview.htm.

8. Kunuk, quoted in Gillian Robinson, *Atanarjuat/The Fast Runner* (Toronto: Coach House Books, 2002), 13.

9. Kunuk, quoted in White, 62.

10. White.

11. Kunuk, quoted in Igloolik Isuma Productions, "*Atanarjuat* Press Kit," http://www.isuma.ca/Press_kits/Atanarjuat_PressKit.pdf.

12. Kunuk, quoted in Doug Alexander, "Zacharias Kunuk Q&A," *Geographical* 74, no. 4 (April 2002): 106.

13. Kunuk, quoted in Svenson.

14. Kunuk, quoted in Mari Sasano, "Inuit Filmmaker Brings his People's History to Light," *Edmonton Journal,* October 6, 2006.

15. Kunuk, quoted in Sasano.

16. Audio interview by Eleanor Wachtel, CBC radio, September 6, 2006, http://www.cbc.ca/radioshows/THE_ARTS_TONIGHT/20060906.shtml.

17. Cohn, quoted in Jason Anderson, review of *The Journals of Knud Rasmussen, Eye Weekly Review,* September 28, 2006, http://www.eyeweekly.com/eye/issue/issue_04.11.02/film/atanarjuat.php.

18. Martha Fisher, review of *The Journals of Knud Rasmussen, Cinematical,* September 9, 2006, http://www.cinematical.com/2006/09/09/tiff-review-the-journals-of-knud-rasmussen.

19. Cohn, quoted in Anderson.

20. This plot summary is adapted from the official *Before Tomorrow* Web site at http://www.beforetomorrow.ca/en/synopsis.php.

21. Kunuk describes some of the techniques necessary for using a video camera in extremely cold conditions in Kunuk, "The public art of Inuit storytelling," *2002 Spry Memorial Lecture,* November 25, 2002, http://www.com.umontreal.ca/spry/spry-kz-lec.html.

Chapter 10

Epigraph. Barry Barclay, "Exploring Fourth Cinema" (lecture presented at *Re-imagining Indigenous Cultures,* National Endowment For The Humanities Summer Institute, Honolulu, Hawai'i, July 2003).

1. Sean Mallon and Pandora Fulimalo Pereira, "Pacific Art Niu Sila: Introduction," in *Pacific Art Niu Sila: The Pacific Dimension of Contemporary New Zealand Arts,* ed. Sean Mallon and Pandora Fulimalo Pereira (Wellington, New Zealand: Te Papa Press, 2002), 7–20.
2. Vilsoni Hereniko, "Indigenizing the Camera" (paper, presented at *The Conference on Globalization and Cultural Diversity,* East-West Center, Honolulu, Hawai'i, February 13–16, 2006).
3. The film is sometimes known as *Tukana: Husat I Asua?,* which translates roughly as "Tukana, what is to be done?"
4. *Te Rua* also introduces the concept of "spiritual ownership" of material and ideational culture, an idea that Barclay has continued to develop. See Barclay, *Mana Tuturu: Māori Treasures and Intellectual Property Rights* (Honolulu: University of Hawai'i Press, 2005).
5. Sarah Chauncey, DVD review of *Once Were Warriors, Reel.com,* http://www.reel.com/movie.asp?MID=8345&buy=closed&PID=10110497&Tab=reviews&CID=18#tabs.
6. Desson Howe, review of *Once Were Warriors, Washington Post,* March 3, 1995.
7. Released over a decade later, the Navajo-made *Mile Post 398* (discussed in chapter 8) also examines the impact of alcoholism on an Indigenous family. The scenes of domestic abuse in *Mile Post 398,* however, do not come close to matching the brutality depicted in *Once Were Warriors.*

Chapter 11

Epigraph. Merata Mita, interview on *First Friday,* television broadcast, Olelo Cable presentation, August 1991.

1. See Whale Rider, "National Outreach," *Pacific Islanders in Communication,* http://www.piccom.org/whalerider/outreach.html.
2. Witi Ihimaera, *The Whale Rider* (1987; repr. New York: Harcourt, 2003).
3. Ihimaera, "Author's Note," ibid., n.p.
4. Ihimaera, "Making of the Film," *Pacific Islanders in Communication,* www.piccom.org/whalerider/thefilm3.html.
5. See chapter 1 for further discussion of *Whale Rider.*
6. Selwyn, quoted in "Shakespeare goes Maori," *BBC News,* December 4, 2001, http://news.bbc.co.uk/1/hi/entertainment/film/1691261.stm.

7. Selwyn, quoted in *The Māori Merchant of Venice* Press Kit, http://homepages.ihug.co.nz/~hetaonga/merchant/Files/MediaKit.pdf, 8.
8. Ibid., 41.
9. Rapata Wiri, cited in Valerie Wayne, review of *Te Tangata Wahi Rawa o Weniti, The Māori Merchant of Venice, Contemporary Pacific* 16 (Fall 2004): 425.
10. Vilsoni Hereniko, "Indigenizing the Camera" (paper, presented at The Conference on Globalization and Diversity, East-West Center, Honolulu, Hawai'i, February 13–16, 2006).
11. David Bevington, Anne Marie Welsh, and Michael L. Greenwald, *Shakespeare: Script, Stage, Screen* (New York: Pearson Longman, 2006), 216.
12. Hereniko, quoted in Lusiana Speight, "Local playwright translates legend to celluloid," *Fijitimes Online*, September 6, 2005, http://www.fijitimes.com.
13. Alan Howard, "Presenting Rotuma to the World, The Making of the Film *The Land Has Eyes*," *Visual Anthropology Review* 22, no. 1 (2006): 74–96.
14. See chapter 4 for further discussion of various audience reactions to *The Land Has Eyes*.
15. Peter Sciretta, "Eagle vs Shark Movie Review," /*Film: Blogging the Reel World*, January 25, 2007, http://www.slashfilm.com/2007/01/25/sundance-eagle-vs-shark-movie-review.
16. Sean Mallon and Pandora Fulimalo Pereira, "Pacific Art Niu Sila: Introduction," in *Pacific Art Niu Sila: The Pacific Dimension of Contemporary New Zealand Arts* (Wellington, New Zealand: Te Papa Press, 2002), 10.
17. Ibid., 14.

Chapter 12

Epigraph. Archie Weller, "Films in Color," *Cinema Papers* 87 (March–April 1992): 44.

1. Aborigine director Bruce McGuinness made *Black Fire*, a 16 mm feature, in the early 1970s. However, to the best of my knowledge, prints were not publicly shown and are not now available.
2. Quoted in Scott Murray, "Tracey Moffatt, *Night Cries—A Rural Tragedy*," *Cinema Papers* 79 (May 1990): 21.
3. Michael Leigh, "Curious and curiouser," in *Back of Beyond: Discovering Australian Film and Television*, ed. Scott Murray (Sydney: Australian Film Commission, 1988), 78–88.
4. Marcia Langton, "Aboriginal art and film: the politics of representation," in *Blacklines: Contemporary Critical Writing by Indigenous Australians*, ed. Michele Grossman (Melbourne: Melbourne University Press, 2003), 109.
5. Ibid., 110.

6. Brian Syron, "The Problem Is Seduction: Reflections on Black Theatre and Film," in *The Mudrooroo/Muller Project*, ed. Gerhard Fischer (Sydney: NSW U.P., 1993), 171.

7. Marcia Langton, *"Well, I heard it on the radio and I saw it on the television . . ." An Essay for the Australian Film and Television Commission on the politics and aesthetics of filmmaking by and about Aboriginal persons and things* (Sydney: Australian Film Commission, 1993).

8. Though primarily a stage actor, director, and teacher, Syron's Australian screen acting included: *Backlash* (1986), *Flight Into Hell* (1985), *The Coolangatta Gold* (1984) (aka *The Gold and the Glory*), and the television series *Pig in a Poke* (1977).

9. Syron, 168.

10. Ibid.

11. Langton, 1993, 55.

12. Ibid., 53.

13. Alan McKee surveyed many reviews and found that reviewers commonly associate "Aboriginality" with social problems. If problems are not the focus then reviewers find films with Aboriginal characters to be about "universal" themes. See McKee, "Accentuate the 'negative': reality and race in Australian film reviewing," *Australian Studies in Journalism* 8 (1999): 139–57.

14. Moffatt's work is held in various international private and public collections including the Museum of Modern Art (NYC), Tate Modern (London), Museum of Contemporary Art (Los Angeles), Museet for Santidskunst (Oslo), Museum of Contemporary Photography (Tokyo), National Gallery of Australia, Art Gallery of New South Wales, Museum of Contemporary Art Sydney, BP Australia, Steve Vizard Foundation, NRMA Collection, and Parliament House Collection Canberra.

15. More about Moffatt's career can be found in Jane Cole's documentary, *Up in the Sky: Tracey Moffatt in New York* (Artarmon, Australia: Beyond Distribution, 1999).

16. John Wojdylo, "Bedevil," *Cinema Papers* 96 (1993): 47.

17. Moffatt, quoted in John Conomos and Raffaele Caputo, "BE-DEVIL: Tracey Moffatt," *Cinema Papers* 93 (May 1993): 28.

18. Catherine Summerhayes, "Haunting Secrets: Tracey Moffatt's be-Devil," *Film Quarterly* 58, no. 1 (2004): 19.

19. Moffatt, quoted in Summerhayes, 10.

20. Moffatt, quoted in Sebastian Smee, "Just don't call me an Aborignial artist," *Independent Online Edition*, April 16, 2001, http://www.independent.co.uk/incoming/article239478.ece.

21. Perkins, "Interview 6," DVD Special Features, *Radiance* (1998, Universal Pictures, Australia).

22. Ceridwen Spark, "Gender and Radiance," *Hecate* 27, no. 2 (2001): 41.

23. Chris Eyre's film about a girls' high school basketball team, *Edge of America*, came out a year later. *The Land Has Eyes* also focuses on teenagers but is set in the 1960s in a pre-Independent Rotuma.

24. See the official home page for the band at http://www.yothuyindi.com/index.html. Many of Johnson's music videos are now freely available on Internet video-sharing sites.

25. Johnson was born in England but spent much of his boyhood in Darwin, including his time in high school. Johnson left upon graduation to learn filmmaking in London, then returned to Darwin in 1990 to begin what would be a near-ten-year-long process of fulfilling his dream of making a feature film about the Northern Territory and its Indigenous people.

26. Sen, quoted in Libby Tudball, "*Beneath Clouds:* A Study Guide" (2002), 7, http://www.metromagazine.com.au/metro/default.asp.

27. Sen, quoted in Daniel Browning, "Ivan Sen Interview," *Message Stick*, May 25, 2002, http://www.abc.net.au/message/blackarts/film/s720711.htm.

28. Stephanie Bunbury, "Beyond black and white," *The Age*, May 19, 2002, http://www.theage.com.au/articles/2002/05/18/1021544084403.html.

29. Ibid.

30. Sen, quoted in "Ivan Sen talks to Dan Edwards, News and Events, *Australian Film Commission* (n.d.), http://www.afc.gov.au/newsandevents/afcnews/converse/sen/newspage_284.aspx.

31. Langton, 1993, 12.

32. Luke Buckmaster, review of *Ten Canoes, InFilm Australia*, n.d., http://www.infilm.com.au/reviews/tencanoes.htm.

33. De Heer, quoted in Michael Gullien, "TIFF REPORT: Review of Ten Canoes & Q&A with Director Rolf De Heer," *Twitch*, September 9, 2006, http://twitchfilm.net/archives/007477.html.

34. This and other stories of the production of *Ten Canoes* are reported in the *Ten Canoes* Press Kit, http://www.tencanoes.com.au/tencanoes/pdf/Background.pdf.

35. Djulibing, quoted in ibid., 24.

36. Gulpilil, quoted in ibid., 25. Broad positive effects on their respective remote communities have also been made on the island of Rotuma through the production of *The Land Has Eyes*, in Bolivia with various videos made by the Center for Cinematographic Training (CEFREC) and Organization of Indigenous Audiovisual Communicators of Bolivia (CAIB), and in the Arctic in shooting both *Atanarjuat: The Fast Runner* and *The Journals of Knud Rasmussen*.

37. John Harding, "Canons in the Camera," *Cinema Papers* 87 (March–April 1992): 42–43.

Chapter 13

Epigraph. Marcelina Cárdenas, "Cultural Creativity on Screen" (symposium, National Museum of the American Indian Symposium, New York, NY, May 12, 2005).

1. Other notable Kurdish filmmakers include the France-based Hiner Saleem, who has made five feature films, and Shawkat Amin Korki, whose first feature, *Crossing the Dust* (*Parinawa la Ghobar* [2006]), follows two Kurds as they search amid the chaos of the United States invasion in Iraq in 2003 for the parents of a five-year-old boy.
2. For the availability of these films, see Kabayan Central, http://www.kabayancentral.com/video.html.
3. For information on the Bolivian-based Center for Cinematographic Training (CEFREC) community, see Carol Kalafatic, "CEFREC/Media in Bolivia," *Native Networks*, http://www.nativenetworks.si.edu/eng/rose/cefrec.htm#open. Concerning Mexican Indigenous video production, see Amalia Córdova and Gabriela Zamorano, "Mapping Mexican Media," *Native Networks*, http://www.nativenetworks.si.edu/eng/rose/mexico.htm.
4. Many of these short fiction films (under sixty minutes) are described on the Web sites listed in note 3 above.
5. See Amalia Cordova, "Rolando Klein Interview," *Native Networks*, http://www.nativenetworks.si.edu/eng/rose/klein_r_interview.htm.
6. Jorge Sanjinés, "Problems of form and content in revolutionary cinema," in *New Latin American Cinema: Theory, Practices, and Transcontinental Articulations*, ed. Michael T. Martin (Detroit: Wayne State University Press, 1997), 62–79. See also, Freya Schiwy, "Decolonizing the Frame: Indigenous Video in the Andes," *Framework* 44, no. 1 (2003): 116–32.
7. The Web site of the Smithsonian Institution's National Museum of the American Indian lists nearly fifty film festivals that either exclusively or preferentially showcase Indigenous films. See http://www.nativenetworks.si.edu/eng/yellow/festivals.htm.
8. Australia, Bolivia, Canada, and New Zealand already have government-sponsored television networks specializing in Indigenous media.

Selected Filmography

"DVD" follows the entries below that are widely available in North American (Region One) DVD format. Further information is provided only for films available from either small or region-specific vendors. Films not available as *Native Features* went to print are labeled "not currently available," but readers should be aware that older titles are frequently being re-issued.

ARCTIC

Atanarjuat: The Fast Runner. Directed by Zacharias Kunuk (Inuit). 2001. DVD.

Bázo. Directed by Lars-Göran Pettersson. 2003. Available from www.trust-film.dk.

Before Tomorrow. Directed by Marie-Hélène Cousineau and Madeline Ivalu (Inuit). 2007. DVD forthcoming.

A Bride of the Seventh Heaven (Jumalan morsian). Directed by Anastasia Lapsui (Nenets) and Markku Lehmuskallio. 2004. Available from http://www.ses.fi.

The Journals of Knud Rasmussen. Directed by Norman Cohn and Zacharias Kunuk (Inuit). 2006. DVD.

The Kautokeino Rebellion. Directed by Nils Gaup (Sámi). 2007. DVD forthcoming.

The Legacy of the Tundra. Directed by Paul-Anders Simma (Sámi). 1995. Not currently available.

The Minister of State. Directed by Paul-Anders Simma (Sámi). 1997. Not currently available.

Pathfinder (Ofelas). Directed by Nils Gaup (Sámi). 1987. DVD.

Seven Songs from the Tundra (Seitsemän laulua tundralta). Directed by Anastasia Lapsui (Nenets) and Markku Lehmuskallio. 1999. Not currently available.

AUSTRALIA

beDevil. Directed by Tracey Moffatt (Aborigine). 1993. DVD and VHS available from http://www.roninfilms.com.au.

Beneath Clouds. Directed by Ivan Sen (Gamilaroi). 2002. DVD and VHS available from http://www.roninfilms.com.au.

Jindalee Lady. Directed by Brian Syron (Aborigine). 1992. Not currently available.

One Night the Moon. Directed by Rachel Perkins (Arrernte/Kalkadoon). 2001. DVD available from http://www.ezydvd.com.au.

Radiance. Directed by Rachel Perkins (Arrernte/Kalkadoon). 1998. DVD available from http://www.ezydvd.com.au.

Ten Canoes. Directed by Rolf de Heer and Peter Djigirr (Yolngu). 2006. DVD available from http://www.ezydvd.com.au.

Yolngu Boy. Directed by Stephen Johnson. 2001. Not currently available.

OCEANIA

Eagle vs Shark. Directed by Taika Waititi (Māori Te Whanau-a-Apanui). 2007. DVD.

The Land Has Eyes (Pear ta ma 'on Maf). Directed by Vilsoni Hereniko (Rotuman). 2004. DVD available from http://www.thelandhaseyes.com.

The Māori Merchant of Venice (Te Tangata Wahi Rawa o Weniti). Directed by Don C. Selwyn (Māori Ngati Kuri and Te Aupouri). 2002. Not currently available.

Mauri. Directed by Merata Mita (Māori). 1998. VHS available from http://www.arovideo.co.nz.

Naming Number Two (No. 2). Directed by Toa Fraser (Fijian). 2006. DVD available from http://www.arovideo.co.nz.

Ngati. Directed by Barry Barclay (Māori Ngati Apa). 1987. VHS available from http://www.arovideo.co.nz.

Once Were Warriors. Directed by Lee Tamahori (Māori). 1994. DVD.

Samoan Wedding (Sione's Wedding). Directed by Chris Graham. 2004. DVD.

Te Rua. Directed by Barry Barclay (Māori Ngati Apa). 1991. VHS available from http://www.arovideo.co.nz.

Tukana (Tukana: Husat i Asua?). Directed by Chris Owen and Albert Toro (Papua New Guinean). 1983. Not currently available.

Whale Rider. Directed by Niki Caro. 2001. DVD.

NORTH AMERICA

American Indian Graffiti. Directed by Steven Judd (Kiowa/Choctaw) and Tvli Jacob (Choctaw). 2003. Not currently available.

Bearwalker (*Backroads* 2000). Directed by Shirley Cheechoo (James Bay Cree). 2002. Not currently available.

The Business of Fancydancing. Directed by Sherman Alexie (Spokane/ Coeur d'Alene). 2002. DVD.

Dancing on the Moon. Directed by Rodrick Pocowatchit (Pawnee/ Shawnee/Comanche). 2003. DVD available from http:// www.harmyfilms.com/harmyhome.html.

The Doe Boy. Directed by Randy Redroad (Cherokee). 2001. DVD.

Edge of America. Directed by Chris Eyre (Cheyenne/Arapaho), 2001. DVD.

5th World (*Fifth World*). Directed by Blackhorse Lowe (Navajo). 2005. Not currently available.

Four Sheets to the Wind. Directed by Sterlin Harjo (Seminole/Creek). 2007. Not currently available.

Grand Avenue. Directed by Daniel Sackheim. 1996. VHS.

House Made of Dawn. Directed by Richardson Morse. 1972 and 1987. VHS.

Imprint. Directed by Michael Linn. 2007. Not currently available.

Itam Hakim, Hopiit. Directed by Victor Masayesva Jr. (Hopi). 1985. VHS available from http://www.eai.org/eai.

Johnny Tootall. Directed by Shirley Cheechoo (James Bay Cree). 2005. DVD available from http://www.johnnytootall.com.

Mile Post 398. Directed by Shonie De La Rosa (Navaho) and Andee De La Rosa (Navaho). 2007. DVD available from http:// www.sheepheadfilms.com.

Naturally Native. Directed by Valerie Red-Horse (Cherokee/Sioux) and Jennifer Wynne Farmer (Shinnecock). 1998. DVD available from http://www.naturallynative.com/home.html.

Skins. Directed by Chris Eyre (Cheyenne/Arapaho). 2002. DVD.

Skinwalkers. Directed by Chris Eyre (Cheyenne/Arapaho). 2002. DVD.

Sleepdancer. Directed by Rodrick Pocowatchit (Pawnee/Shawnee/ Comanche). 2007. DVD available from http://www.harmyfilms.com/ harmyhome.html.

Smoke Signals. Directed by Chris Eyre (Cheyenne/Arapaho). 1998. DVD.

A Thief of Time. Directed by Chris Eyre (Cheyenne/Arapaho). 2004. DVD.

A Thousand Roads. Directed by Chris Eyre (Cheyenne/Arapaho). 2005. Not currently available.

Tkaronto. Directed by Shane Belcourt (Métis). 2007. Not currently available.

Tushka. Directed by Ian Skorodin (Choctaw). 1996. Not currently available.

Selected Bibliography

Alexie, Sherman. *The Lone Ranger and Tonto Fistfight in Heaven.* New York: HarperPerennial, 1993.

Alexie, Sherman. *Reservation Blues.* New York: Warner Books, 1995.

Alexie, Sherman. *Smoke Signals: A Screenplay.* New York: Miramax Books, 1998.

Allen, Paula Gunn. *The Sacred Hoop: Recovering the Feminine in American Indian Traditions.* Boston: Beacon Press, 1992.

Barclay, Barry. *Mana Tuturu: Māori Treasures and Intellectual Property Rights.* Honolulu: University of Hawai'i Press, 2006.

Brown, Dee. *Bury My Heart at Wounded Knee: An Indian History of the American West.* New York: Holt, Rinehart & Winston, 1970.

Carpenter, Edmund. *Oh, What a Blow That Phantom Gave Me!* New York: Holt, Rinehart & Winston, 1972.

Churchill, Ward. *Fantasies of the Master Race: Literature, Cinema and the Colonization of American Indians.* San Francisco: City Lights Books, 1998.

Collins, Felicity and Therese Davis. *Australian Cinema After Mabo.* New York: Cambridge University Press, 2004.

Howard, Alan. "Presenting Rotuma to the World, The Making of the Film *The Land Has Eyes.*" *Visual Anthropology Review* 22, no. 1 (2006): 74–96.

Ihimaera, Witi. *The Whale Rider.* 1987. Reprinted, New York: Harcourt, 2003.

Krausz, Peter. "Screening Indigenous Australia: On Overview of Aboriginal Representation on Film," *Australian Screen Education* 32 (n.d.): 90–95.

Kunuk, Zacharias. "The public art of Inuit storytelling." *2002 Spry Memorial Lecture.* November 25, 2002. http://www.com.umontreal.ca/spry/spry-kz-lec.html.

Langton, Marcia. "*Well, I heard it on the radio and I saw it on the television . . .*" *An Essay for the Australian Film and Television Commission on the politics and aesthetics of filmmaking by and about Aboriginal persons and things.* Sydney: Australian Film Commission, 1993.

Leuthold, Steven. *Indigenous Aesthetics: Native Art, Media, and Identity.* Austin: University of Texas Press, 1998.

MacDougall, David. *Transcultural Cinema.* Princeton, NJ: Princeton University Press, 1998.

Mallon, Sean, and Pandora Fulimalo Pereira, eds. *Pacific Art Niu Sila: The Pacific Dimension of Contemporary New Zealand Arts.* Wellington, New Zealand: Te Papa Press, 2002.

McLuhan, Marshall. *The Gutenberg Galaxy: The Making of Typographic Man.* Toronto: University of Toronto Press, 1962.

Pilkington, Doris (Nugi Garimara). *Follow the Rabbit-Proof Fence.* 1996. Reprinted, New York: Miramax Books, 2002.

Rose, Wendy. "The Great Pretenders: Further Reflections on White-shamanism." In *The State of Native America: Genocide, Colonization, and Resistance,* edited by Annette Jaimes, 403–21. Boston: South End Press, 1992.

Singer, Beverly R. *Wiping the War Paint Off the Lens: Native American Film and Video.* Minneapolis: University of Minnesota Press, 2001.

Wood, Houston. *Displacing Natives: The Rhetorical Production of Hawai'i.* Lanham, MD: Rowman and Littlefield, 1999.

Index